To Barb:

My Mother always told me, "If you tell the truth you don't have to remember what you said."

The book is full of the truth with a stretch here and there!

Thanks for your friendship

Bill Wellman

"It's Made to Sell- Not to Drink!"

by
W.F. "Bill" Wellman

Bloomington, IN
authorHOUSE®
Milton Keynes, UK

AuthorHouse™
1663 Liberty Drive, Suite 200
Bloomington, IN 47403
www.authorhouse.com
Phone: 1-800-839-8640

AuthorHouse™ UK Ltd.
500 Avebury Boulevard
Central Milton Keynes, MK9 2BE
www.authorhouse.co.uk
Phone: 08001974150

First published by AuthorHouse 06/15/06

ISBN: 1-4259-4544-9(sc)
ISBN: 1-4259-4543-0 (dj)

Printed in the United States of America
Bloomington, Indiana

This book is printed on acid-free paper.

"This book is dedicated to my mother and father. It's too late for them to approve it, but I promised them I will tell it all like it happened!"

Your #2 Son,

Bill

Prologue

The title of my book needs an explanation. This was pointed out to me while having lunch with my good friend, Len Dryfus, when I had dropped a seed with him, hoping he would help me with the design of the book cover.

Len asked, "What does your title mean?" The title of my book, "It's Made To Sell, Not To Drink," came from my father, Guy Wellman, Sr. I have called his many sayings, "Guys Laws". They were the many treasures of wisdom my older brother and I heard growing up while living over a bar. Then Dad shared more of them with me when I decided to leave Indiana University to go into business with him and my mother.

The Author of "Guys Laws", Guy Wellman, Sr. – 1945 at the Blue Note in Chicago

It was during my first week of tending bar in the Palace, Dad told me his theory on drinking, "It's made to sell, not to drink." I questioned his logic and asked, "I hear what you are saying, but you drink!" He didn't hesitate when he answered, "Do as I say, not as I do."

Guys Laws were nothing but good old fashioned common horse sense. Example: "It's just as easy to hire a good looking waitress as an ugly one." Another example: "When you are tending bar and you serve a customer that first drink, he is your responsibility. It is up to you if he needs to be told he is cut off because you think he has had enough to drink – 86 him. Once you have cut off his drinks you may have the additional responsibility of driving him home." I always considered a drive home was reserved for only a very, very good customer.

"Guys Laws" have stuck with me throughout my life and I feel his simple honest logic helped me in many ways, so my title, "IT'S MADE TO SELL-NOT TO DRINK" is logical.

CONTENTS

Chapter One

$ BASEBALL $
For a living?

Baseball has been a tradition in my family since before I was born. It all began with Dad...an undersized catcher with a very strong arm, lots of baseball knowledge, and a high performance hitter to all fields. Another plus for him – he was on the cocky side, but when you are good, a little cockiness is okay. Guy Wellman, Sr., was born in Michigan City, Indiana on July 10, l895. He was one of the five children (three sisters and one brother) of Kate and Ira Wellman. I never saw my grandfather, though I know he was a railroad conductor, and my grandmother kept a small grocery store in Waterford, a town that now belongs to history located between LaPorte and Michigan City.

Grandma Wellman, Age 97

When Dad was 15 years old, he and his older brother Ray had a pony. He would ride the eight miles to Michigan City to play baseball with semi professional teams. Because he was always the youngest team member, he would hang around the team and learn from the older players.

Because baseball was the major sport then, Dad always told my older brother Guy and me how important baseball could be to our livelihoods. Nearly every saloonkeeper wanted to sponsor the town's top team. The factories also got into sponsorship offering good paying jobs with fringe benefits to the best baseball players in Northwest Indiana.

The reasons for having the best baseball team were recognition and publicity. What else was there to do back in the early twenties? Television was not around yet and baseball was by far the most popular game in the country. It was the National Pastime.

Still in his teens, Dad went to work for the Rumley Company (eventually Allis Chalmers) in LaPorte, Indiana. He became the team catcher, the position he was to take almost every time he walked onto a ball field. He actually got the job with Rumley because he could play baseball and, he soon found out, twelve more good baseball players were hired strictly for their baseball skills, and for no other reason. It seemed to be a very important practice for management to hire in this fashion.

If you look up the baseball players listed in the Old Timers Association Hall of Fame in LaPorte, Indiana, you will find many of them played on this Rumley Company team.

While working at Rumley, my dad met a very attractive, trim, young lady who also worked in the foundry. Her name was Leona Schultz. Their romance developed quickly. My grandmother passed a story about the time Dad came to visit. It was dinnertime and, since the Schultz family members were all very good eaters, my mother had two plates of food in front of her. Before Dad took his seat at the dinner table, my mother shifted one of her plates over to her brother Elmer's place. She did not want her future husband to know she was, or ever thought of being, a heavy eater. A lot of things happened back in the early twenties that are right on target in the "2000's." Being over-weight will never change.

On October 4, 1920 my folks were married in Benton Harbor, Michigan. They spent their weekend honeymoon at the House of David compound and, unbelievably, the House of David offered my dad a job playing baseball with their #1 traveling team. Dad and Mom had just registered for a room when Francis Thorpe, the manager of their Barnstorming Team approached my dad with an offer: "Son, you're Guy Wellman and I have been watching you play ball. I would like to make you an offer to join our team..." Dad was excited and proud his natural ability had brought him this recognition. But he was smart enough to know how to answer Mr. Thorpe: "I'll let you know before I leave in two days..."

Mr. & Mrs. Guy Wellman Sr. 1920 Wedding Picture – check out the haircut!

The next few honeymoon days must have been interesting for young Guy Wellman and his new bride. Mr. Thorpe had made my father an offer of $150.00 per month plus all expenses, with an additional $50.00 per month if he would grow a beard, and all my dad would have to do was what he really loved to do – play baseball!

In 1920, this kind of offer made Dad feel like he was going to the BIG LEAGUES, but there was another person now involved in the negotiations. She was a strong German bride, seven years younger, but with a strength that would always keep Guy on the straight path.

It was huge money, but living out of a suitcase was not what Leona Wellman had in mind. She was an old fashioned girl from a very strong family background and having a family and a house was much more important to her than baseball and a beard. So, when dad told her of Mr. Thorpe's offer, there was no hesitation. She said NO!

Now let me give you a little history about The House of David and its baseball team, which was equivalent to the top AAA Teams of today.

Benjamin Purnell and his wife, Mary, established the Israelite House of David, a religious community, in 1903 in Benton Harbor, Michigan. The purpose of this colony was to gather the twelve lost tribes of Israel for the "In-gathering" to await the Millennium. Purnell, a sports enthusiast, encouraged the playing of sports during the wait. The House of David started playing baseball around 1913 as a weekend recreation. By 1915 the team was playing a more grueling schedule against local semi-pro teams. By 1920, it was well known around the country, earning money for the colony, and using the team as a way to preach to potential members.

Benjamin Purnell, founder of the House of David

A Young Queen Mary

While the team was on the road, the colony established a home team, a girl's team, and a junior boy's team. The players were led by manager Francis Thorpe, and the teams were originally comprised of members of the colony. The House of David Baseball Team was always an attraction because of their long hair and beards, a doctrine of the religion. It would draw substantial crowds wherever the team played. By the early 20s, in need of participants

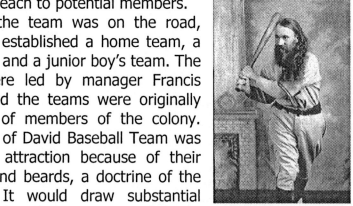

Typical House of David baseball player

with better playing abilities to keep the crowds interested, the House of David was in the business of hiring players not of the faith. These ringers were required to grow a beard, and some played for the team for many years. This fit Dad perfectly. He was considered a real ringer in 1920. He definitely was not of the faith and could grow a beard in one week.

The House of David became the biggest industry in Benton Harbor, Michigan. It ran a tourist resort and amusement park; farm and fishing industries; and entertained many with its bearded traveling baseball and basketball teams.

Diamond House

King Ben Purnell made his original fortune as a broom-maker. In 1898, with the help of a $75,000 gift from a carriage maker and his personal fortune, he purchased 103 acres on which were built five houses. The Diamond House of the House of David compound is where Guy and Leona Wellman spent their honeymoon.

King Ben was a shrewd businessman, and set high goals for the cult. The Detroit News estimated that it made over a million dollars per year. Huge profits were possible because cult members donated all labor. King Ben preached to his followers that when the cult reached the total of 288,000 members, they would all gather on the shores of Lake Michigan and would go to heaven as a group.

The King knew that the figure of 288,000 was impossible to reach because the group had to practice celibacy. Children could not be allowed because the number of members was "fixed."

Ben accepted all that comes with wealth. He always rode a white horse and had a custom built 65-foot yacht, which he called "Morning Star." His followers enjoyed no such luxuries, so the young men turned to sports.

King Ben on his favorite white horse

King Ben died in 1927 during a court trial charging him with being an imposter, defrauding cult members and using his position for immoral purposes. Other charges included perjury, obstruction, and breakup of families, failure to educate children, teaching disloyalty to the government, forced marriage, inadequate food, clothing and shelter for members, and failure to rest on Sunday. Followers hid his body for four days thinking he might still come back to take them all to heaven. When this did not happen, they took the body to an embalmer who used a non-poisonous fluid just in case King Ben chose to come back at a later time. His wife wept and blamed enemies for his death. Members displayed his body in a glass case, which attracted long lines of curious viewers.

My many questions on dad's offer to play baseball for a living with the House of David are still unanswered. Did my mother know that the cult favored vegetarianism? Did she have any idea that children were not allowed because old Ben had set the number at 288,000 members? Did Dad know that they were to practice celibacy? That just doesn't sound like my dad. If Dad were considered a ringer, none of the rules would apply to him anyway.

Before finishing my House of David episode, I have to tell a side story I remember from 1937. The Pontiacs, a semi-pro team from Valparaiso, Indiana had booked a game against the House of David to be played at Browns Field at Valparaiso University. A huge crowd gathered to see the bearded wonders perform their magic before the game. They were called the Pepper Team, three ball players fielding the ball from a batter at close range. They were very quick with their throws and their fancy passes behind their backs. They had a red-haired short fellow who really captured the crowd's attention as he performed his smooth act. I didn't realize until they received a standing ovation, and the star of the show removed his fake red beard, it was Dad dressed in a House of David uniform. It was clear he would have been great on tour with the House of David but I still think Leona made the right decision when she said "no" to that offer back in 1920.

"Pepper Game" 1937 – Browns Field, Valparaiso

It did not take Dad long to receive his second offer. A good friend, and a very good baseball pitcher, named Chief Ben Ranier, took a job as a guard at the Michigan City State Prison. Chief was the name given to him by his baseball friends because he was a full-blooded Indian with a great curve ball. My son Scott would describe this chief as a "woo woo" Indian, not a "dot head" Indian.

The Chief knew the warden had hired him because the warden had the same desire as the saloonkeepers and the factory CEO's - to field the best baseball team in town. The Chief approached the warden, telling him that if he was serious about building a team and bringing home the trophy of the league from Northwest Indiana, he had to build the team from the middle up. That meant a good catcher – pitcher combination, a great center fielder, followed by a good double play combination. The Chief then told the warden about this scrappy catcher who could manage this future powerhouse behind the ivy covered (not really true) walls.

The warden made my father an offer similar to the House of David's. Security with the job was tops on the list, full time work, but with no guard duty involved. Dad would manage the team, keeping the ball players in line and out of trouble, and provide maintenance for the best manicured field east of Wrigley Field.

Michigan City Prison Baseball Diamond before the ivy covered walls

The first thing that Dad did was to give tryouts to the inmates to see how much talent there was inside the prison and, then he followed with a recommendation to the warden that three other outsiders be offered guard jobs. It was quite a coincidence that two of the three new guards were the slickest double play combinations in Northern Indiana. The other guard was a center fielder who could also hit home runs.

1921 Northern Indiana Champions

One rule the warden put in place Dad could not explain: "At no time will there be more than (4) prisoners on the field at one time."

I am sure Dad was enjoying his life style – and why not? At the age of twenty-five managing a team inside the Michigan City Prison with five hand-picked ball players to bolster the old theory of building your team right up the middle and, plenty of competition for the other nine spots on the team. Interestingly, six out of the nine inmates were imprisoned for murder.

Competition was keen among the inmates because once a team member, your lifestyle immediately changed. Fringe benefits inside the wall were really cherished. As Dad said, "No one was ever late, or missed a practice, and some of these guys would kill to make this team." A big advantage was the schedule – all home games, no time on the outside – and it was baseball all year round. During these two years, Dad never drew guard duty.

Guy Wellman - center

It did not take long to bring home the 1921 Trophy for the league championship. Dad sent a penny postcard to my grandmother in Waterford. It read, "Here is the cup that we fought for all summer. It doesn't look big to you, but pretty big to us, Guy."

Two years in prison (guard duty?) must have been enough, or maybe the challenge was gone after the 1921 league championship, but, whatever it was, it did not take Dad long to accept another offer he received from two young lawyers in Kouts, Indiana. Pete Lyons and Pat Crowe asked Dad and Chief Ranier to come to Kouts to put together another Indiana powerhouse. They offered the two of them $50.00 per game each, plus $1.00 per strikeout. Dad said the Chief never got less than eight strikeouts per game, but he would usually get twelve to fourteen. Two games a week and extra pay for strikeouts put Dad on what he thought was the top of the baseball world. "I thought I was in the Big Leagues once again!"

Speaking of Big Leagues, Dad had an offer to go with Philadelphia in the National League during these early years, but the lure of Kouts and the potential for more money then the national league was offering, had convinced Dad not to make the move. I have to wonder if Mom had anything to do with that decision. To her, the house and family were still better than a suitcase and a beard – and anything was better than living in Philadelphia! I believe W. C. Fields has something like this on his tombstone: "I would rather be here than in Philadelphia."

Kouts, Indiana, 1924 – population 700

I asked my Dad to explain the theory of two young, successful attorneys offering baseball players this kind of money to put together a semi-pro team, in a town of less than 800 people. His answer was simple, "They will make money with the team."

I did not see it at first, but later on it came to me. A baseball game was a big event and all of the communities had teams; Hebron, Boone Grove, LaPorte, Wheatfield, North Judson, Valparaiso, Michigan City, Wanatah, on and on. They were all proud of their teams. In fact, the fans, at least some of them, were proud and confident enough to make a bet on their team each time it took the field. Gambling has always been there, and evidently it was BIG in Kouts. Pride was also

BIG, but money was BIGGER. I have always been sorry that I did not get a chance to ask my father if gambling had anything to do with Michigan City and the warden's desire to be the best in his league. We will never know.

Dad often talked about the pride that Kouts had in the early 1920's. The Kosanke family, who owned the funeral home and Turner Edus, a construction contractor, both contributed substantially to the baseball team. Pride also showed up in number of fans who attended the weekend games – over 2,000 people would watch a ball game. Of course, what else was there to do? No television, only radio, but a live baseball game with "pride" and gambling involved – now that was HUGE." Only in America!

In the 1920's, the Ku Klux Klan was very strong in Porter County and Dad told me the story about arriving at the ballpark, which was on the south side of the Kouts High School, and how, on several occasions, the Klan constructed a gallows behind the backstop because several team members were Catholic. He also told me that the gallows were never used.

Dad played against Satchel Paige on three different occasions, in LaPorte, Kouts, and in the Michigan City Prison. The Vidette Messenger interviewed him in 1976 and he was asked what it was like to face a pitcher from the big leagues. He said, "Sometimes you can hit better against a pro than against some local guy who can hardly pitch."

In that same article, Dad told about the first game he played for Kouts. This story has always stuck in my mind. Dad was warming up the Chief before the game and the other team was taking infield practice, when Dad was hit with two baseballs simultaneously! One went to the side of his face, thrown wildly from the first baseman to the catcher of the opposing team and the pitch from Chief Ranier hit him directly on the nose, and Dad looked dead. He spent the night with Dr. Sam Dittmer because there wasn't a hospital. Quoting my dad in the interview, when the reporter asked him what his treatment was, he said, "Treatment? I just had to eat soup for two weeks."

During the eight years we spent in Kouts, Dad operated a "billiard" parlor, which meant he had poker and euchre (Indiana Bridge) games along with a few pool tables. I always thought it was great to tell people my folks operated a billiard parlor. To me it sounded first class!

Baseball wasn't the only sport in Kouts. My dad was also the local fight promoter. Boxing was not legal in Illinois, but it was in Indiana. Dad used a big canvas tent as the arena, and every so often a fight card was put together and fans would even come by train from Chicago to Kouts to see a boxing match. Dad would charge $.75 admission and hire fighters from Chicago, Hammond, and East Chicago and pay them $2.00 to $5.00 to fight Porter County residents in six to eight three minute rounds.

One of the most popular local fighters was Red Schultz, father of ex-councilman Tony Schultz of Valparaiso. Red was fast, and a former Golden Glove Champion out of LaPorte. One night in the arena, the eight round main event was Red fighting a fellow from Chicago. In the 7th round, Red ducked back to avoid a punch and hit his head on the main tent post that was in the corner of the ring. He knocked himself out and scared Dad to death because it took 50 minutes for Red to come around. This event ended Dad's career as a fight promoter. He was not known as the "Don King of Kouts" in the 1920's, but he was a promoter on everything from organizing a party in a bar to running a baseball team.

I discovered later on that in his many years of tending bar, when Dad would say lets buy so & so a drink, it was nearly always the start of a party. But, when the party was at its peak, Guy Wellman, Sr. was nowhere to be seen. He disappeared because of his ulcers and his health – but in his mind, he was still promoting.

In 1939, I was second-string quarterback on the Valparaiso High School freshman team. We played a game one Saturday morning inside the walls of the Michigan City Prison. We lost the game, but I got to play the last half so for me it was a great experience. They had the goal posts wrapped in green and white crepe paper for Valparaiso, and red and white for Michigan City High School, and there were printed programs listing names, numbers and weights of each player – it was just like the big teams.

With one minute to the end of the game, I took a kickoff and ran down to the 5-yard line before they caught me. We did not score, but as the game ended a prisoner called me over to the fence and asked me if I was related to Guy Wellman. I told him that he was my dad. He then said, "If you had scored a touchdown, these guys would have taken down the bleachers and put them back up again." Then he said something that really made me feel good: "Your dad was one of the best ball players ever to play in here, and on top of that he was a great Guy."

My last prison story took place in 1950. I was being paid to play fast pitch softball and we played a game inside Michigan City Prison. This time we played against the inmates. During the first few innings the prisoners found out that our pitcher, Kelly Gott, was the Chief of Police in Valparaiso. There was one prisoner who kept saying the same thing over and over: "Chiefy, you can't touch me in here." The chief was not too happy about this discovery, but he held his temper and we escaped with a victory.

Charlie Grimm, Guy Jr. and Gabby Hartnett

It is time I talk about

baseball and my older brother Guy Wellman, Jr. He was born in Michigan City, Indiana in 1921, which gave him three years of experience on me because I came along in 1924. Guy's first claim to fame took place in 1927 in Kouts. We lived in a small two-bedroom bungalow on the main street of Kouts, and at that time we had a small shed/barn behind the house. Guy discovered cigarettes and matches at the age of six and when Dad found him hiding under his bed, after the firemen had extinguished the fire and the shed was leveled, I thought he would be strung up by his feet. But Dad handled the punishment like he always did. He gave him a lecture on smoking and matches and that was the last we heard of the shed. I never could remember what we kept in that shed anyhow.

Dad's advise about baseball opening doors to make a good living must not have impressed me as much as it did brother Guy, but one other thing also came into play, a thing called ability.

Guy Jr. played four years of high school baseball while I only had the opportunity to play two. During my junior and senior years, our high school dropped baseball for some reason that was never explained. It was a rumor in V.H.S. that since the star left handed pitcher, Walter Molinder had graduated, Coach John Wiggins felt he was facing a disaster and took the easy way out. Now that was a rumor. Lucky Strike Green went to war along with VHS baseball.

During my junior and senior years, I was hired ($5 a game) to play with a semi-pro fast pitch softball team from Hebron, Indiana called the Johnson Seeds. I was always amazed that I could make money doing something that I absolutely loved doing. Maybe Dad was right!

Brother Guy really must have been listening to Dad when he preached to us that baseball could always open many doors and you could make a good living at baseball. Because Guy is now 84 years old and he still is working with the Los Angeles Dodgers by running three of their Fantasy Camps each year at their official spring training camp in Vero Beach,

FL. I recently asked him when he was officially going to hang it up and he said, "It's an unwritten rule that if the uniform fits you keep going."

After having a great high school athletic career, Guy received a full scholarship to Indiana University in 1939 where he earned his numerals his freshman year in football, basketball, and baseball, followed by winning "I" Letters in basketball under Coach Branch McCraken and in baseball with Coach Pooch Harrel. In those days, athletes were encouraged to go out for more than one sport. Guy's senior year he decided baseball was where he should put all of his energy, along with being on the Dean's list as a top student.

He was captain of the baseball team and was given the Gimbel Award in 1943 followed by AG Clevenger Award in 1997. This award is presented to living "I" Men who, as alumni, have made outstanding contributions to Indiana University through service to the athletic program.

Big Brother graduated from Indiana in 1943 and immediately as a second lieutenant in the Big Red 1 Infantry Division headed for Germany and World War II where he was awarded the Bronze Star. To catch the full story of where his career took him, I'll repeat a story that was in a special edition that was written by Tom Riggs, writer for the Press Journal, written on March 4, 1989, from Vero Beach, FL. "Congratulations to our World Champion Dodgers." The caption in the story was: "Field Coordinator is some kind of Guy."

If there is one guy who can tell what's going on when and where at Dodgertown, it's Wellman. Guy Wellman, whose title in Los Angeles Dodgers' player development department is field coordinator, does just that – coordinate the minor leaguer's use of the Dodgertown fields and facilities each spring. Each spring training morning he posts a schedule in the minor league clubhouse. Something like 10:00 AM meeting; 10:30 A.M. stretching on Field 2; 10:45 pepper and easy throwing; 11:00 AM fundamentals – maybe run downs on Half-Field 1; pitcher's covering first base on Field 1; 1:00 PM batting practice on Field 2; pitchers throwing; then running and extra work.

The routine varies depending on what instruction is needed, depending on the need of the big-league club, which might require a player or two to round out the roster for an intersquad game, depending on the number of minor-leaguers in camp. "Our job is to make sure that each individual gets the proper instruction that he wants and that he needs," said Wellman. To make best use of the time and space available, work on fundamentals is done in groups rotating from fundamental to fundamental.

The Dodgers have 17 minor league instructors and coaches to go around, and Wellman sees to it that they are in the right place at the right time to provide the instruction. This spring the number of minor-leaguers in camp will peak at 147.

The title "field coordinator" has more involved than spring training scheduling. It's a year-round duty."

"I'm in charge of the coordination of all teaching by our minor-league instructors," Wellman said. "Seeing to it that all our minor league teaching and instruction is all on the same level, the Dodger way."

Guy Wellman, left, brings former Dodger greats like Duke Snider to fantasy camp

Wellman also runs the Dodger's Fantasy Camps and their Arizona Instructional League operation.

"He surrounds himself with good people and he lets those people use their abilities," said minor league pitching instructor Dave Wallace. "You have a free rein, as long as you run it through him. He's well aware of everything that is going on. He's a tremendous communicator."

As a player Guy was a good fielding, light hitting catcher. "I was like most catchers today," said Wellman. "I hit over 300 once in a class C ball, the higher I got up, the harder the pitching got to be."

Wellman signed with the Cincinnati Reds in 1946 after spending two years overseas in Germany, and then he was drafted by the Brooklyn Dodgers. "I was here when DodgerTown in Vero Beach first opened," Wellman said.

Guy Wellman Jr. – Indiana University 1943

He made it as high as Class AAA, but once again Uncle Sam sent Major Guy Wellman a telegram asking him to give a hand in the Korean Campaign.

While Guy was playing in St. Paul AAA, three pretty fair catchers were with the Los Angeles Dodgers – Roy Campanella, Bruce Edwards, and another Hoosier Gil Hodges. All three are in the Hall of Fame.

He has remained associated with the Dodgers over many years. He was a player manager in South Dakota in the summer time Basin League for college players and former pros, he saw fit to recommend and sign Frank Howard to the Dodgers.

By 1960, Wellman was working fulltime with the Dodgers. He has been an area scout, the Midwest scouting supervisor, a big league scout (a position he handled from his Downers Grove, Illinois home by attending White Sox and Cubs games in nearby Chicago), and a minor-league instruction coordinator.

The scouting and scheduling his past and present baseball jobs required a harken back to his World War II days, when he was a battalion S-2 intelligence officer in charge of maps and reconnaissance. "Everything came to you," he recalled. "If you were scouting a battle or planning a battle, it all came back to you."

I remember the day that telegram arrived. Frances, Guy's wife, started to cry thinking their lives would be interrupted.

There was no need for tears because his assignment was just 18 miles away where he was to be responsible for ROTC in Gary High Schools. This gave him the opportunity to coach football at Valparaiso University in the morning and ROTC in Gary in the afternoons. He was among the first Americans to cross the Rhine River on the Lunderdorff Bridge in the final stages of the war. "The Germans forgot to blow it up," he said. "That led to the Ruhr pocket. That was one of the big breakthroughs."

Wellman, who goes about his work with an infectiously positive attitude, finds more parallels between his military days and baseball than the importance of scheduling and information gathering. The parallels also exist in high school teaching and coaching that he has done. "It's all teaching," he said. "Whether I was in the infantry, where you had to teach 'em how to fire arms and how to clean 'em or here." When a pupil makes good, Wellman gets the typical teacher "high."

"Seeing players develop, seeing young coaches and managers move up the ladder in baseball, I get a bigger kick out of this than anything," he said.

Other organizations have shown interest in Wellman. In 1985, Wellman said the Kansas City Royals offered him the player development director's job.

"It would have been a good opportunity and I would have liked to have done it," Wellman said. "But with the ties I have with the Dodgers, I didn't want to leave."

It was during these many years with Los Angeles that Guy has captured three World Series rings and two National League Championship rings. He has been inducted into three

Hall of Fames – Downers Grove High School, Valparaiso High School, and Valparaiso University – and he is very close to the big one: Indiana University. Guy was also sent to Japan and Australia to give baseball clinics.

The Los Angeles Dodgers were like a big family. They were all close. Tom Lasorda always used the line, "When I cut my finger, I bleed Dodger blue."

When my first grandson Guy Wellman (named after my Dad and Brother Guy) was having a problem because his parents had split up, Tom Lasorda wrote a letter to Guy when he was 14 years of age. The letter was great and it did help.

Tom Lasorda, 1992

Letter from Tom Lasorda to grandson Guy

LOS ANGELES Dodgers®

1/19/92

TOM LASORDA

1000 ELYSIAN PARK AVENUE
LOS ANGELES, CA 90012-1199

Dear Guy-

I've been meaning to write to you for some time, although I never met you, I heard all about you from your grand-father and his brother guy whom you were named after.

Guy, I found out that you were having a hard time getting adjusted to life, and things have been pretty tough for you.

Well I want you to know that when I was your age, I had problems getting adjusted to life. Then one day I made up my mind that I wanted to be a Major league pitcher. So I set my goals and then I began to work hard to get my education and play baseball. Well, I made the big leagues as a pitcher and now I am the manager of the Los angeles Dodgers.

Guy what I want you to do. is to make up your mind on what you

LOS ANGELES Dodgers®

2

TOM LASORDA

1000 ELYSIAN PARK AVENUE
LOS ANGELES, CA 90012-1199

want to do when you grow up. Then study hard and get a good education, as that is something which will be very important in your life.

No matter how rough things are you must make up your mind to grow up and be a successful person. You can be anything you want to be, all you have to do is work hard to achieve your goals.

Guy, when we come to Chicago to play the Cubs, why dont you call me at the Hyatt Hotel on Wacker St. and I would like to invite you to see a game with the Cubs as my guest.

Well Guy, if you can find time, please write to me and let me know how things are in your house. If ever I can help you out, please call me. Good luck Guy, and may God Bless you.

Your friend
Tom Lasorda

In 1928, Guy Wellman Sr. got another offer; this time from a wealthy insurance man in Lowell, Indiana, who wanted Dad to move to town and help build the reputation and pride of a semi-pro baseball team.

Due to the Chicago Black Sox scandal, former big leaguers were facing the local teams, so it was getting harder to build a team. These players were playing wherever they could because they were banned from the majors. Dad played against Hippo Vaughn and Buck Weaver. Weaver ended up playing shortstop for a team in Chesterton, Indiana for quite a few years before he retired.

We moved to Lowell, but we were only there for one season, and for another billiard parlor. The one thing that stuck in my memory about Lowell was the water: it smelled like rotten eggs. Mom had to force us to take a bath because you usually smelled worse after the bath.

Our next move was to Valparaiso, Indiana in 1929. Dad opened a billiard parlor at 21 Washington Street and called it "The Club."

The days of being paid to play baseball were winding down. The money just was not there like it used to be but, my dad's desire to play was not winding down. He played for the Pontiacs, a team managed by George Buck Bowman, the owner of the Pontiac garage and dealership in Valparaiso.

There were many nights that I would see my dad cutting the end of a lemon off and then tape the lemon to his injured finger. The next day the sore finger would look like a prune. The swelling was gone and Dad was ready for the next game.

$ BASEBALL $
For A Living?

When I would have a friend over to stay all night, I always wanted to show off my dad's hands. From all of the games where he was the catcher, his fingers had been jammed many times from foul balls and they looked like someone had taken a hammer to them.

When anyone would ask my dad why he had wanted to be a catcher, he would say, "No one else wanted to put on the tools of ignorance (meaning the equipment) and I knew that if I learned that position, I could make a living playing baseball for a good many years. He did just that!

Chapter Two

THE CLUB

Just like the movie "The Sting"

Baseball lost its entertainment dominance, its sponsors and fan loyalties and no longer provided a comfortable living for the Wellman family. After a year in Lowell, we headed for the big city – Valparaiso where my parents bought an ongoing business from Walter Bosel.

The business was a billiard parlor (what else?) with a few pool tables and always occupied card tables for the playing of buck euchre and poker.

It wasn't legal, but home brew (beer) and liquor were also sold on request. The national prohibition law in 1926 prohibited the sale of intoxicating liquor, but that didn't slow up my dad.

PROHIBITION IS AN AWFUL FLOP,
WE LIKE IT.
IT CAN'T STOP WHAT IT'S MEANT TO STOP,
WE LIKE IT.
IT'S LEFT A TRAIL OF GRAFT AND SLIME,
IT WON'T PROHIBIT WORTH A DIME,
IT'S FILLED OUR LAND WITH A VICE AND CRIME,
NEVERTHELESS, WE'RE FOR IT.
PROHIBITION by Franklin P. Adams, 1931

In 1933, my father received one of the first 3-way liquor licenses issued in Valparaiso. It was for "The Club" at 21 Washington Street. The Club was a two-story building with a pool room/restaurant on the main floor, and a small two-bedroom apartment in the front of the second story. Behind the apartment was a large, wide-open room, which could have been used in the movie set for The Sting: a movie with Paul Newman and Robert Redford.

Gambling was the major activity in and above The Club. The "house" (operators of all card games) would make its money by pulling a "drag" (money) out of each card game.

Center Building is the Club Tavern / Bookie

The amount the operator would "drag" would depend on the size of the pot. This is the way the owner would make his expenses and profit. There were many times when my dad would play for the house as a poker player or he would bank a player to play for the house. This was considered a good way to start a great night of poker.

I remember one of the poker players Dad would hire named Rags. He was in his late sixties and always wore a suit and a tie. The things that intrigued me about Rags were his hands. They were thin with lady-like softness. It was fun to watch him shuffle and deal the cards. He just seemed to flow and never flustered. He was a perfect poker-faced player.

The other poker player who really hooked my interest was a Cherokee Indian who actually lived in Chicago but was known as the Indian Doctor from Tremont. His office was on the south side of the tracks of the South Shore Rail Road at the Tremont stop on U.S. 12.

This sketch by R. Ramsey Smith captures the exact setting as I remember it when I was eight years old. The one story building had a sign on the roof which could be read by riders on the South Shore train and the larger billboard was read by the westbound traffic heading into Chicago on U.S. 12.

Tremont Medicine Man (Late 1930's)

The sign itself was a showstopper, especially to a very impressionable eight-year old. The Indian with a war bonnet always got my attention. It read: "Medicine Man Knows..." followed by "Knows Barks – Roots – Berries – Herbs – Seeds – Leaves..." followed by, "See Him and be Convinced." By the way, the "Doctor" was considered an excellent poker player and I respected him as a great storyteller.

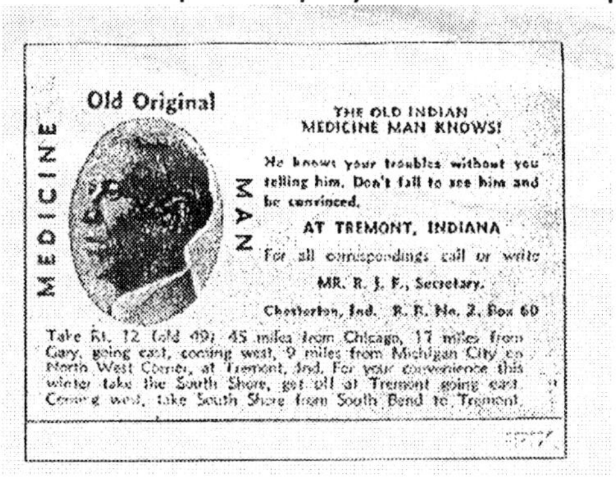

Old Original Medicine Man

About three to four times a month the Doc would attend a Friday or Saturday night poker game above the Club Tavern, accompanied by a beautiful black German Shepard dog called "Topay."

Doc told me the story about how some one in 1926 broke into his office and ransacked the place and even worse, the thief took his beautiful dog "Topay." But history had a happy ending, according to this column from The Chesterton Tribune of May 27, 1926.

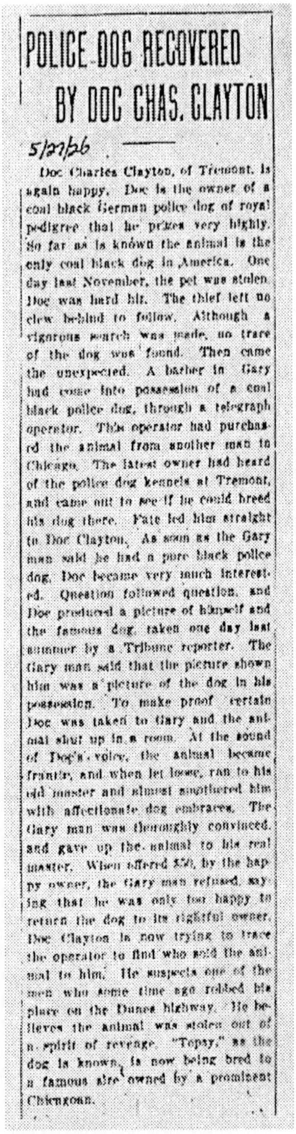

POLICE DOG RECOVERED BY DOC CHAS. CLAYTON

5/27/26

Doc Charles Clayton, of Tremont, is again happy. Doc is the owner of a coal black German police dog of royal pedigree that he prizes very highly. So far as is known the animal is the only coal black dog in America. One day last November, the pet was stolen. Doc was hard hit. The thief left no clew behind to follow. Although a vigorous search was made, no trace of the dog was found. Then came the unexpected. A barber in Gary had come into possession of a coal black police dog, through a telegraph operator. This operator had purchased the animal from another man in Chicago. The latest owner had heard of the police dog kennels at Tremont, and came out to see if he could breed his dog there. Fate led him straight to Doc Clayton. As soon as the Gary man said he had a pure black police dog, Doc became very much interested. Question followed question, and Doc produced a picture of himself and the famous dog, taken one day last summer by a Tribune reporter. The Gary man said that the picture shown him was a picture of the dog in his possession. To make proof certain Doc was taken to Gary and the animal shut up in a room. At the sound of Doc's voice, the animal became frantic, and when let loose, ran to his old master and almost smothered him with affectionate dog embraces. The Gary man was thoroughly convinced, and gave up the animal to his real master. When offered $50, by the happy owner, the Gary man refused, saying that he was only too happy to return the dog to its rightful owner. Doc Clayton is now trying to trace the operator to find who sold the animal to him. He suspects one of the men who some time ago robbed his place on the Dunes highway. He believes the animal was stolen out of a spirit of revenge. "Topsy," as the dog is known, is now being bred to a famous sire owned by a prominent Chicagoan.

Tribune Article – "Police Dog Recovered..."

The story that really hooked me was told by the Doctor without cracking a smile. I always tried to hang around the poker game because I was used as a "go-for" and of course, I would make money in tips. When the Doctor came with his dog, I would spend time with "Topay" because he was a beauty and very friendly. The Doctor told me that he had trained his dog to use the inside toilet facilities, but he was having a problem getting him to flush the toilet. Of course, I went for the story hook, line and sinker!

Every time the Doctor joined the game I would ask him if I could see his dog go to the bathroom. He would say something like, "You just missed it" or "If he has to go he will let me know and I will look for you."

It took me a year to figure out that an Indian Medicine Man had hooked me "big time" and I'm sure he had a few good laughs at my expense. But if you were eight years old and a Cherokee Indian Medicine Man tells you this tale, wouldn't you believe it?

This article was written in 1991 with the headline:

"See Him and Be Convinced." It was probably in the early 30's that Gladys Rizer relates how her aunt came to their home in Tremont and asked her Dad, "What would you think if I married the old Indian?" Glady's Dad laughed and said, "Well, if you can turn over and see that face in bed, it is all right with me."

Doc, the Indian Medicine Man, was a familiar figure along The Tremont Road. This full blooded Cherokee went by various names: Doc Bercier and Doc Clayton, among others. He was tall – well over 6 feet – and considered by some to be handsome, though his face was pockmarked. Gladys Rizer never saw him in Indian regalia, but she only remembers him dressed in a conservative suit and wearing a broad rimmed hat.

Doc married my Aunt Lillian and "it was the most wonderful thing that happened in my family. He was good to us. He bought an eight-grave lot in the Chesterton Cemetery when another of my aunts died. My grandmother and my parents are buried there as well as Aunt Lillian (1947). Doc hoped to be buried there, too, but it wasn't allowed at that time. After he put up Aunt Lillian's stone, he came to me. He was crying and said, "They won't let me be buried there," He said, "They called me a nigger."

Doc eschewed the medicine show circuit. He had a serious intent concerning his remedies, and while he may have had an aura of magic about him, he believed firmly that natural products – herbs and berries, and wintergreen, especially wintergreen – were the best panaceas for what ails you. Doc would say, " I can tell you by looking in a person's eye what the problem is," he would say.

Dealing in patent medicines caused Doc some run-ins with the law, as well as with the American Medical Association. So he would take off periodically for his family's home in New Orleans. Upon returning, he would have adopted a new name allowing him to elude authorities and critics until they caught on to him again.

Doc attempted to keep a low profile regarding his occupation. Still he had a keen sense of the need for advertising and used billboards (Dean White would have liked Doc) and fliers to tout his products – "SEE HIM and be CONVINCED..."

Success in his practice and a growing clientele (many society names from Chicago) allowed Doc to enjoy some luxuries. He bought one of the first Chryslers equipped with automatic drive. It was nearly his undoing!

His first trip was to the Chesterton State Bank and with his new possession curbed near Railroad Park (now Thomas Centennial Park), he entered the bank to conduct his business. According to a witness, "He got into his car, started the ignition, went over the curb and around the band stand, wove in and out of the trees, finally coming to rest against one of them."

Gladys Rizer remembers: "Doc was connected with a pharmacist in Chicago. It was local gossip his herbs were mixed with wine. Whatever was in his tonic helped people."

It has also been reported that those persons of the "temperance" persuasion enjoyed tonics of this variety. Under the label of "medicine," a generous spoonful allowed them a temporary sense of wellbeing.

Mrs. Knobb was the doc's associate. Gladys remembered: "Her husband had been a medicine man, a friend of Doc's. I worked in the store taking care of the mail order business and he would help Mrs. Knobb make this salve. It would take almost all night. I'm not sure what was in it, but I know that Doc liked to use mulberry and huckleberry leaves a lot."

She continued: "One day a woman brought her son into the store. He had been in a motorcycle accident and had very bad burns on his legs. The mother pleaded: 'None of the doctors will treat him. They think he is going to die.' Doc turned to Mrs Knobb and told her to get some of the salve and they applied it to his burns. It worked!"

Doc was probably well over 100 when he died in 1951. He was buried in New Orleans. Before he died he had taken in an associate whose name was "Jack" Johnstone. After Doc died, new fliers were printed and they stated, "The Old Original Indiana Medicine Man's Wonderful Remedies Now Handled by 'Jack' Johnstone, Indiana Medicine Company. " Today, Doc would probably be dispensing his wintergreen painkiller from a natural foods store."

The fourth paragraph of a Chesterton newspaper article inspired my investigation of the Chesterton Cemetery. My three visits have been friendly, rewarding, and a source of interesting stories told to me by Mr. Ralph Brooks and his wife Delores. Mr. Brooks started to work as a helper at the cemetery at the ripe old age of fourteen. At the age of seventeen the Chesterton Cemetery Association asked Ralph to fill in as the temporary manager while they looked for a full time person with more experience. Ralph is now eighty six, which means he has held this temporary position for sixty nine years. I doubt if the association is still looking for someone with more experience. When you see his office, you know it is just the way Mr. Brooks wants it. He has a very comfortable chair located in the corner and I'm sure he knows exactly where everything is located. On my first visit, I introduced myself to Mr. and Mrs. Brooks and told them I was writing a book. I told them how the Indian Doctor from Tremont had hooked me [age eight] into believing his dog Topay was smart enough to use the inside facilities but he was having trouble getting him to flush. Their expressions, told me I was talking about someone they knew and knew well.

After they showed me the gravesite of Doc Biercer's family and I had taken a couple of pictures of the head stone, both of them were anxious to tell me their personal stories about the Indian Doctor. Delores did most of the talking. When she was eight years old, her Father was bedridden with rheumatoid arthritis and a friend recommended the Indian Doctor stop in for one of his rare house calls. Doc gave Delores' father the once over, packed him down with the famous green salve, then ordered him to get out of bed, and walk around. Immediately Delores' mother said, "Doc, he can't do it, he has too much pain." The Doc insisted as the man struggled and finally started to walk, while producing beads of perspiration and lots of groans. Delores finished the story "Dad continued to use the magic green salve and led a normal life."

Delores remembered another episode. After they had been married a couple of years, Frank developed a severe case of ulcers and a local doctor prescribed a soft diet with lots of milk. This treatment didn't ease Ralph's condition. Delores recalled childhood memory of Doc Bercier and how he magically helped her Dad. Once again the Indian Doctor from Tremont was asked to make another house call. After Doc examined Ralph he immediately took him off the soft diet and returned him to a regular menu but he included his "Blood Zone" tonic on a daily basis. Once again the amazing Indian Medicine man came to the rescue of the Brooks family. Ralph's ulcers were finally under control. Before the Doc left, he looked at Delores and shocked her when he said "I see we are going to have an addition to the family with a little papoose." Delores responded, "I haven't told anyone I'm pregnant, how did you know?" The Doc answered, "I can see it in your eyes." Before Delores gave birth to their first child, she was presented with a gift, a hand made wooden cradle made by the Indian Medicine Man from Tremont.

During my last meeting with Delores and Ralph in the office of the Chesterton cemetery, Ralph told me about the old article in the Chesterton newspaper which quoted Doc Bercier: "They won't let me be buried there; they called me Nigger." Ralph was angered by the story. "I have never refused anyone burial in this cemetery and the article was wrong saying the Doc purchased an eight plot site. There are only six plot sites and all six of the Berciers' were filled." I promised both Delores and Ralph, if they would allow me to use their names in my book, I would try to right the story by telling their side of it. You be the judge.

The Indian Doctor's name turned up one more time in my life. I was discharged from the Marines on Nov. 10, 1945, with no idea of what to do when my Dad suggested that I should consider going to school in Chicago to learn how to service and repair slot machines. This sounded exciting so I did it.

Two weeks later Dad called and told me to come home. The era of slot machines in Porter County was over, he said. County officials had shut down the slot machine business.

During the time that slot machines were in operation, my dad had a partner from Chicago with the name of Al Stern. Mr. Stern was also a pharmacist in downtown Chicago. But he also had a sideline. He furnished a lot of the drugs for the famous Indian Doctor in Tremont.

To this day, I still wear the diamond ring that Mr. Al Stern gave my dad after their "tour" of operation of slot machines in Porter County ended.

Now you know the rest of the story about the famous Indian Doctor from Tremont!

My brother Guy and I had one of our first dogs when we lived above The Club tavern. His name was Tonto named after the famous Lone Ranger's sidekick.

When we first got Tonto, our bartenders, in all of their wisdom, decided he would look much better with his tail cut short rather than going with the natural look. I also think they came to this conclusion after the bar was closed and they had a few drinks.

Unfortunately, they carried this off with a pair of tin snips. When they wacked his tail off, Tonto bolted and ran through the basement of The Club as fast as his short legs would take him.

When they finally caught him, the dog was weak from the loss of blood. So they took him across the street to the funeral home where the mayor was preparing a body for the funeral. The mayor was sober and he put embalming fluid on Tonto's tail. That stopped the bleeding and actually saved the dog's life.

It took Tonto several weeks to recover. Rather than take him outside, we opened the living room window which faced south onto an arched roof that was tar-papered. This turned out to be Tonto's play area and of course, his bathroom.

Mom would make the two of us clean up the roof every Saturday. I didn't tell the Indian Medicine Man about this area, but, of course, his German Shepard "Topay" was used to the "inside facilities," or so he told me.

In 1938, Mom and Dad woke the two of us at 4:00a.m. and told us to get dressed quickly. "The Court House is on fire and the hot cinders and debris are landing on the roof next door right on Tonto's play area." We dressed fast with the thought of being burned out of our apartment. As we were leaving, I saw a fireman on the arched roof with a shovel scooping and throwing hot embers to the sidewalk below.

Porter County Courthouse before fire

The next day we returned to our apartment with no damage to either building, but the Porter County Court House was badly damaged. It was completely gutted with the clock tower on the ground and only the main walls standing. The newspaper, the "Vidette Messenger," told the story about the LaPorte fire truck that tipped over on State Route 2 on the way to the fire, killing one fireman. At 10 years of age, the memory of this fire remained with me for many years.

Another lasting memory came later at the dedication of the new and refurbished Court House. I was taking my third ride in the very small elevator of the Court House on Dedication Day in 1937 when it stopped between floors for almost three hours. There were six people stuck in a very small space and one of the girls became ill. It was not a pleasant experience. I remember being so happy to crawl out of that small space. To this date, I have walked up the stairs every time I visit the Court House.

On a very hot summer night, my brother and a couple of friends wanted to spend the night at Johnson's Beach. I raised so much fuss that Mom said, "If you are staying over night, I'll let you go under one condition." "What's that?" Guy said. Mom explained in no uncertain terms that the condition was that his younger brother had to accompany him. Guy reluctantly agreed. So off we went to check out the girls on an overnight on Lake Michigan's shoreline.

The four of us built a bonfire at Johnson's Beach and settled in for the night. At 2:00a.m. Dad surprised us. He said, "Boys, I have to take your friends back to Valpo because there's been an accident in the family. We have to go to your Aunt Ethel's house in Waterford."

On the way to Waterford, Dad explained what had happened. Our cousin Dick Kunkel was 21 years old and had just been promoted to Sports Editor of the Michigan

City News Dispatch. He was writing a three-part story on sailing as a beginner on Lake Michigan.

There were three of them in the sailboat when a storm came up before they could return to harbor. The boat capsized. According to the two survivors, they only had two lifejackets on board and since Dick was an excellent swimmer, he told the others to take the jackets while he tried to swim to the breakwater.

When we arrived at the lighthouse in Michigan City, they had just recovered our cousin's body. It was just daybreak when we drove by our Aunt Ethel's house. Then, Dad turned the car around and continued driving only to return 15 minutes later. He told us to wait in the car as he approached the front porch. We had no idea that Aunt Ethel was sitting on the porch when we drove by the first time. She had recognized Dad's car, so I guess Dad wanted to collect his thoughts first.

Then we heard a scream that to this day still haunts me. That's when Dad told Aunt Ethel about Dick's death.

Dick had a bright future as a young sports editor, but tragically he only wrote part one of the three-part sailing story. I'm sure one very important part of his completed series would have covered boat safety and having a life jacket available for every person aboard.

Our apartment was small, so my older brother Guy and I slept in one bedroom and mom and dad were right next to us with a connecting door. There were many nights that we would hear dad come to bed and start his nightly coughing spells. They were strong and long and at the ages of nine and twelve we were always pleasantly surprised to see dad alive the next day.

My first brush with the death of a friend came one night when we were wakened at 2 a.m. Walter Bosell was in the bathroom with both Mom and Dad and we could hear them talking about internal bleeding and how the blood looked like coffee. Walter was my "buddy" and I usually got the opportunity to travel with him whenever he would go out of town. By seven o'clock the next day my good friend was across the street in the mayor's mortuary.

My dad believed the mayor's theory on gambling went something like this: "Gambling is going on and will continue to go on, so we will have our own people run it. No outsiders." According to Dad there was never any kind of a pay-off to the mayor, he stuck by his theory.

The open horse bookie was very professionally run by having the Western Union ticker tape machine located in my parent's bedroom. A fellow by the name of Gill Johnson was usually the only one in that room. He sat at the table/desk and announced the races from the beginning to the end.

The open room had chalkboards hanging on the wall so as the odds would change, or the results would come in, the board operator could make the changes and post the results. Telephones were also important to the operation because Dad had special customers who would call in to make their bet. One that I remember well was Mrs. "B." She had a running account that was settled every week. Mrs. "B" lived on Washington Street and came from one of the better families in town. She was also considered to be one of the better handicappers in Valparaiso.

Big Bud Gott ended up as my dad's partner in the Bookie. He seemed to be the numbers man and had the ability to handle situations. It was a daily routine six days a week: the scratch sheets were picked up at the railroad station and distributed free or sold to certain customers throughout the community. The entire bookie business was well run and seemed to have a place in the community. This last statement would rustle a few of John Wolf's feathers, but I will only say "Amen" to that.

Because of the "business" activity, my brother and I often made our own decisions. We went to Meaghar's drug store for a banana split and did this regularly. The drug store was the site of a hot story and it went something like this: the owner, James Meaghar, had his small office on an open balcony over-looking the entire store, including the great soda fountain. Legend is that this actually happened. There was a small, self-contained hot peanut stand at the end of the soda fountain and one busy day Mr. Meaghar, in a very loud voice, shouted to his two employees, "Would someone please get the man by the nuts." According to the late Chicago Tribune critic, Will Leonard: "Legend, of course, is something that can be believed in, in whole or in part." Well, this story moved around the town like wild fire.

It was during this period in my young life that movies were big and heroes were looked for and found. One of my early heroes was "Wild" Bill Wellman. He directed one of the first huge technicolor films, "Wings." I would go to see that movie for five straight nights just to see my name on the screen. In fact, I would see the start of the late show just to see it twice a night. Follow these great nights with a banana split at the drug store and my evening was complete! Life was simpler in those days.

The first day I saw Broncho John Sullivan walking on Lincolnway in Valparaiso, I knew he was someone important. He was always dressed in a dark suit, white shirt, and a thin string tie with a 10-gallon Stetson covering his long white hair. His mustache gave him the look of how a real true Wild West hero should look. When I was nine years old, I was privileged to see Broncho John Sullivan's son John "Texas Jack" Sullivan's Wild West show when it performed in Valparaiso in the empty lot near the Pennsylvania railroad where R. W. Pool is now located. The owner of the vacant lot was one of the original poker players above The Club tavern, Mr. Goddard. The same man owned the building where our dog Tonto played while recovering from his tail-clipping episode. Texas Jack was considered to be the best trick shot artist in the world and appeared as a stunt man in many cowboy movies out of Hollywood. Quoting from the "Broncho John Sullivan's Memories of Half a Century", as told to and recorded by his son, "Broncho John fell in love with the Vale of Paradise and started to use Valpo as his eastern headquarters."

First known photo of Broncho John Sullivan-cowboy, Indian scout, army quartermaster and showman. Born 1859 and died in Valparaiso, 1951

In 1884 Dr. Carver proposed a second Wild West show to operate independently of the Buffalo Bill show. Broncho John was a member of the "Buffalo Bill's Wild West Show" as one of the longhaired cowboy riders, ropers and shots. Dr. Carver asked Broncho John to be his aide and to be in charge of all cowboys, Indians and livestock. They used about thirty-five Indians with the show. The Indians were not long removed from the bloody war trails and were full of queer ideas and moved to "dig up" the tomahawk upon the slightest provocation. Broncho John was the only one who could handle them, as they had known him in their own country and trusted him.

True Friends: Broncho John and Buffalo Bill

In the routine course of the new show, the tour finally arrived in Valparaiso in 1884 for a series of exhibitions in the fair grounds. These shows were usually put on in ballparks, fairgrounds, or parks where there was a walled enclosure and seating arrangements.

From the start Dr. Carvers Wild West Show seemed destined to encounter bad luck and adverse weather conditions and in 1884 the outfit hit the rocks and was stranded. Among those stranded were Broncho John's wild animal friends: a huge Rocky Mountain black bear named "Uno," a very majestic bald eagle called "Abe," a pet deer and a team of exceptionally large elk with gorgeous spreads of antlers.

Dr. Carver and the rest of the company followed the line of least resistance and quickly vamoosed to Chicago, but there were about thirty-five Indians with their squaws and papooses left behind in Valpo. They were mighty pathetic and in desperate circumstances. They looked to their friend Broncho John to care for them.

They made camp for nearly three weeks in Indian teepees near the Pennsylvania depot while Broncho John succeeded in arranging for the government to furnish transportation. This was July 1884, one year before my dad was born.

During this period some amusing incidents occurred. The Indians had no funds with which to purchase food and stark hunger was their lot. At the end of the first week it was noticed that a number of the town's pet dogs had mysteriously disappeared. By the middle of the following week dogs were becoming scarce in Valparaiso and had begun to disappear from farms ten miles away. It was whispered about that the dogs were finding their way to the boiling pots of the Sioux Indians. At the time, it took a lot of diplomacy on Broncho John's part to avoid an Indian war in Valparaiso.

In his "Memories," Broncho John mentioned the many friends and chums he made in Valparaiso, some whose names I recognized: Al Heineman, John Sievers, Pete

Horn, Pat Clifford, Dan Kelly, Chan and Charlie Sager and Doc Powell. Two names that never made the "Memories" were of young men who were caught several times playing cowboys and Indians in Mr. Sullivan's shed behind his house on Erie Street where he stored his stage coaches. The guilty culprits were a young Harley Snyder and a small Dick Beach. They were never punished too harshly because they returned to the scene of their crime several times.

My final story about one of my heroes, Broncho John Sullivan, is of his desire to leave his stagecoaches for the historical value they would have after his death. Porter County is missing the boat with such an important part of history right at its fingertips and no one seems to see it.

"Broncho John" Sullivan's Red Concord Stage Coach

The stagecoach in storage should have a prominent spot in the new Welcome Center to be located in Porter County on State Road 49 north of Chesterton. This is exactly what Broncho John Sullivan had in mind when he gave the coaches to the county.

During the serial on HBO called Deadwood, both Broncho John Sullivan and his son John "Texas Jack"

Sullivan, were mentioned as friends of Wild Bill Hickok (1837 – 1876) and Calamity Jane.

The short story that I am about to tell is a true story and it happened because my brother Guy and I were on our own a lot while Mom and Dad ran the business. The horse bookie and card room was separated at the end by a partition wall that did not go all the way to the very high ceiling and, along the wall was a small storage room that backed up to the ladies rest room that serviced the tavern below. The partition wall was made of "beaverboard" (that is somewhat of a joke) that was soft enough that even young boys could punch peepholes by simply using a screwdriver. My brother was nine years old and I was six . . . when we poked some peepholes in the storage wall directly in front of the ladies restroom.

I was relating this story to my mother when she said, "I have heard you mention that you would like to write a book. What would you put in a book that would be interesting to other people?" When I got to the part of telling her where the peepholes were located, I realized that I had her complete attention. I continued by saying that after many nights of sitting at our posts and keeping records, the two of us came to the conclusion that when ladies go to the restroom, they rarely come up the stairs by themselves. There were usually two at a time, and we also took notice that only one out of four groups would close the door. I looked at Mom and her mouth was wide open and she seemed to be a little shocked.

One night we were at our posts and two ladies were using the facility and they left the door wide open. Our two pair of young, lustful eyes were less than four feet from the two ladies and we were glued to our peepholes. During our watch, one lady complained to the other, "Damn it, there is no toilet paper." My brother was a little quicker and older and since we were in the storeroom, he grabbed a roll of toilet paper and tossed it over the short

partition where it hit the floor and the standing lady picked it up and gave it to the sitting lady. After that, the standee turned to the wall and said, "Thank you." Then I stated, "Mom, they still didn't close the door."
My mother, shaking her finger said, "Before you get the book printed, I need to read it!"

The peepholes in the storage room were the ones we used most, but we also had several holes in the wooden floor that would give us a good viewing in case there was a fight in the bar. This seemed to happen regularly and we knew by the sound of the shuffling chairs when it was "fight time."

Dad hired a bouncer who was considered to be one of the toughest men in Valparaiso. His name was Ed, better known as "Big Ed." It only took about three weeks to crown a new king of the hill and Ed quit the business.

Dad had his own theory about how to run a bar. First, he always felt that anyone who could handle drinking and be sociable could drink, and age did not enter into the picture. George Beach was eighteen and considered a customer, even though the law specified that to be in a bar you had to be 21 years old. It was called "Guy's Law."

"Guy's Law" also clicked in when two customers had a dispute that couldn't be settled. The entire bar would go outside the back door where the two participants would settle the argument. When the fight would go to the outside arena, my brother and I would come down the back stairs to watch the fight. Our parents would be so involved that they would not notice two young fight fans with great seats.

I realize that sex entered my thinking at a very early age, because a car dealer in Valparaiso (Buck Bowman) told this story many times. Western Union had a school directly next door to The Club and most of the students were young girls from 18 to 30 years old. I was walking with my dad and Buck Bowman when (according to Buck) I said, "Buck, do you see those two girls in front of us? Well, the tall one is putting out!" Some place at the early age of six I heard someone say that, so I thought it was worth repeating. Maybe we spent too much time at those peep holes because Buck told the story to everyone in town!

There was another experience that sticks in my memory. I always walked the two blocks home from Gardner Elementary School for lunch. Mom would fix me a sandwich and a bowl of soup and, while she was doing this, I would on occasion slip behind the bar and draw a snit (small glass) of cold beer. If there were customers at the bar, they would not tell my mother, they just thought it was cute and funny to see a young squirt drinking a little beer.

In the years when bars were just getting started, Indiana had a few unique laws. One was that women were not allowed to tend bar unless they were married to the owner. Another was that women were not allowed to sit at the bar. This seemed to be one of Indiana's very unusual laws. A third law was "no drinking on Sunday." So, to see my mother tending bar during the day time just did not seem right, but she did an excellent job when it came to unusual situations.

One noontime, I had just finished a liverwurst on rye with just a touch of cold beer, when a big fat lady called Dimp came in the front door. She headed right for the end of the bar, where her boyfriend Harold was lapping up a few brews. Dimp did not say one word, but she picked up Harold's half empty beer mug and hit him on the top of the head with it. The blood and the beer were running down Harold's smiling face, and he started to laugh as Dimp walked out the door without saying one word.

My mom took Harold into the kitchen and pulled out the first aid kit. She cleaned him up and gave him her home-taught first aid treatment. The damage to Harold's head was considered minor and it only took away about twenty minutes of his drinking time.

When I first started to tend bar at the Palace, Dad gave me this advice: "When you serve a customer a drink he becomes your responsibility, and as long as you continue to sell him booze he is yours. If you think he has too much to drink, you should "86" him (cut him off)." There were many times that we would make arrangements to drive a good customer home after he had lost a "bout with the bar." Another one of "Guys Laws" was never buy a drunk a drink.

The definition of a "26 girl." Twenty-six was a popular dice game that was a permanent part of The Club's décor. The 26 table was designed like a small blackjack table, covered with green felt. It was high enough that the "26 girl" would sit on a bar stool while the customer would stand in front of the table. This table was against the wall and a floodlight hung over it to show off the table, but mainly to show off the "26 girl." This girl always seemed to be good looking. I am sure this came from another one of "Guy's Laws." He always told me it is just as easy to hire good looking people as it is to hire ugly ones, and the good looking ones will make you more money.

I have set the scene to finish my "26" story. It was lunchtime and I was home having my favorite liverwurst on rye. At this time I am thirteen and my older brother is sixteen. I am halfway through lunch when Guy Jr. bursts in the back door, at the very same time the good-looking Spanish "26 girl" is coming down the back stairway. They met at the backdoor at the same time and this girl, named Rita, laid a tongue swallowing wet kiss on Brother Guy.

At the very same time my brother Guy was having his mouth massaged, Mother popped out of the kitchen and grabbed Rita by the hair, spun her around like a top, and followed up with a tongue-lashing I will never forget. Guy went up the stairs like a shot while Mom continued to lash out at Rita. I enjoyed the whole episode. It made my dry sandwich go down with ease, and while Mom was working over Rita, I slipped behind the bar for a little snit.

I never heard Mom follow up with a lecture to her 16-year-old son. I thought he would be "dead meat," but I think Mom saw him as an innocent bystander. I am sure Guy had a few thoughts about Rita after his chance meeting at the back door.

It was during this period that The Club turned into an entertainment/nightclub. My dad sent Ernie Roach to a bartender's school in Chicago. Ernie was about 6'3" tall with premature gray hair. He was good looking and smart. Each week Ernie would return to work on Friday's and Saturday's with a new mixed drink. He would always try the drink of the week out on Hymie Magid, a young heavy-set Jewish fellow who sometimes stayed overnight by sleeping on a cot in the horse-bookie's upstairs. Hymie was well liked by everyone and he loved to sing. He also was given the pleasant chore of picking up the entertainment on weekends.

Sam Linkemer was another good Jewish boy, also well liked by the night people of the town, who dealt in the sale of alcohol as a lubricant. His singing voice was never the quality of Hymie Magid, however. Entertainment and drinking were new to Valparaiso, but it seemed to hit the spot on weekends. The same band was always at The Club to backup whatever entertainers were booked. The members were Walter Carr on piano, Dick Marks on guitar, and Roy Wheeler or Tracy Havens on the drums. I can still remember looking at Ray Wheeler's drum set. It actually had Band-Aids on the face of the snare drum to patch several holes.

This band featured a trumpet player who was well known in Los Angeles and Chicago, Ted Bullock. When Ted was short of cash, he would float a loan with my mother and leave a mouthpiece from his trumpet as collateral.

The band always had a sign on the stage in front of a stuffed cat. The sign simply read FEED THE KITTY. It seemed to work, because they were always able to divide up their take at the end of the night.

To my brother and me, the entertainment never could hold our interest like the fights or the peepholes. Extra bartenders always seemed to be part of the entertainment at The Club. Buck Fife was one of the most unusual and interesting.

My folks could not understand how Buck would come in sober, work a complete shift, and leave half in the bag though no one ever saw him take a drink.

At the age of 13, I wanted to know and understand everything about the bar business. So, I did my own investigation into the mystery of the intoxicated bartender.

Indiana had another unusual law that stated, "When you empty a liquor bottle, it was mandatory that you immediately break the bottle." I hid in the basement and watched Buck bring down a bucket full of empties. He then used a heavy metal rod to tap out the bottom of each one. It did not take long to solve the mystery! Each empty bottle had a good inch or so of lubricant that he poured into one bottle and then, after disposing of the broken bottles, he drank his mixture. This practice by Buck got him the title of being one of the neatest bartenders on the night shift. I never told my parents about how Buck salvaged the dregs of the bottles to keep his bartender conversation at its peak.

Buck Fife was, at one time, a great pitching prospect and was signed by the New York Yankees. However, on his second off-season he had a car wreck in front of the high school where he hit a huge tree and he was almost killed. When he was asked about the huge hole in his head, his response was, "It's just a hole in my head where half of my brains leaked out."

My brother Guy and I seemed to learn many lessons during this period of our lives. Neither one of us were smokers or drinkers. We both learned from Guy's Laws that *"It's made to sell, not to drink."*

In the Wellman family, when it came to discipline, it was Leona Wellman who was in charge. For instance, if we misbehaved in the back seat of the car, we could expect Mom to take off her shoe while driving and take a swipe at the guilty party.

Once we were returning home from a doctor's appointment in LaPorte on State Route 2 when the back door flew open and I flew out hitting the pavement. I bounced a few times like a rubber ball. Amazingly, I landed on my feet!

I almost got back to the car before Mom came to a complete stop. She put me in the front seat and headed to Porter County Hospital located on Jefferson Street across from the Valparaiso Public Library.

I was a mess. When I was cleaned up, I didn't have any broken bones, but I sure had sore muscles. My face looked like I had been attacked with an Urschel meat grinder.

There was a rumor that my older brother had pushed me out of the car. Frankly, I couldn't recall what happened, so I didn't make an issue of it. Once again, Mother proved that she could handle pressure and any situation. She didn't even swing at me with one of her shoes!

THE CLUB
JUST LIKE THE MOVIE "THE STING"

By the time I was 16 years old, I had a fair understanding of what it took to run a first class bar. I also was gaining on my knowledge of the gambling business as well. Both enterprises had to be run just like any business. But both faced the very real possibility that the political atmosphere would change for any number of reasons, and that sufficient pressure would be put on the powers in charge to suggest that it may be best to shut down one or the other of the enterprises for a while.

This same political atmosphere shut down horse betting in 1939 in Lake County, Indiana. One thing led to another and Mr. Sammy Mullins, who had an apartment on 5th Avenue in Gary across the street from Horace Mann High School, approached my Dad about joining him as a partner in a betting parlor just across the county line. Their plan was simple. They rented a building on U.S. 20 called Camp 20 and started a horse bookie business as close to Gary as you can get and still be in Porter County.

I worked at Camp 20 a few days a week during the summer just doing odd jobs and I enjoyed watching the customers. Horse betters are cut from a different cloth. They try to come up with different kinds of handicap systems to beat the odds. There are good handicappers and there are bad ones, but to make a living off of betting on the horses is almost an impossible feat.

Saturdays at Camp 20 seemed to attract a special customer. Most wore short-sleeved Hawaiian shirts and Panama straw hats. I mentioned this to my Dad and he didn't hesitate to respond: "Those fellows are all Priests out of the Gary, East Chicago area." He added, "They are usually great customers, but not good handicappers."

I wasn't at Camp 20 on the Wednesday that the Indiana State Police made a raid, but I heard my dad tell my mother they allowed the customers to leave. It was a real break for my dad that the Lieutenant in charge was a very good customer and a friend. His name was SUDS and when he approached Dad, he said, "Guy, put your money in the waste basket and put a newspaper over it. Walk out of the back door like you were one of the customers. Come back tonight to pick up the money. Go!!"

Dad didn't question SUDS and when he returned at 10:00 pm the money was just where he left it. But Camp 20 had just ended a short lived but interesting life. Because gambling didn't expand in Porter County, folks couldn't count on it as a vocation or a source of recreation for that matter. Gambling in the next county over also encountered a different but similar outcome.

Big Bud Gott jumped at the opportunity to build a small block building to house a betting parlor just off of the old U.S. 12 in Porter County. This time my good friend Murph Shauer (Valparaiso Movie Magnet?) decided to go to work there for the summer.

It was during the second week that they discovered on opening the door a bomb sitting on the counter with some kind of timing device. The bomb didn't go off, but the message got to the owners. Management decided that the border business wasn't as good as they thought it would be. So Valparaiso became the only safe place to operate the bookie business in those days.

Even so, the bookie business seemed to disappear from the Wellman family when The Corral opened its doors. But it didn't leave town. Big Bud Gott continued to operate in what was locally known as "The Hole." This was in the basement of the Block Hotel located on the south side of the main street adjacent to Philly's Confectionary and the well known Premiere Theater.

I have the feeling that Mother had a lot to do with my dad not being involved with "The Hole." Her intuition was always good and I think she realized that times were changing. My guess is she thought the Mayor's attitude about gambling should be relegated to the past. He once said: "We are going to have gambling, and we will run it with local people and not outsiders." It turned out that Mom was right on.

Whether run by the locals or outsiders, gambling was fast approaching its end in Porter County. In 1950, the open bookie room was to leave Valparaiso, and it's never returned.

My last personal contact with "The Hole" came on the night Liz, my wife, and I were on our honeymoon in Chicago. It was in 1948 when we were married in Crown Point, IN. Our good friends Jim and Betty Eason stood up for us and the reception (four people) was held in Clems Bar located on the square. The menu included ham sandwiches on rye and whisky sours. We paid in cash (no credit cards) and the new bride and groom headed for the Windermere East Hotel located near the Field Museum close to the outer drive in Chicago.

At 2:00a.m. our hotel telephone woke us up. Evidently my best man returned to Valparaiso and ended up at The Corral where he proceeded to have a number of drinks and tell everyone where the bride and groom were staying in Chicago.

The voice sounded like it was coming from someone talking in a barrel when he said, "Bill, this is Diz. Are you giving Liz the biz?" This call was repeated two more times before I convinced the caller that it was funny the first time, but the third call should be the last.

Diz was the nickname for Diz Beiers who worked in the horse parlor above The Club when I was growing up. He worked for "The Hole" and he made the calls to us from there. Diz had a father who dealt in real estate. His yard sign has always remained with me:

"A.C. BEIERS FOR LAND THAT YOU DESIRES
UNITED STATES AND CANADA."

Betting on horses in open rooms finally came to an end. But there were always a few bookmakers around who would take a bet without being bothered by the authorities.

When Guy was leaving for his first year at Indiana University, Dad's advice has stuck in my memory. He said, "Keep your peter in your pants and you will get along just fine." Knowing what college life was like, I am sure that my brother broke that particular one of Guy's Laws many times during the next four years in Bloomington.

During my high school days, my best friend was Bob Wilson. I spent many nights at the Wilson home under the watchful eyes of his parents, Sadie and Zeb.

Bob's Dad was an engineer on the Pennsylvania Railroad, operating two runs in and out of Chicago five days a week. The train was nicknamed, "The Dummy." It didn't know which way it wanted to go, I suppose.

I remember Valparaiso had a large roundhouse, which enabled the train crew to turn the steam engine around on the huge turntable for the trip back to Chicago.

Sadie, Bob's mother, "saved" my life many times when I returned to civilian life. It occurred every time I joined returning veterans celebrating their homecomings. If I lost the bout with the bar, Sadie would come to the rescue with her famous "pink" tonic. Believe me, I was grateful for her assistance.

Before entering the service and still in high school, Bob and I worked for Tom Marimon as filling station attendants. We pumped gas, checked oil and even washed windshields. This job was a great learning experience for two active 16-year-old boys.

It was 1942 when the two of us entered into a partnership. We bought a 1920 Model T convertible from Ike Skinner for $8.50. It is still a mystery to me how we arrived at this "high" price.

We had this feeling when we bought this car. We asked ourselves, "Do you think we were taken?" This car looked better in the over grown field than it did sitting on the paved lot at Marimon's garage.

Tom gave us permission to pull our vehicle into a main stall in his garage. It was obvious to all of the employees,

Bob Wilson, Bill Wellman – Before!

Wellman and Wilson had no idea how to tackle the major job of converting "an almost nothing" to "a working something" on wheels.

We started the process while one of the older mechanics watched. It didn't take him long to say, "You guys have no idea what you are doing." Then he said, "Move over and let me show you how."

The transformation from a wreck to a cool looking black convertible with bright orange spoke wheels took a month. The process reminded me of the story in Tom Sawyer when Huckleberry Finn conned many people to paint Aunt Polly's fence while he watched!

Both of us were excited and proud of the outcome. A neat 1920 automobile, free and clear!

We called it a convertible, but neither of us had enough money to purchase the canvas to cover the frame.

If it rained, we would turn on our newly installed electric windshield wipers and snap the roof frame up into place, just for laughs.

The 1920 Model T Ford didn't have a heater. When necessary, we pulled up a couple of floorboards to expose the hot manifold, giving us enough heat to keep our feet warm and almost dry.

Bob Wilson – After!

In 1938, Mother convinced Dad to buy a house at Wauhob Lake four miles from Valparaiso. I'm convinced she thought Brother Guy and I had enough education by living next to a horse bookie and over a bar since 1933. It also could have been too much access to our peepholes and the 26 girls.

I drove "our" car the four miles to the high school on a daily basis while my partner and I shared it on weekends for a variety of short adventures in and around the Vale of Paradise, "Valparaiso."

One trip that sticks in my memory occurred on a trip to Hebron for a fast speed softball game. Bob and I invited Shirley Foster and Kate Hippensteel to join us on the 14-mile adventure.

I was driving on State Road 2 heading south around 40 miles per hour, when the front right tire came off and shot past our car into a cornfield. Bob ran after it in hot pursuit as soon as the car stopped. We had to retrieve the tire and put it back on the wheel using a nut lug from each of the other three wheels.

Fortunately, we arrived in time for the game. Mr. Johnson gave me $5 for playing, which covered our expenses. The return trip was uneventful and we ended the day at Sievers enjoying the soda fountain's famous milk shakes. What a great time we had in those simpler days!

In April 1943, I surrendered my 50% interest in the car to Bob as I headed for San Diego and Boot Camp. Later I heard a rumor that Bob sold the car for $65.50 when he left for the Army. I think he still owes me my share!

Moving to Wauhob Lake, north of Valparaiso, was great for me because I loved to hunt and fish. But brother Guy had other interest, which kept him form learning how to swim. The lack of not being able to swim gave us a scare as five of us took a small boat to the center of the lake for a little fun!

We were in the deepest part of the lake to take advantage of cold and clean water. Guy was showing his best imitation of Mark Spitz as he "dog-paddled" around the boat, made a grab for the boat and missed! As he went down twice I sprung into action. Grabbing the oar, I leaned out to give him something to hang onto as he came up for the third time and gave him a "shot" to the head (accidentally!) We pulled him into the boat coughing, sputtering and swearing. He actually thought I hit him on purpose.

This story on being a swimmer showed up when Guy moved west.

Guy's baseball career took him to Ogden, Utah where he was a player/manager for a couple of years. He also was hired as an assistant football coach at Weber State. They evidently liked him as a football coach because in order to keep him they needed to offer him more money. The only opening on the budget was the need for a head swimming coach. This news broke me up! A swimming coach who couldn't swim! He took the job.

I asked him how he was going to handle this job and he told me the first meeting with the swim team went like this, "The first rule that I must insist on, when we win our first meet and all of the following victories, NEVER – NEVER throw the coach in the pool."

Rumor around the campus was, Coach Wellman has a very unique ear infection and it could be fatal if he was dumped in the pool!

It amazed me that he could be the head swim coach and not be able to swim a stroke. Weber State had a winning season his first year.

Guy and his wife Francis were going to celebrate their 50th wedding anniversary in Flat Rock, North Carolina. Daughter Connie made all of the arrangements. During the celebration I presented Guy with a brass platted oar inscribed, "TO BROTHER GUY – IN MEMORY OF YOUR SWIMMING LESSON!"

My graduation class was the class of 1943, Valparaiso High School, Valparaiso, Indiana. My brother Guy labeled this class as the first class in the history of the school to rebel against authority. He may have been right.

We had a total of 126 seniors and all of the boys knew that unless they had a health problem we were all headed for the draft immediately after graduation. Then, patriotism was so thick you could cut it with a dull knife. It seemed like everyone wanted to enlist as soon as possible.

I wanted to be among the first to go. So in January 1943, I decided if I joined the Marine Corps., I would get into the war faster than the rest of my classmates. So I gave my goodbyes to the rest of my teachers, friends and family and four of us hopped on a Greyhound bus and headed to Indianapolis to enlist in the Marine Corps.

Gene Hart and Dick Eason were one year older than my friend Jack Cavell and myself. The last thing on my mind was the possibility that I wouldn't pass the physical examination. I was in great condition with very little body fat on a very young hard body.

While I was going through this "not so tough" physical exam, a Navy doctor informed me that I had failed and that I had high blood pressure. This came close to putting me in a depression, but the only thing that saved me was, we really didn't understand depression like we do today.

The bus ride home was one of the longest Indianapolis to Valparaiso trips of my life. My three friends – Gene, Dick and Jack – were already on a train headed for boot camp in San Diego while I was headed back to high school and all those folks I had left behind.

The desire to join the Marine Corps. was stronger than ever. The next day I went to see Dr. Malcom Fife, our family doctor, to check on my condition. Yes, Dr. Fife was the father to Buck Fife whom our family regarded as the neatest bartender to ever work in The Club tavern located on 21 Washington Street.

Dr. Fife was about 5'6" and weighed about 140 pounds. He was a retired Army colonel from World War I. When I told him that a Navy doctor had turned me down because he said I had high blood pressure, he cut loose some language that I had never heard before even in The Club on a party night. I won't share his exact words, but they went something like this: "Most f...... doctors who join the service do so because they couldn't make it in the real world and this son of a ..... was so far off in turning you down for high blood pressure."

Then this former military doctor gave me a small bottle of liquid with the following instructions: "The next time you take the trip to Indy, I want you to take a teaspoon of this secret formula one half hour before you are to take the exam and you will have the last laugh on that boob Navy swab jockey who is masquerading as a doctor."

In April 1943, I quit high school for the second time and jumped aboard a Greyhound bus to give the Marine Corps. one more chance to turn me into a "mean fighting machine." To make sure I was covering all bases, I arrived in Indianapolis on Tuesday, April 12, and stayed over night in the Washington Hotel, which was known as the skinniest hotel in town. At that time, Indianapolis was known as "Indy no place."

Before going to sleep, I reminisced a little, thinking that it was only a year earlier that my good friends Bob Wilson, Breezy Johnson and I stayed in this very same hotel for the weekend attending the state high school basketball tournament at Hinckle Fieldhouse. The most exciting thing we did was to drop balloons filled with water on unsuspecting workers on the street below. No one was injured and no arrests were made, fortunately.

There was nothing to distract an eighteen-year old in Indianapolis in 1943 so I had turned in early knowing that the physical was to start at 8 a.m. The following morning, I ate a light breakfast and pulled out Dr. Fife's secret potion. Since I didn't have a spoon and my desire to pass the physical was so strong, I tipped the small bottle up and swallowed twice as much as Dr. Fife had prescribed.

When my turn came to see the same Navy doctor who had turned me down in January, I had persuaded myself that my blood pressure was perfect and I was convinced that he couldn't possibly remember me. In fact, I was so relaxed that I came very close to failing the eye exam. I was almost giddy when I raised my right hand as I was sworn in as a United States Marine.

The trip back to Valparaiso was one of the shortest in my life. I was so excited that I had passed my physical and made it into the service, rather than being drafted.

My first telephone call after arriving in Valparaiso was to Dr. Fife to tell him the good news. The doctor's answer went something like this: "I told you that f...... son of a b.... didn't realize that you have what I call an athlete's heart which means that when you get f...... excited, the adrenalin runs high. Then it settles down in a short time. That bonehead better stay in the navy because he will be swallowed up in the real world."

Now, I'm leaving high school for the second time in two and one-half months. I am really excited and looking forward to getting aboard a train at the Grand Trunk station and heading for boot camp in San Diego.

My folks took me to the train station and we said our goodbyes for the second time. I boarded the train heading for what I thought would be excitement and adventure.

The trip to California was fast. George Neely was on the same train heading to Navy boot camp also in San Diego. Every time I see George he reminds me of our anniversary day in April waiting for the train to pull into Valparaiso. This somewhat reminded me of the tension and excitement in the movie, "High Noon."

Valparaiso Train Depot – April 1943

Chapter Three

WORLD WAR II

The first day of boot camp was most impressive and was purposely designed to let us know exactly what would occur during each one of the next 70 days of our lives as Marine Corps recruits. Sgt. Rawlinson let us know without a doubt from that moment we belonged to him and our "asses" were in his charge every minute of every day. We were Platoon 386 USMC.

I had a paralyzing fear of this man. The scar that began at his right ear and ended under his chin made him even more intimidating. (Our corporal told us the scar was a souvenir of a bayonet wound suffered during the Nicaraguan Campaign.) It didn't take me long to realize Sgt. Rawlinson was teaching us to survive, how not to get killed.

To this day I can remember my first Marine Corp payday. We stood in line to get into the barracks, and then stood at attention in front of the sergeant to pick up our pay. Addressing the sergeant as "sir" came next. When he handed me my pay, I saluted and said, "Thank you, sir." He stopped his routine and looked up at me: "Son, don't you ever thank anyone for any pay. You worked hard for this money and there is no need to thank anyone." I said, "Thank you sir," and got the hell out of there.

In my platoon there was a big kid from Chesterton, Indiana with the name of Warren Boo. The sergeant fell in love with the name Boo. He told Warren the first day, when I yell Boo, I want you to jump and if you do not jump high enough, I will be the first one to tell you.

We had a celebrity in our platoon: the big band leader Dick Jergens. There was no preferential treatment for Dick during boot camp, but he went directly to special services after we finished our ten weeks. Our paths would cross again in 1970 when I signed a contract with the Dick Jergens' Big Band to play a one-night stand at Bridge VU Theater in Valparaiso, Indiana. When I asked Mr. Jergens about boot camp, he did not remember me, but he did remember our sergeant.

Another member of our platoon I cannot forget did not make it the ten weeks. He just seemed to disappear after about six weeks. His name was Merrcer and he had the unique ability to use his top bunk as a piece of equipment using the rafters to show everyone how he could give himself oral sex by being almost double jointed in the top bunk. He was really proud of this little trick, but I am sure it did not impress our sergeant. There were many times over seas that I thought about Merrcer, and I finally came to the conclusion that Mr. Merrcer wasn't a dumb Marine anymore, he was a sick civilian.

The ten weeks went by fast. I was in the best shape of my life, at 18 years of age the sins of over eating and over drinking had not yet affected my body. I did not give the sergeant an excuse to single me out for any of his little punishments. I was a good Marine. One of his punishments was for the smokers. If he caught someone throwing a cigarette butt on the ground, he would give them a needle and a long thread and send them throughout the camp (during their free time) to collect 200 to 300 butts to string onto the thread, making a big necklace of cigarette butts.

If someone dropped a rifle on the ground, they could count on sleeping with it, and then standing in front of their barracks with their rifle in hand, repeating over and over for one hour, "This is my gun (grab their crotch), this is for shooting, this is for fun."

One of the sergeant's favorite punishments was saved for really dumb stunts. I never had to do this one, but it seemed like someone would screw up once a week. The punishment was that they had to circle the barracks for one hour with a bucket over their head and a stick in their hand. Each time they would hit the bucket they would yell out, "I am a shit head." The other platoons always enjoyed seeing someone make fools out of themselves, and, of course, the sergeant felt like every punishment was getting us ready for things to come that would not be humorous.

We had finished the rifle range and we were headed into our final weeks when the sergeant taught me a personal lesson that really stuck with me. During one of our training days, he caught me without my helmet. His explanation went something like this: "Wellman, you have to learn that your helmet is really an important part of your equipment. When you are in the field, it is your bathtub and your sink for shaving. You must wear it in the field at all times. It could save your life." This infraction would be remembered later on in Okinawa.

The bayonet course was the sergeant's favorite and when he demonstrated he would say, "When you stick the bayonet into the son-of-a-bitch, make sure that you twist it to do more damage. If it gets stuck, don't screw around trying to pull it out, shoot it out and kill the Jap bastard." As you can imagine, this wisdom stuck with us.

The final days of boot camp were really exciting. I was going to be able to go home on furlough, and our platoon graduation coincided with the decision by the Marine Corp to issue a stripe to some boot camp graduates. They were short of non-commissioned officers in the corp., so they gave PFC stripes to 20 out of our platoon. I was one of the 20 and I was surprised and exceptionally proud.

The old timers were shocked that young *jar-heads* would be given a stripe right out of boot camp. I really couldn't understand the logic. Why didn't they issue the stripes to the veterans who were overseas and had battles under their belts? It did not make sense; but I was so proud to have that first stripe put on my uniform I felt like I was the chosen one and almost believed that I really deserved it!

Home on a thirty day furlough, dressed in a Marine uniform and a PFC stripe on my sleeve; what more could a 19-year-old want? The thirty days flew by and then I was in communications school in Camp LeJeune, North Carolina. I decided that on weekends I would go to Wilmington for "R and R." It did not take me long to figure out if I went to a church on Sunday morning and then just stood around for a while looking homesick, some family would ask me to come home for Sunday dinner. About 75% of the time, the family would have a daughter who was 18 to 20 years old. Fifty percent of the time she was nice looking, but 100% of the time the Sunday dinner was great.

PFC W. F. "Bill" Wellman

After several successful weekends, I told my friend Dick Warren how to work the "church scam." He came with me to church the next week and after church we split up and stood around with that sad homesick look and, sure enough, it worked like a charm for both of us. The same family started asking Dick back for Sunday dinner on a steady basis, and I found out that after the war he married the girl from Wilmington and became Vice President of Transportation of National Steel in Portage, Indiana. I felt like I was responsible for this marriage because of my church scam. What a cupid!

In December 1943 we got the word we were being ordered overseas. No more furloughs. No more R and R, and no more Sunday dinners with 50% of the girls being good looking.

My last night in the United States was December 31, 1943 in San Francisco. They gave us leave on New Years Eve and we were told to be ready to board the aircraft carrier, USS

Saratoga, at dawn on New Year's Day 1944. My days of living above a bar had taught me that my father's advice was, "It's made to sell, not to drink." When I had asked him why he drank, he bounced back with, "Do as I say, not as I do." I really never had been drunk; in fact, I did not drink at all. Now here I was, 19 years old, it was our last night in the good old U.S.A., and I got hooked up with some of the older Marines, like 20 or 21 years old. This was their second trip overseas.

The next morning I had a hangover so bad that I prayed to God that if he would just save me from this horrible death, I would never drink again. I really think that hangover had a lot to do with my giving up drinking later on in life.

The USS Saratoga was originally converted to an aircraft carrier in 1922 and was launched on April 7, 1925. This ship was 888 feet long with a beam of 106 feet. It had a top speed of 33.91 knots, a crew of 2,111 and a capacity of 81 aircraft. This was a "shakedown" cruise and the captain got his ship up to 32 knots! It was like a city and we were guests in one of the Navy's finest carriers.

USS Saratoga

It was very easy to get lost on the Saratoga, but in my physical condition I didn't move too far from the head! My hangover turned into seasickness and I didn't eat for four days, except for pieces of bread my buddies would bring back to me from chow.

It was during these four days of near death that an older swab jockey came up to me and said, "Did you hear what happened today at chow?" Of course I said "no" and he continued, "Well, one of your jarheads was going down the ladder when the cook was going by carrying a huge pot of soup into the galley for chow, and this Marine got sick and threw up right into the soup kettle. It made the cook so mad he served it anyhow." This little story turned my stomach the other way and I continued on my hunger strike.

We landed in Pearl Harbor on January 4, 1944, and were there for two weeks. It was during this time that I got my first experience in guard duty. A first lieutenant came up to me and said, "Sergeant, do you know how to handle a forty-five?" My answer was, "Yes sir, I have had training." He then said, "Great, follow me." He took me into an office where another lieutenant was standing guard over a young Marine private. The lieutenant handed me his forty-five and said, "If he tries to leave this room, shoot the son-of-a-bitch." I said, "Yes sir," and took the side arm. The two officers said they would be back in a couple of hours. This young Marine was about 6'2" and weighed over 220 pounds. I was 5'9" and tipped the scales at 155 pounds.

Nothing was said for a little over and hour and then he looked at me and said, "You know I could take that pistol away from you at any time and stick it in your ass." I looked at him and said, "You are forgetting one thing. I have this piece (while I waved the forty-five), and I know how to use it. Did you ever see the size hole this thing makes when it comes out the other side of a body? Now just sit there and I will forget what you just said." The officers came back in an hour and forty-five minutes with two Navy shore patrol and took the prisoner away. The first lieutenant asked me if I had any problems and of course I said, "No sir." The truth is, I almost wet my pants I was so nervous and I have often wondered if I would have had the courage to shoot another Marine if he had tried to take the forty-five away from me. Who knows? The incident went on my record that I served on guard duty and it would show up later on after my overseas adventure.

The city of Honolulu didn't impress me in 1944. It seemed to take on a carnival atmosphere and of course, it reminded me of Norfolk, VA, where there were signs in some yards that stated, "Sailors, Marines and Dogs Keep Off."

It was January 1944, and I found myself standing in line waiting in front of a whorehouse near Honolulu, Hawaii. Twelve of us were waiting like we were going to see a movie in a sold-out theater.

I had no idea what the experience would bring. But I did know I was 19 years old and many miles from Valparaiso, Indiana and I was trying to act like my macho buddies. Not knowing what the future would hold in a time of war, it was not a difficult decision at all.

The line moved slowly, but the smiles on the other Marines as they departed encouraged me to stick out the wait. When it came to my turn to actually enter the house, I walked into a neat living room with over stuffed furniture, carpet on the floors, and pictures on the walls. It could be a living room anyplace in the USA. As I waited along with two other "jar heads," I caught myself thinking, "What the hell am I doing here." This thought disappeared when the Madam tapped me on the shoulder and said, "Son, it's your turn. Come with me." I followed like a very obedient puppy down a dark hallway to one of several bedrooms where she gave me a porcelain wash basin filled with warm water, a bar of soap, and a small clean towel.

The next instructions were, "Son, drop your drawers and give yourself a washing. Your young lady will be with you in a few minutes." Once again, I followed her instructions as if they were given to me by Sgt. Rawlinson in "boot camp." Then I set on the edge of the bed in my Marine issued green shorts eagerly waiting for my next orders.

The elderly lady (I would guess 40 – 45 years old) entered the room once again and said, "Drop your shorts and milk it down for me." I jumped up and proceeded to follow her wishes. I evidently passed her final inspection. Then she asked, "What kind of treatment are you looking for?" I could feel my face flush as I said, "M'am, this is all new to me.

Would you work with me and head me in the right direction. I'm not sure what I'm looking for..." Her next statement really confused me when she said, "I would suggest the Silk Handkerchief Trick!" I must have had that "down-on the Indiana-farm look" when I responded, "What does that consist of?"

Her answer must have unhinged my jaw. My mouth was wide open as I listened to her words: "The girl will take this silk handkerchief and tie as many knots in it as your want and then she will proceed to stuff it up your fanny and then she will perform oral sex (she didn't use that term) and when you are ready to have an orgasm, you will tap her on the shoulder and she will quickly pull the end of the scarf out of your backside (again, she didn't use that term) very fast like a rip cord." I'm sure the look on my face made her want to ease my fright as she quickly added: "I guarantee you will never forget this young lady and the treatment you are about to get." I even shocked myself when I said, "Okay, I'm game but what does all of this cost?" There was a tone in her voice that allowed no room for negotiations when she said, " Five dollars for the oral sex (she did not use that term) and two dollars per knot up to ten knots."

I had enough cash to cover the event, but none of this was in the budget of a staff sergeant. Because I was still thinking about this, I asked my "new found friend and adviser" the following question: "What would you suggest I do?" Her answer was a surprise. "I would not take 10 knots on your first try. I would start with five knots." Once again I agreed with her terms and found my cash hidden in my left sock and paid her my $15. The contract was set.

As the Madam walked out, a young attractive oriental looking girl walked into the room. She looked to be about the same age as her customer sitting on the edge of the bed. I now know why they call them "professionals." This young lady gave her instructions and I gave her my best puppy obedience. She knew her trade well and I was out of the bedroom in 20 minutes.

As I left the house, I walked gingerly past my buddies still in line. Frankly, I was feeling the pain of a rug burn in my posterior when one of them asked: "How was it?" I didn't hesitate to say: "It was great and I suggest both of you go for the 10 knots on the silk handkerchief trick."

It took me three days to get over the "rug burn" sensation. I never had the opportunity to return and if I had I would not have endured the "10 knot" experience. That affair would have put me in sickbay for a week.

I understand that people are reluctant to talk about their wartime experiences. Like so many others, I had my share of combat, from Kawai to Midway, from the Marshall Islands to Tinian, from Okinawa on Easter morning, and more. There are events that I choose to remember and others I choose to forget.

But that time in Hawaii so many years ago is an experience that only young soldiers or marines would remember, even treasure. It was part of a remarkable time of my life and I remember it like yesterday.

Onto Midway Island...

ON FEBRUARY 25, 1944 eleven other marines and I boarded the Merchant Marine ship named the John Owen and headed for a five-day cruise to the "exotic" island of Midway.

The John Owen had been around for a very long time, so accommodations were not what you would call first class, but the chow was excellent.

On our first day the crew taught us how to man the antiquated gun power on the old ship. We knew nothing about firing a ship's artillery, but they gave us enough instruction to make us dangerous. We practiced a couple of hours in the morning, followed by lunch and then additional practice in the afternoon. The third day we were attacked by two Japanese planes, and had a chance to put our four practice sessions into action.

There was very little chance that we could even scare the two planes with our firepower, let alone bring one down.

My assignment on our crew was called "hot shell man," which meant that as the shells popped out of the breach of the gun, I would catch them and throw them overboard. I was given a pair of insulated mittens that covered my arms up to the elbows to avoid burns. My job was to keep the deck free of debris so as the crew moved around they wouldn't break or sprain an ankle.

During this short attack, one of my buddies called my name and as I returned to my task as hot shell man, I caught the next shell just two inches below my left eye. The blood flew like the air coming out of a punctured balloon. I dropped my mittens and headed below deck looking for a corpsman or a doctor to sew me up.

While "Doc" was doing a eight-stitch-sew-surgery job on me, he told me two interesting things. First, he said, "I am really not a doctor, but I am a cook and what I'm doing to you is the same as trussing up a turkey for Thanksgiving." Then he said, "Son, you just earned the easiest Purple Heart that I have every seen. I will put this down in the ship's log, so consider it done."

I thanked the Doc and went back up to rejoin my buddies, but the short attack was already history and there was very little damage done to the John Owen, and I assure you that those two planes did not receive a scratch from twelve "jarheads" and their fire power. In fact, we didn't even give them a scare. We were very lucky that they weren't armed with torpedoes or we would have taken a direct hit.

As far as my purple heart, the records from the self-taught doctor ended up at the bottom of the Pacific Ocean. We learned later from Tokyo Rose that the John Owen was sunk on its very next trip to the USA.

On the fifth day of our cruise we pulled into the harbor and I stood on the deck and looked down at Midway Island.

There are no hills, valleys, streams, or hula dancers on the island.

Midway Island is an atoll with a coral reef roughly six miles in diameter enclosing a shallow bay containing several islands. The two principal islands are named Sand Island and Eastern Island.

Sand Island is about 2¼ miles by 1¼ miles and Eastern Island is about 1¼ mile by ¾ mile. Both are flat and sandy and about twelve feet above sea level. The atoll is about 1,300 miles west and a bit north of Hawaii.

THE BATTLE OF MIDWAY

In June of 1942, a large Japanese task force approached Midway with intentions of taking the island. Its strategic location was recognized as a valued prize by the Japanese forces, and an all-out attack was mounted, causing heavy damage. However, our troops stood their ground; the Japanese were met by aircraft carriers and Midway-based aircraft. The ensuing battle ended in a crushing defeat for the Japanese and marked the turning point of the war in the Pacific.

The air-raid tunnels constructed during this time served as our housing, and remained intact for several decades, serving as a reminder to all Midway residents the importance this tiny island had played in recent history.

I am not sure what I was expecting when I reached Midway Island, but whatever it was put me into a "funk." We were told of an unwritten rule in the "Corps" that no one was allowed to stay on this island for more than 14 months. This was easy to understand after I had finished just a couple of months. I thought we were being punished by being assigned to a safe zone. The 12 of us were assigned to the 16th AA Battalion, but we continued to train for landings on some unknown island.

Our living conditions contributed to our morale problem. We actually lived underground in bunker type sleeping and eating areas because we were told to expect an attack any night. The attack never came. Almost nightly, when the weather was clear, one plane would fly over us, but just out of range. It was a game meant to get on our nerves and keep us from having a good night's sleep.

Every night we would listen to the radio and hear our "favorite" personality, Tokyo Rose. She would say things like, "Hi, boys of the 16th AA Battalion. Do you think your government has forgotten you? The plane is a little late tonight, but it will get you out of your comfortable beds in your dreary underground bunkers." She knew more about what we were doing than we did. We laughed at many things she said, but we also marveled at how accurate her information was about our training and the names of the ships in the harbor.

Tokyo Rose was a young Japanese American woman, born in the United States and a 1940 graduate of the University of Los Angeles, with a degree in zoology. In 1941, Ikuko Toguri sailed for Japan without a United States passport, telling friends she was going to visit a sick aunt and then study medicine.

Tokyo Rose

She appeared in front of the United States Consul in Japan to obtain a United States passport so she could return to the USA for permanent residence. Before she got the passport, the Japanese attacked Pearl Harbor.

In 1943, Toguri began her career as a broadcaster for Radio-Tokyo. This job was to bring notoriety and eventually result in her 1949 conviction for treason. Her program, known as Zero Hours, became a big part of Japanese psychological warfare, designed to lower our morale.

This was a typical program that we would hear six days a week. She called herself, "Orphan Annie," "Your favorite enemy Ann," or "Your favorite playmate and enemy Ann."

In 1944, I heard the broadcast and it came across like this: "Hello boneheads. This is your favorite enemy, Ann. How are all you orphans of the Pacific? Are you enjoying yourselves while your wives and sweethearts are running around with the 4 F's in the States. How do you feel now all your ships have been sunk by the Japanese Navy. How will you get home? Here's another record to remind you of home." She would then play a ballad that was meant to make us homesick.

The name Tokyo Rose was given her by the U.S. Armed Forces. The Japanese thought they could make us feel homesick, but we really made fun of her. Her choice of music wasn't too good, but her Christmas selections came close to lowering our morale. We would sing along, "I'll be home for Christmas, just you wait and see. I'll be home for Christmas in 1953." And then we would open another beer.

Midway Island had very little vegetation, but some of the Sea Bee's had taken a vine they called 'Scaviola." They ran it through a washing machine ringer and produced a juice that, when mixed with raisins and any kind of fruit and allowed to ferment, became "white lightening." The taste was not too good, but the final results were about the same as cheap, very strong bourbon. I tried it and decided it was best to keep my eyesight. I stayed with beer!

The same Sea Bee's made news back home when they braided a piece of rope and made it into a tail for the only milk cow on the island. The cow had lost its tail in an accident and these sharp thinking Sea Bee's sympathized with her frustration because she couldn't swish away the flies. Even Bill Veeck would say, "That's great PR, boys."

We had nothing but time on our hands on Midway. Swimming and fishing was big, but I never thought I would enjoy bird watching to the extent I did.

One of the older Merchant Marine sailors on the John Owen told us that we would see birds fly backwards and hear birds moan like babies in the night. I took this with a big grain of salt, because a Cherokee Indian had already got me on his story about his German Shepard using the toilet, but we soon would learn he was telling the truth.

The big bird of the island was popularly called the Gooney bird. Its real name is the Laysan Albatross. Pairs mate for life and build elaborate, mound-like nests to which they return each year. The Gooney stands about 18" tall, weighs about 5½ pounds and has a 7' wingspan.

They perform an entertaining courtship dance, bobbing up and down and strutting around. This activity would go on for several weeks prior to mating.

An Albatross chick is covered with big downy feathers and gets really silly looking when the feathers fall off as the bird matures. Awkward on land, but truly graceful in flight, these birds glide effortlessly on the wind and fly great distances, as many as 3,200 miles in 10 days.

Laysan Albatross and chick

We were told not to harm the birds, nor to eat their eggs. Telling Marines not to eat the eggs was a challenge. Everyone tried the eggs once, but not a second time. Gooney birds feed entirely on fish, so the eggs tasted too fishy and are not too good in an omelet!

There is also a black-footed Albatross that prefers to lay its eggs in more remote areas. This bird is very aggressive. If you walk too close to a nest, its owner may growl at you, bite your pant leg, and even throw up on your boot. The Gooney is well known for this because that's how they feed their young: digesting fish and feeding their young by regurgitation.

The last bird that I remember is the red-tailed tropicbird. This is the bird sailors told me flies backward. I thought this was unlikely, but I found out later this bird was extremely ungainly on the ground and extremely agile in the air. It can fly backwards! I saw some tuck their twin red tail feathers underneath their body and actually do it! This actually happened before we were off duty and before we started drinking our beer.

Speaking of beer, it became a custom that after a few beers someone would grab a young Gooney and force a half of can of beer down its gullet. These birds were always clumsy when walking, but under these circumstances, they were a riot to watch. We had too much time on our hands!

On May 15, 1944, we received notice we were to board another Merchant Marine ship, the "Henry Burg," and return to Pearl Harbor for reassignment. The Marine Corp never seemed to want you to know where you were going until aboard ship. It reminded me of the old saying at the time: "Loose lips sink ships."

We stayed in Honolulu only two days, but once again I got the worst end of another hangover. "Sometimes you beat the bar, but usually the bar beats you..." was a favorite saying. I was sick as hell when we crawled up the side of a ship called the "Nordam" in full battle gear. One more time I talked directly to God and pleaded with him to save me. I knew I was about to die from a hangover. I felt better when it was announced we were headed for the "Garden Island" of Kauai. This was less than half of a day away. We were headed for heaven - KAUAI – THE GARDEN ISLAND.

The short trip was uneventful, and the difference between this beautiful island and looking down at Midway Island was like night and day.

Our first home on the Garden Island was a tent city located on the west side of the island, near a quaint town called Hanapepe, which means "boy crushed by falling rock."

Something that has stuck in my memory about Hanapepe was a "PINK" movie theater location on the main street called "Aloha Theater." In 1995, my wife Liz and I were sent to the Hawaiian Islands by my boss Dean White to locate the right hotel for Whiteco Outdoor Company to use as a one-week incentive trip for 80 couples. We looked at hotels on all of the Hawaiian Islands, but we also had a chance to retrace some of the paths that I took back in 1943, 1944, and 1945. Please understand that not all of my paths were retraced on this trip!

Aloha Theater, Hanapepe Kauai (Liz)

During our 1995 revisit to Hanapepe, as we were walking down its main street, Liz asked, "What landmarks are we looking for you might remember?" The first thing I remembered was the pink movie theater.

It did not take us long to locate it, because the main street is only four blocks long. There it was, a very faded pink building with the small marquee hanging precariously at a dangerous angle from the main part of the very small building. Near the roofline and still visible was the name, "Aloha Theater."

Finding this building gave me a thrill. It was 51 years ago when we treated ourselves to a movie and newsreel in the pink Aloha Theater.

We were just about to leave Hanapepe when I spotted two old - timers sitting on a bench enjoying a six-pack. I approached them and asked: "On June 4, 1944, I had a Sunday dinner at the Lihue Hotel. Can you tell me if it is still in business and how do I get there?" Then I showed them a copy of the menu from that very day.

"Two Old Timers"

The ensuing conversation soon became a friendly argument. Neither of these old-timers remembered the hotel, but both were really impressed with the menu. The cost of the entire meal, from soup to dessert, was $1.25. By the time our conversation ended and the six-pack was finished, one of the bench riders came out to our rented car to meet Liz. This old-timer was no fool and before our conversation ended, he gave Liz a little kiss on the cheek to end my day of memories of 51 years ago.

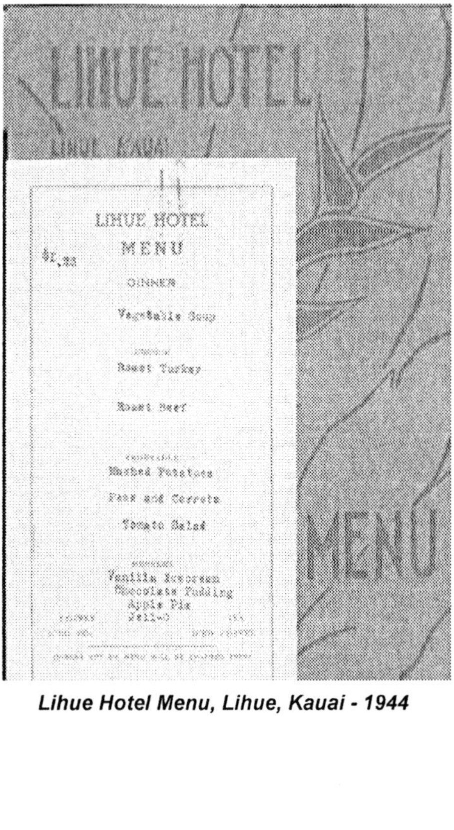
LIHUE HOTEL
LIHUE KAUAI

LIHUE HOTEL
MENU
DINNER
Vegetable Soup
Roast Turkey
Roast Beef
Mashed Potatoes
Peas and Carrots
Tomato Salad
Vanilla Icecream
Chocolate Pudding
Apple Pie
Jell-O

MENU

Lihue Hotel Menu, Lihue, Kauai - 1944

At the time we arrived on Kauai, on May 25, 1944, we had no idea how long we would stay. It turned out to be seven months and yes, it was seven months in paradise.

After two weeks in Tent City, we talked Captain Rock into moving because our radar equipment needed to be higher up to make sure the technical bugs were fixed. We knew we were headed soon to some island invasion.

The "12 minus 2" high above Hanapepe

The captain made the arrangements for our group of 12 technicians to move to Hanapepe Valley Lookout. Rolling green hills and quaint farms with lush vegetation surrounded our camp, which was located high above Hanapepe and the beautiful west coast of Kauai.

Our tents were pitched in a beautiful pasture, which was protected at the entrance by railroad rails to stop cattle from moving from one field to another. For seven months, we lived under ideal conditions. The weather was fantastic. I have never been anyplace in the world to compare to this island. San Diego was close, but Kauai is the clear winner.

Bill Wellman – "Let's play two"

Our camp was made up of 12 non-commissioned men without an officer on site except every other Saturday. Then Captain Rock and Jack Rex, from New York, would inspect our camp. Jack was a technical sergeant with six stripes, so he was in charge. I was a staff sergeant with four stripes. Dick Warren from Pennsylvania and John Ramos "Garcia" from California also held the rank of staff sergeants. Art Weber from Washington D.C., and Tex McLaughlin from Lubbock, TX were three-stripe sergeants. Pete Sowell from Virginia, Jack Allen from Michigan, and Al McGowan from Texas were all corporals. Louis Pfarr and Kirkjohn, both from Baltimore, were private first class and our cook, Tim Kennedy from Tennessee, was a corporal.

There were inspections every other week, which gave us a lot of free time to make trips to points of interest. I was amazed at the waterfalls cascading down Mt. Waialeale's mile-high crater, washing its walls virtually spotless. This water combines to form the only navigable river, the Waialua, which meanders past the famous Fern Grotto on its lazy way to the sea.

We took trips to the Waimea Canyon and saw deep pastel valleys unequalled in the world. Mark Twain called it the "Grand Canyon of the Pacific" and with good reason.

There were times when we would drive one of our trucks to the north side of the island to visit Kilauea Lighthouse and the bird sanctuary atop nearby Crater Hill, followed with a stop at Hanalei with its magnificent half-moon bay. This is where Puff the Magic Dagon was discovered to be "living," according to Peter, Paul and Mary, the famous 70's folk singers.

We also took some night excursions to an Army warehouse halfway between our camp and Hanapepe. Through some investigation by our cook, we learned there was a large walk-in cooler that housed fresh meat for the Army's top brass. The investigation also revealed that on Saturday nights the two guards were absent from their posts for two hours. So our first quick trip got us a side of fresh beef and four boxes of whatever else we could take with us. The beef was great, but it had to be eaten in one week, before our Saturday inspection by the stern Captain Rock. He would not think it humorous to steal supplies from the Army, so we ate steak or some cut of beef for every meal. The four mystery boxes gave us control of the toothpaste and toothbrush market for the rest of the war.

It struck me one Sunday, as I was passing up my "scam" of going to church and standing outside looking like the homesick Marine that I really was, if it worked in Wilmington, N.C., wouldn't it in Kauai?

My first attempt was at a beautiful little church in Lihue. Dick Warren and I both had staked out an area after the church service and were approached by a beautiful 80-year old lady named Mrs. Whittemore.

Church Scam – Mrs. Whittemore

She invited us to her house for Sunday dinner. During dinner, I was trying to figure out the odds of a 18 to 20-year old girl living under the same roof. Her son was the head chemist at a huge sugar cane plantation, but he was a bachelor. It looked like my little game would be dinner only, until events took a turn for the better. A 16-year old maid entered to serve dessert.

The Grand Lady – Mrs. Whittemore

She was Portuguese-Hawaiian and didn't wear shoes, but she had discovered t-shirts and lipstick. She was 16 but looked 20 and she was a beauty. The war scene was looking up and Sunday church and the "lonely look scam" had survived another challenge.

The visits to Mrs. Whittemore's became part of our weekly routine. The "Grand Lady" of Kauai always had plenty of fresh milk to serve all the members or our unit. I continued my quest of getting to know more about the true culture of the island by becoming friendly with the young, attractive maid.

Yehudi Menuhin – the Violinist

I convinced Dick Warren to escort Mrs. Whittemore to the far side of the island to a special concert by the famous violinist of the time, Yehudi Menuhin (1916-1999).

This concert was a big event for the island because Mr. Menuhin was the century's most beloved violinist. He was once described as the best-loved individual in the history of the performing arts. Dick agreed and Mrs. Whittemore was excited about the concert and exceptionally happy that a couple of U.S. Marines were to escort her to this grand event.

The evening of the performance I told Dick I really was not feeling up to it, so I would take a pass. I asked him to tell Mrs. Whittemore how disappointed I was to miss such an event.

My timing was impeccable. As the concert party pulled away from the house, I moved in on a prearranged date with the maid. Things were looking good. One hour for transportation to and from the concert and 1½ hours for the concert gave me a grand total of 2½ hours away from the watchful eyes of Mrs. Whittemore.

There are times when well-laid plans take a fall. The maid and I were just getting to know each other when in walked the concertgoers. Dick Warren told me later that I looked like a surprised Cherokee Indian on the warpath when Mrs. Whittemore walked into the living room and said, "Well, we did not see the concert, but it seems Mr. Wellman has recovered his health and has been entertained this evening."

I had not allowed for a severe storm hitting the far side of the island and cutting off the electricity.

Mrs. Whittemore seemed to forgive me, but I noticed she seemed to watch my moves in her home a little more intently than before.

My dating of the maid continued, but we met during her time off and not at the Whittemore homestead. The pink theater in Hanapepe was one spot that seemed safe from Mrs. Whittemore's watchful eye.

The Bob Hope Show

The war seemed far away, and our training seemed to become more natural to us every day. It was July 24, 1944, when we were told the Marines had invaded the island of Tinian. We knew our time was getting closer. Just before Christmas we had a chance to come off the rolling hills of Hanapepe Valley Lookout to attend one of Bob Hope's Christmas shows. It was a real thrill for all of us to watch Bob Hope and Jerry Colona, and the beautiful singer/dancer, Patty Thomas.

Jerry Colona

Tears pooled in our eyes as the song White Christmas was sung by the more than 18,000 gathered in a sugar cane field just before Christmas in 1944. There was one line in the song we changed every time we heard it. "I'll be home for Christmas – You can count on me – I'll be home for Christmas in 1953."

During the show and in the middle of Bob Hope routines, a small steam engine pulling a dozen flat beds filled with cut sugar cane chugged through the edge of the makeshift arena. It took several minutes to pass and soon as it finally disappeared, Bob Hope said, "What the hell was that?!"

Patty Thomas

As I watched this great show, I didn't imagine that 34 years later I would have the privilege of interviewing Bob Hope on Dean White's radio station WZVN in Lowell, Indiana. I would also sign the contract for Mr. Hope's appearance on stage at the Holiday Star Theatre. The years were 1982 and 1984, and the tickets sold for $17.95 each.

The seven months in Paradise were coming to an end, but we would remember them and many things, like the visits for fresh cold milk at Mrs. Whittemore's, and of course, the Portuguese-Hawaiian maid.

On December 24, 1944, we boarded a ship called "Afoundria" and headed for Pearl Harbor. Sometime during the next three days, the ship, which we were to transfer to, blew up, along with two others. The scuttlebutt was that all three were side by side, and all three sank in a domino effect. We never heard if this was accidental or sabotage, but this tragedy probably saved our lives.

We stayed aboard the "Afoundria," and then we were given liberty on Christmas Day, 1944, with orders to be back aboard by midnight. There were many hangovers aboard ship the day after Christmas. Guy's law – "It's Made to Sell, Not to Drink" – was starting to make sense, so I took in nothing but non-alcoholic beverages. I remember how I felt like I was going to die on the "Saratoga" and I had no desire to go through that feeling again.

We pulled out of Pearl Harbor on December 26th and headed for Eniwetok. The trip took us eight days, and we pulled into the harbor on Jan. 3, 1945. We stayed aboard the ship, except for two days of practice using a landing craft and hitting the beach. On January 7th, we pulled out of Eniwetok and took a five-day trip to an island called Tinian.

We were told later by Captain Rock that when the three ships were sunk in Pearl Harbor our plans were changed. Those three ships were to be in the first wave of the invasion on an island called Iwo Jima on February 19, 1945.

Iwo Jima

Luck was on our side on this one. "Iwo Jima received as much preliminary pounding as any island," according to Admiral Nimitz. "It was incredible that this ferocious bombardment had little effect. Hardly any of the Japanese underground fortresses were touched. Twenty-one thousand defenders of Japanese soil burrowed in the volcanic rock and anxiously awaited the American invaders."

We sent more Marines to Iwo Jima than any other battle – 110,000 Marines in 880 ships. The convoy took 40 days aboard ship. At 18:30 p.m. military time, the order came down, "Land the landing force." Once ashore the Marines were bedeviled by the loose volcanic ash. Unable to dig foxholes, they were sitting ducks for the hidden Japanese gunners. Confusion reigned on the beaches. The Marines fought above ground, while the defending Japanese fought from below ground. The Marines rarely saw a Japanese soldier.

Easy Company started with 310 men and suffered 75% casualties. Only 50 men boarded the ship after the battle. This was the company that raised the American flag on Iwo Jima remembered by famous photographs and immortalized by the monument in Washington, D.C. This battle was won by the "inch-by-inch" tenacity of the Marines.

Over the years I have tried with no success to find out about the loss of the three ships that we were to board to go to Iwo Jima. There is not doubt in my mind that we would have been in on the first wave and the odds would have been heavy for us not to walk away alive.

Tinian was the home base for the newly developed long-range bomber called the B-29. The Sea Bees, then 15,000 strong, had built eight runways that were each 1 ½ miles long, and at least a city block wide.

Our camp was located high above the airstrips and since we did not have an officer with us full time, we did not follow all of the rules. Our "head," or toilet, was designed without a cover around it, but we had built a two-seater set-up some 30 inches off the ground like a throne.

Kirkjohn's Movement – Tinian 1945

Kirkjohn always carried his trombone with him and he had the habit of practicing when he was sitting on the "throne." We called it "Kirkjohn's Movement."

The first week during his daily practice session a jeep went by with a one-star general and two Navy nurses. Of course,

Kirkjohn waved to them. That afternoon we had a visit from Captain Rock. It was an unpleasant time for us, I assure you. Of course, our "concert hall" was wrapped in canvas from then on.

We carefully counted the B29's as they took off for a bombing raid. In fact, it was a sad exercise, watching the departures and waiting for their return. Then we counted the landings to learn how many didn't make it back. Many times we watched anxiously and helplessly as one of those big planes limped home.

It was March 9, 1945, and we knew that something BIG was going to happen. At 6:15 p.m., the airstrips on Tinian were as active as we had ever seen them. We learned later that by 8:15 p.m. 334 B-29s had been launched from Guam, Saipan and Tinian.

The information got back to our camp the next day that the 334 B 29's made up three 400 mile long formations that roared above Iwo Jima and Chichi Jima on their way to bomb Tokyo, Japan.

It was a great feeling the next day when we got the good news that the "Tokyo Calling Cards" – M 69 napalm bombs – had found their targets.

About a week later we got the full story that General Curtis LeMay hatched the plan to fly from the three Mariana Islands. His purpose was to attack Tokyo at 5000 feet so the anti-aircraft guns couldn't adjust quickly enough. His plan was masterfully and lethally executed. The estimate that this bold strike would cost 70% of the B-29's taking part in the raid was wrong. General LeMay lost only 5% of the original 334 planes.

Japan estimated between 90,000 and 100,000 people were lost the night of the attack. The newspapers back home had headlines that stated: "Center of Tokyo Devastated by Fire Bombs;" "B-29's Fire is 15 Square Miles of Tokyo." I didn't hear any reports from Tokyo Rose, but we had other things to worry about.

We had the feeling that our time would come with a landing – like we had practiced over and over. Our next move found us aboard LST 803 for a one-day trip to the island of Saipan. There we received more instruction on a daily basis until we pulled out of the harbor at Saipan, headed for the biggest battle of the war on the island of Okinawa.

Some of the instructions we received had to do with our health. "Do not eat their vegetables; they use their own waste to fertilize everything and although the vegetables will look great, we tell you not to take a chance." The nickname used was "honey carts." This was a two-wheel wagon that was used to spread the human excrement over their gardens. I must say it sounded terrible, but the vegetables were huge!

We pulled out of Saipan on March 26th and headed for a six-day trip to Okinawa. The weather turned bad and the first night we hit the tail end of a hurricane. It did not last long, but some chains snapped on some of the heavy equipment and we lost two trucks and the three Marines who were sleeping in them. It was fortunate that the trucks were not from our unit, and the lost Marines were not from our group of 12. Frankly, I was so scared that I even forgot about being seasick.

It was Easter Sunday, 1945, when we gathered on the deck before dawn to have a pre-sunrise church service before boarding our landing craft.

SPOTTING ERNIE PYLE

Just before we boarded our landing craft we spotted a PRESS sign on another landing craft. Someone recognized the great U.S. war correspondent and Indiana native Ernie Pyle. We waved at him and he returned the wave. He was considered to be the top writer for both the Army and the

Marine Corps. He wrote about what the war was really like. He made the American public feel the war, telling its story not from the views of the brass, but through the eyes of the common foot soldier and Marine at the front lines. The one who was grimy, wet, scared and homesick; the one who may not have been able to bathe for weeks or even take off his socks, let alone change them. Pyle described the advantage of going six weeks without a bath. "If you don't bathe for a long time, the fleas don't bother you," he wrote.

World War II war correspondent and Hoosier Ernie Pyle (center) talks with Marines on a Navy transport ship while en route to the invasion of Okinawa in 1945

Unlike some of the correspondents who stayed safely behind the front lines, Pyle took a shovel, dug a foxhole, and shared our experience. Ernie Pyle was "embedded" with the military during World War II before "embedding" became popular in more current conflicts.

Ernie Pyle wrote about the Army soldiers and Marines – not who was winning or losing. He told homey anecdotes and used real names and addresses.

On April 18th, we received the sad news that Ernie Pyle had been killed by Japanese machine gun fire on the island of Ie Shima. His death was a personal loss and hard to take, remembering the wave he gave us on Easter morning before we landed at Okinawa.

Some of his comrades erected a simple plaque that read, "At this spot the 77th Division lost a buddy, Ernie Pyle – April 18, 1945."

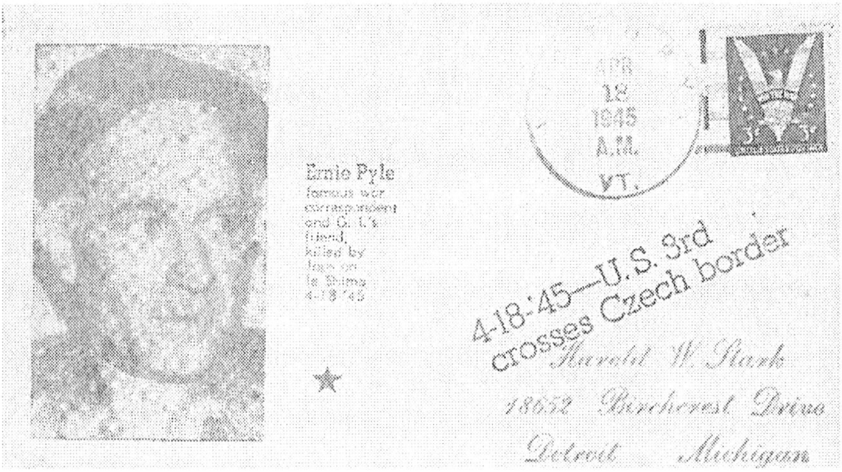

Commemorative Patriotic Stamped Envelope honoring the day Ernie Pyle was killed. Courtesy of Bill Nangle, Executive Editor of the Times

When Liz and I made our trip to retrace some of my adventures, we made a point to go where they had buried his body: The National Memorial Cemetery of the Pacific at Punchbowl Crater in Honolulu.

His grave was marked by a simple marker, one of which he would have approved. President Harry Truman insisted on announcing the correspondent's death to the nation. He said, "No man in this war has told the story of the American fighting man as the American fighting man wanted it told. He deserves the gratitude of all his countrymen."

If you have a full tank of gas and you live in Chicago or Northwest Indiana and would like to learn more about Ernie Pyle, I urge you to drive to Dana just east of Indianapolis near the Illinois/Indiana border. "Ernie Pyle State Historic Site" is located at 120 Briarwood in Dana.

If you take the trip, you will see a pair of World War II Quonset huts that look somewhat out of place sitting next to the old-fashioned two-story white farmhouse in Dana where Ernie Pyle grew up. This small town amid the cornfields of west-central Indiana is a fitting location for the Ernie Pyle State Historic Site, which chronicles the life of the Pulitzer Prize winning WW II correspondent and the people and places he wrote about.

Ernie Pyle was born in this house on Aug. 3, 1900. He was the only son of Will and Maria Pyle. Today, his restored birthplace holds family memorabilia and period furnishings, though not all belonged to the Pyles. There was no running water or electricity when he was growing up.

The museum's multi-media exhibits are centered around his words, designed to have the same affect as his writings did almost six decades ago.

Actual vintage WWII photos form the backdrop of many displays. Visitors can pick up field phones to hear local newspaper writer William Windom echoing Ernie's words from his newspaper columns.

There is a jeep, which Pyle thought was such an important part of war life. He wrote the jeep was "...as faithful as a dog, as strong as a mule and as agile as a goat."

Also there is the raggedy Army coat with the elbows out Ernie wore to tea with the First Lady, Eleanor Roosevelt, as described in one of his articles. Also on display is Pyle's wool knit cap, press credentials and a movie script of the film, "The Story of G.I. Joe." There's the rifle, which was taken from a Japanese prisoner. Pyle wrote, "My own contribution to the capture consisted of standing to one side and looking as mean as I could."

The trip also teaches visitors about the great people of WWII in a way that facts in textbooks can't begin to communicate.

Like many Marines and Soldiers, I felt I had lost a personal friend when I heard Ernie Pyle had been killed.

The other death to hit us hard was on April 12, 1945, when the news came that President Roosevelt had passed away. Young men cried in small groups as the word flew along the front lines. Death seemed to be coming in bunches and the morale was not too good. I was now 21 years old and I had started when I had enlisted in the Corps when I was 18.

When you are 21, and have been trained by the United States Marine Corps, you believe that nothing bad can happen to you and you will live forever.

The church service on Easter morning is the only time I can remember when I seemed to concentrate on every word the Chaplin was saying. I also knew that all of our months of training were coming to an end.

Our landing craft did some maneuvering for a few minutes, but all at once we were headed straight for the beach. No matter how many times we made practice landings, my biggest fear was the first step off the end of the ramp. I was more concerned about being dropped off in water over my head than being shot. You cannot imagine the good feeling when my feet hit the bottom of knee-deep water.

All of our portable radar equipment was carried ashore in six telephone carts by our 12-member team.

The plan was to hit the beach, dig foxholes and prepare to have all hell break loose. It did not happen! We moved off the beach like we were having a practice landing session. No shooting! No Japs!

Okinawa landing Easter morning - 1945

The mission of our 12-member team was to seek high ground before we started to put up our little black tents and our equipment.

The higher the ground, the further away we could track incoming enemy planes. If we had a perfect site, we would be able to pick up incoming aircraft 80 miles out from our location. The equipment was capable of using an IFF system, which means Identification Friend or Foe. The aircraft would show up on our screen as a blip, but if it were one of ours, the IFF system would show a pulsating blip below the signal. No blip meant that it was one of theirs.

Easter morning went right into afternoon and the III Amphibious Force, went straight across the island, which was only eight miles wide.

Our team picked a high spot about four miles up from the original beachhead, and started to set up our radar unit. At this point no one had fired or been fired upon during this Easter morning invasion.

The team worked well in setting up our equipment and we were tracking enemy bogies before the sunset; so, our next chore was to dig in to protect our camp and try to get some sleep.

At approximately 10:30 p.m., we were calling in "bogies" from all directions and within minutes, we had a ringside seat to watch the harbor light up like Chicago on the Fourth of July. The attack continued for over four hours. At one time, a ship exploded and lit up the sky. We found out later that the ship was the "New Mexico," and it had taken a direct hit from a Kamikaze pilot.

The first night was coming to an end. We took our turns at guard duty and tried to catch a few hours of sleep. The next morning I was awakened by the first rays of sunshine through the holes in my pup tent. I discovered first-hand that digging below the surface and having your shelter above ground could and would "save your ass." The first chance I got, I dug my foxhole deeper by six inches, just in case.

After a few days, we became a little too cocky about our safe area around our equipment, so we decided to check out the territory around us. We had been instructed not to go into caves, and that if we found a civilian or soldier sleeping, never roll him over. The orders were to just kill him, because he could be booby-trapped.

Three of us who went into our first cave, which was located near our camp, decided we would feel much safer at night if we knew what was around us.

It only took a few minutes for the first test of what to do when confronted with a sleeping Japanese soldier. The light from someone's flashlight was held on his head and I did not think twice when I shot him. The flashlight seemed to be bouncing all over the cave, and we got out of there fast.

Two hours later, John Garcia showed me a flag he took off a body near our campsite. It appeared to be the same cave, but I told John I was not about to roll a body over just for a flag. Curiosity got the better of me the next day, so we revisited the same cave and I took a wallet and watch off of the dead soldier.

Inside the wallet was a small amount of Japanese paper money and a picture of what looked like a mother and daughter. It did not bother me, because the entire situation could have been reversed and I could have been the one shot.

Mother and Daughter

On the third day we had our first casualty, a Marine named Kirkjohn from Boston. From our early days, he was warned about not wearing his helmet, but for some reason he always wore a "piss cutter" instead.

The second rule he broke was to never go out of camp alone; we were to have someone with us at all times. But on this day, he walked into the mouth of a cave when he ran into three Japs. As he turned to run, one of them shot him in the back of his head and he stumbled and fell about 15 feet below the opening of the cave, where he grabbed a small tree. When we heard the shots, we ran through a small valley, 30 feet below the opening of the cave. Kirkjohn would occasionally shake the tree, so we knew that he was still alive. Four of us worked our way up the side of the hill until we reached him. He was still conscious, so we half carried and half slid him down to the valley where we could carry him back to a casualty area.

It was in the valley that I discovered I had left my carbine near the little tree. I also had a 45 automatic, so I decided not to go back for the carbine right away.

It took us an hour to get Kirkjohn to an area where a doctor could look at him.

Flamethrower results

I talked John Garcia into coming with me to work our way back to the spot where I left the carbine, but it was gone so we called for some backup with a flamethrower. When help arrived, we lobbed six hand grenades into the cave and then the flamethrower unleashed its awesome power, as we worked our way into the cave.

We killed four enemy soldiers and I found my carbine. The Japs had found where I left it on the ground. The wooden stock was completely burned off, but I took it back to the camp and I was issued a new one that same day. The next morning John Garcia and I went over to see how Kirkjohn was doing. We were told he did not make it through the night. This was our first, but not our last casualty.

Two days later we were told that a few of us were going on a night patrol with Captain Crawford. When you are in the Marine Corps, you are an infantryman first, then you are a technician or a cook second, so being called to do a night patrol was part of the job.

Night patrol results

My memory of Captain Crawford was a twenty-mile overnight hike he took us on in the swamps of North Carolina during training. I also remember he was a real fitness nut.

The night was long and I thought it was wrong to penetrate enemy lines when visibility was non-existent. It sticks in my mind that we could hear the Japs talking as they passed by. The next morning we had lost two more of our people, but there were many dead Japs.

Art Weber was a former detective from Washington, D.C., and we considered him the old man of our group at the ripe old age of 28.

This next incident happened as we were working our way back to our base camp. It was like watching a movie, but we could not yell or give him a warning without giving away our position.

I spotted Sergeant Weber walking down a path some 30 yards from where we were located, and as he turned a corner he ran directly within six feet of a Japanese solider coming from the opposite direction. Both men jumped into the weeds and we heard the muffled sound of a hand-grenade. By the time we made our way up to Art's location, we found a dead Jap, but we also found Art with the top half of his right ear missing.

We took him to a first-aid station and we said goodbye because Sergeant Weber had just gotten a one-way ticket back to the USA.

This was the last time I saw Art Weber, but in 1948, I ran into an old friend of mine from Valparaiso, Russell Glover, who was a detective on the Washington, D.C. police force. He knew Art and told me he was still active as a detective. The story I told him solved a mystery around the station.

Evidently Art never talked about his experience overseas, so the rumor was that someone had chewed the top of the detective's ear during a night raid. Russell was going to go back and give "the other side of the story."

We had a visit one day from a one-star Army General and his entourage of two other officers and a sergeant. The quote of the day came from the General when he said, "It is nice to have a cold K ration with the boys in the field every once in a while." He did not stay too long, after he found out what went on in our black tent.

"Goat Dinner"

After eating cold rations for several weeks, we got brave and roasted a young goat. The meat tasted great the first couple of times, but someone decided to make gravy. It was too sweet and I decided I had eaten my last goat meal.

It was the 10th of May when we were ordered to break up camp and make a move closer to the capital, Naha, Okinawa. As we were moving, several of us investigated a house.

Bad mistake! I got the worst case of fleas you could imagine. The only thing that seemed to kill them was washing with naphtha soap and also washing my clothes with naphtha. The only benefit of visiting the house was the wooden bowls I found. I used them instead of my issued utensils. I still have a bowl on my bedroom dresser that reminds me of some of those meals. No more goats!

Shrine Camp

Our next camp was just outside of Naha, the capital of Okinawa. We made our "home" in one of the religious shrines. It was dry and seemed to be a good location near an airport.

On May 16th, Captain Rock came by our camp and called me over to his jeep and informed me I was to pick up my gear, say my goodbyes, and he would drive me to the beach where I could be escorted to a hospital ship headed back to the U.S. What a surprise!

I did not want to ask too many questions because I thought it might be a big mistake. I did not want to say something wrong and screw up the orders. This completely surprised and shocked me, as it did the remaining seven members of our close-knit group. Saying goodbye to people that I might not ever see again was tough, but I would be stretching the truth if I didn't say I was excited about the possibility that I could be on my way home. Someone was watching over me and I thought my luck was running out, so the timing was perfect.

Easter Morning Okinawa – 1945

"The First Wave"

Easter Morning Okinawa - 1945

III Amphibious force moves across Okinawa eight miles the first day

Okinawa – 1945

Heavy Equipment on the road to Naha

Okinawa – 1945

House full of fleas along with wooden bowls

My first night aboard the hospital ship was unsettling. Here I was eating things like fresh bread and drinking milk, and still trying to figure out why I was going home. I finally found out that I had been taking a lot of quinine. At sickbay they had informed me that I had malaria almost a year ago. I took so much quinine that my skin had a yellow cast and it was the joke of our group that I was going to join the enemy because of the yellow color of my skin.

The paper work on my malaria had just caught up to me at the outskirts of Naha and I was headed home.

Clean sheets were issued to me aboard the hospital ship, but I slept little. I couldn't figure out what the lights where and just where the hell I was!

I thought we were reversing the trip when the hospital ship headed for Saipan. The first day out of the harbor was one of my saddest days aboard a hospital ship. I was one of eight walking patients so we were given burial detail immediately. The first day we buried eight at sea. Since I was only 5'9" I was the last one closest to the rail on the side of the plank that held the body in a weighted body bag. At a given signal, the Marines on the far end would raise their end of the plank, allowing the body bag to slide under the American flag. This was "burial at sea."

This was a daily routine for the eight walking patients. On the five-day trip back to Saipan, we buried a total of 14 very young Marines. When you have the position on the rail, you get to have that final look at the black bag as it hits the water. Not a pretty sight, I assure you, but it was one that I would never forget. Every time I hear taps I remember those 14 young Marines buried at sea.

I watched the flag pass by one day,
It fluttered in the breeze.
A young Marine saluted it.
And then he stood at ease.

I looked at him in uniform
So young. So tall, so proud.
With hair cut square and eyes alert
He'd stand out in any crowd.

I thought how many men like him
Had fallen through the years.
How many died on foreign soil
How many mothers' tears.

How many pilots' planes shot down?
How many died at sea.
How many foxholes were soldiers' graves?
No, freedom isn't free.

I heard the sound of Taps one night,
When everything was still,
I listened to the bugler play
And felt a sudden chill.

I wondered just how many times
That Taps had meant "Amen."
When a flag had draped a coffin
Of a brother or a friend.

I thought of all the children,
Of the mothers and the wives,
Of fathers, sons and husbands
With interrupted lives.

I thought about a graveyard
At the bottom of the sea
Of unmarked graves in Arlington.
"No, freedom isn't free."

Anonymous

We picked up a few more patients from Saipan and then headed for Entiewtok. Six days later on May 28th, we pulled into the harbor only to refuel and pull out the next day, heading back to Pearl Harbor, where we dropped off some of the more seriously injured.

We had several Marines who had lost their sight and many were missing a leg or an arm. Not a happy group, but deep down they knew they were headed home. The war was over for them.

On June 8th, we were headed east for a five-day trip to good old San Francisco. The excitement really hit a frenzy stage when we went under the Golden Gate Bridge. The band was playing everything we knew as the ship pulled into the harbor. "Happy Days are Here Again" and "God Bless America" brought out a few tears from all of us. The only one that they missed was "White Christmas." But I did make it home before that line that we replaced: "I'll be home for Christmas, Just You Wait and See, I'll be Home for Christmas in 1953."

The walking eight patients on burial details were immediately told that we had 45 minutes to catch a civilian train headed for San Diego. No new clothing was issued, so we looked like prisoners of war as we got ready to board the train. Calling home was the first thing that I did as soon as I found a pay phone.

When I got my mother on the phone, I made the mistake of saying, "Mom, I did not hear what you said, will you say that again?" Mom started to cry and the next thing I heard was the voice of my Dad. I said, "What's wrong with Mom?" He then gave me a little shock when he asked," Did you loose your ear?" I followed with, "No, I did not lose anything." Where did you hear that, Dad?" He answered: "We heard a rumor that you had your ear shot off from Frank Leachman when he came home last week."

It took me a long time to figure out how my parents heard that rumor, but I finally decided that my old friend Frank Leachman must have heard about my good buddy Arthur Weber losing his ear, and I must have been mistaken for Arthur in the story. It did not take me long to convince my Dad that it was the telephone connection that caused me to say," Mom, what did you say?"

The trip to San Diego on a regular train was interesting because the civilians looked at the eight of us as if where were prisoners of war. My dungarees were threadbare and even had holes in the knees, but we knew we would be issued all new clothing as soon as we arrived in San Diego.

When I arrived in Valparaiso on June 18th, two days after my 21st birthday, I could not get over that it took me 28 days aboard the same hospital ship to come from Okinawa to San Francisco. During the 28 days I got to know some of the non-critical patients, but the memory of seeing and hearing those 14 body bags slide under the flag and then hit the water still woke me up nights.

My next 30 days were in and out of uniform because I was home on furlough being treated like a hometown hero back from the war. The furlough went by fast and the next thing I knew I was headed for Norfolk, VA, where my old record of being on guard duty in Pearl Harbor caught up with me. I landed at the Naval Brig on guard duty. I really disliked the duty, so I immediately put in for a transfer. I was shocked when I received my transfer within three weeks, but the shock wave wasn't finished because I was transferred to another brig at Camp Peary in Williamsburg, VA.

This camp was the original Sea Bees boot camp that was turned into a prison for both prisoners of war from Germany and our own Navy and Marine Corps prisoners.

Weekend leave from Camp Peary was as dead as a "waitress's kiss." On any given night the sidewalks were rolled up and stored away by 7 p.m. If we had the time, we'd take a trip to Washington, D.C., which was known as the "action" place. We had heard there were six females to every one male. Great odds for a Sunday church scam! I found out the overseas ribbons and a very homesick look would still get you an invitation to Sunday dinner. Add this to the 6 to 1 odds and I had solved my problem of "where to go on leave" at Camp Peary, VA.

30 day leave – June 1945

Chapter Four

PARTY TIME

A Try at Education

November 10th is the Marine Corps birthday and it was on this date in 1945 I received my honorable discharge at Camp LeJune, NC.

The dinner served every year at this time was always special, but this year was especially special, for in addition to the great food, an invitation was extended to sign up for another four years. For me, it would mean a promotion from staff sergeant to tech sergeant...going from three stripes up and one across to three up and two across. At that time in my life, if I had been offered a general's star, I would have turned it down.

When the United States Marine Corps handed me my discharge, I also received a ruptured duck pin, which signifies that you are no longer in service, and a replica of the pin on a small yellow patch to be sewn onto the front of your uniform in the event you wore it after going home. I still have both my greens (with my ruptured duck) and my dress blues hanging in my closet. I would have to shed 45 pounds to fit into them now.

I returned home early because the government was discharging service men according to a point system. Points were given for overseas time, with additional points for each engagement. My trips to Midway Island, landings on to Tinian, Saipan, Marshall Islands, and the Easter morning invasion of Okinawa put me out in front to go home first.

It is worth repeating the story that hit the newspapers when we landed in San Francisco. The late President Roosevelt's widow, Eleanor, suggested strongly: "All returning Marines should be sent to a camp for rehabilitation before they are turned loose on the public." This news item did not set well with any of us!

As one of the first veterans released on the unsuspecting public, I deemed it my duty to help each returning warrior celebrate his return to civilian life. The next few months are not too clear in my memory, but I did find out that although I was not a good drinker, I did have the ability to bounce back from some terrific hangovers with the help of lots of Anacin tablets.

Dad asked me what I was going to do with my life and I told him, "I haven't a clue." It was then he gave me a diamond ring given to him by a partner, Al Stern. Al Stern was a pharmacist working out of Chicago, and his connection with Northwest Indiana was his furnishing the famous Indiana Doctor of Tremont most of his illegal drugs. What comes around goes around.

Mr. Stern and my father had about fifty slot machines scattered throughout Porter County. The attitude at the time was best stated by the Mayor of Valparaiso who was quoted, "If there is going to be gambling, and there will be, we will have our own people run it, not anyone from the outside."

It was Dad's suggestion I attend a school in Chicago to learn how to repair slot machines. This sounded fine with me so I started my informal education. School was in its second week when I received a call from Dad: "It's all over. Come on home." Evidently, some one in authority decided that the slot machines would have to go.

My next move fooled everyone, including myself. For some reason I had an idea engineering was something that I would like to do. To prepare myself, I decided to go back to Valparaiso High School to take some courses that would prepare me for entering Valparaiso University when the next semester started.

During this blur in my life, drinking seemed to be part of social life, so I started to celebrate homecomings for veterans I didn't know and didn't even care to know.

My decision to pursue an engineering degree was a mistake. I just wasn't ready to settle down. In fact, there were many mornings before school I would have to stop at the Old Style Inn to pick up my books from the previous night's celebration. But the GI Bill was paying, so I continued to party.

To catch up with my lack of education, I was required to take a course called "Grammar O (Zero)." The name was embarrassing enough, but it was a requirement for all freshmen who "goofed off" in English classes in high school.

I fondly recall that the O (Zero) Class was taught by a short trim young lady with a big chest named Miss Allen. I could tell immediately that my lack of concentration in high school could get me in trouble in this course unless I took steps to cover my lack of class preparation.

Miss Allen wasn't a looker, but I soon discovered she made up for her lack of looks with other talents. Our relationship worked out well because Miss Allen didn't want it known she was dating a student. Faculty frowned on extracurricular activities with students, even though I was a couple of years older than my professor. I wasn't too keen on being seen in public with her, so our secret worked for both of us.

For the time being the first education crisis seemed to be solved, but the storm clouds were still gathering.

I decided to try out for the baseball team. Don Warneke, the coach, was a 6'11" former basketball player at Valpo who knew as much about coaching baseball as I did about engineering. But I got caught up in the excitement of the game so almost all of my efforts were directed to making the team as the starting second baseman. Meanwhile, I continued to keep on the good side of my Grammar O instructor. With so much of my time geared toward making the baseball team, I made a decision to drop a history course, since it was taught by an older male professor and I didn't have a plan to "protect" my grade in history.

One of my favorite friends on the baseball team was our only catcher in 1945, Abe Gibron from Michigan City. Abe attended Valparaiso University for one year and then transferred to Purdue where he made All American in football and then went on to play professional football. He played All Pro five years in Cleveland and later coached the Chicago Bears for three years.

Abe still holds the record at Valparaiso University. We played Notre Dame a double header and he struck out nine out of ten times! He still holds another record - no one could keep up with Abe at the buffet table.

It was a week before our big game with Illinois and I was checking the bulletin board. My name was conspicuous by its absence on the traveling squad.

I headed straight to the coach's office. Looking up at someone 6'11" when you are angry adds to your feeling of frustration. The anger didn't lessen when he told me that I was scholastically ineligible for this upcoming road trip to Illinois and if I had a complaint I should take it directly to the president, O.P. Kretzmann. I could tell by his attitude that coaching baseball would not be his lifetime career. I also could tell our conversation was over.

I really thought I had my tail covered as far as staying eligible. My Grammar O (Zero) grade was extremely better than my test grades, but I presume my "homework" must have helped. I had dropped the history class before the grades came out so I assumed I was covered. I came to the conclusion that the school, some how, had made a terrible mistake. Surely, somebody would have to straighten out the whole mess or I would have to go to the Grievance Committee of the Veterans Affairs to plead my case.

Meeting with President O.P. Kretzmann was like having an audience with the Pope. His office was located on the old campus and the atmosphere was very stiff, stuffy, and formal.

His secretary invited me to have a seat in his office and I was told he would be with me in a short time. When he entered the room, I sprang to my feet like I was reporting to Captain Rock. The president's dress seemed to be identical to the priest at the local Catholic Church and this was before it was popular for Lutheran ministers to dress like Catholic priests.

His first statement threw me a curve. "Bill, how are your parents?" I thought he would start out in a different direction like apologizing for the terrible mistake the university had made and how it all would be made up to me. That isn't what happened next. After a few more comments about my folks, he said, "Bill, what can I do for you?" This shocked me because I thought he was keeping his hand on the pulse of the welfare of the veteran's problems. I started to explain that someone had made a terrible mistake with my academic standing and I needed to have it corrected so I could join the traveling squad for the "BIG" game coming up Saturday at Springfield against Illinois.

I decided not to mention that my grades were all passing and how well I was doing in my Grammar O (Zero) class.

The president seemed to take in my story with interest. In fact, he excused himself as he made a telephone call. After he hung up, the pleasant smile seemed to disappear. He said, "Bill, did you drop out of a history class last week?" I immediately jumped to the offense. I gave him what I thought was a great explanation of why I had dropped the class and how dull the professor (male) was. I added that I dropped the class before the grade period ended so it wouldn't affect my grade.

Upon completing my case summary, OP gave me a lecture of how many hours of classes must be carried to be a full-time student and to be eligible to participate in athletics. "Bill, by dropping the history class, you are considered a part-time student, and therefore, you are ineligible to participate in our athletic program. This is effective immediately."

After his explanation, I came up with one of those "brilliant" statements. "If I'm not eligible to play baseball this weekend. I think it might be the right time for me to leave this school." The president fooled me one more time. He simply said, "I agree with you. I think you should leave."

The "homecoming" parties continued, but the classroom distraction was out of the way. In fact, I seemed to be catching up on some much needed sleep.

I received an invitation for a weekend visit to the campus of Indiana University where I was pleasantly surprised to find out that this school was very serious about their parties and the welcome mat was out to veterans. This weekend convinced me that I.U. was the right place for me. Because of my past experience, I made several changes to assure that a new start would relieve me of the pressure that seemed to come with higher education.

My experience at Valparaiso taught me engineering wasn't for me. Besides, it interfered with extracurricular activities and my "homecoming parties." So I decided to follow in those big footprints of my older brother and enter Indiana's School of Education. This sounded pressure-free, especially physical education. That was it! I would become a COACH and a teacher.

My mother and father both agreed with my decision to go south to pursue my education. I really think they were ready for me to fly the coop. This didn't hit me until many years later when my wife and I had three children of our own. Our son at the age of 42 asked to stay with us a few weeks when he was getting on his feet. He came with a young beautiful

Great Dane named Miles and it only took a few weeks for me to say to my bride, Liz: "How long is he staying? It's not the dog that is the problem. It's the dog's master. The dog minds."

In any event, I loaded up my new 1946 Maroon Ford coupe with my meager belongings, including a baseball glove and spikes and headed for a new chance at education in Bloomington.

I checked into Indiana University and was assigned living quarters in an old Navy portable housing building on the east end of the campus. Things didn't get off to a great start because there were no doors on the rooms. I had the feeling of de-ja vu all over again. It instantly brought back memories of USMC boot camp. I had the feeling that I had not progressed very far, but it was a new chance. So I took it in stride...well, almost.

If I were going to follow in the footsteps of older brother Guy, I came up with the idea of looking into a fraternity. He was a member of the Acacia House, and of course, in keeping with his legacy, I attended a couple of rush parties. The first thing I noticed, they had doors on all of their rooms. This alone convinced me that I needed to make the move from my barracks. So I informed my good friend Don Findling that I was going to move into a more modern building with doors.

I soon discovered being a pledge in a fraternity might be beyond my age and experience. When you are a freshman and a pledge, you are pretty low on the totem pole. You are assigned a fraternity father type to give you advice and counsel on educational matters.

James "EARS" Sparks was assigned to me. He was from a small town in Indiana called Bloomfield. Jim told me there were two Jim Sparks in his town. If I ever wanted to mail him a letter, I was to put "EARS" on the envelope. The U.S. Post

Office would make sure that he got it. No need to ask why, as the nickname was very obvious.

The situation got interesting when an 18-year old with big ears is trying to be a father figure to a 23-year old Marine veteran with five silk handkerchief knots under his belt. EARS and I got along just fine. In fact, I think after a couple of months, the roles were reversed. I became more the father to my fraternity brother.

My problems with English at IU started to raise its ugly head so I started to look around for a solution to this problem once and for all.

The government under the G.I. Bill of Rights had tests for veterans coming back from the Great War and if you passed the test, you would be given so many hours of credit in English and other subjects. My problem was passing this test. I knew I couldn't make it on my own so I found a very bright fraternity brother named Bill Thompson. I offered him $10 to take the English examination under my name. He agreed and I paid him in advance.

My plan was not perfect. The evening of the test my clone was in the process of taking the test when he saw a student being asked for his identification as he handed in his exam to one of two proctors running the tests. This set my substitute into a panic because he looked nothing like my picture on the I.D. He was white, with an Afro haircut, and glasses that resembled the bottom of soda bottles.

He threw his crumpled test into the wastebasket and started to leave when one of the young proctors asked, "What are you doing. I have to account for every government test?" As he leaned over to pick the test out the basket, my man made a brilliant move. He bolted out of the room and headed back to the Acacia House.

When he told me his story, I assured him not to worry because I wouldn't drag him into my problem. Still he was a nervous wreck!

The next day I had a telephone message that the Dean of Students, Colonel Shoemaker, wanted me to be in his office at 2 p.m. I once again assured my test taker he was in the clear but I thought my educational days at Indiana University were to be short lived.

Colonel Shoemaker was a very short man about 5'7" who was in charge of the ROTC when my older brother Guy had enrolled at the university in 1939. Of course, Big Brother was in ROTC from the get-go. He also was on the Dean's List from the get-go.

Dean of Students
Raymond L. Shoemaker

There was something unusual about the Colonel. He always wore dark glasses both inside and outside so it was almost impossible to see his eyes. I was about 10 minutes early, but the Colonel made me wait until 2:30. When he walked in, I jumped out of my chair as if I were still in the Marine Corps. The Colonel immediately said, "At ease, son." This was followed by, "Tell me about your Brother Guy, where he is, and where has he been." I gave him the "catch-up" on Guy, including his Bronze Star and the big German capture by the Big Red One, and told him about the new German Lugar he gave me when he came home. My story took 15 minutes, but the Colonel then went on for 45 minutes telling me that Guy was a great military man as well as a great student. After the stories, he looked at me and said, "Tell me son, why did you walk out on this government test?" I tried to explain that my grade in English was not too good and I thought I wasn't doing well on the test and, if I failed the test, it would affect my present grade. At this point, I felt that the Colonel's eyes were directly looking into mine when he said, "That is the part that bothers me most. You only finished 80% of the test and you passed. If you had completed the test, we would be asking you to teach English here at Indiana." Then he said, "I want you to get out of here and I don't want to see you again." The Colonel had me and he gave me a big break and let me go. I really think I should thank Brother Guy for the favor from Colonel Shoemaker.

I was in a happy mood when I hit the front door of the Acacia House. So I looked up my friend-and-substitute-exam-taker. I gave him the results of my meeting and I told him the pressure was off, I had received six hours of credit in English. My next statement even shocked me when I said, "Would you consider taking the history exemption exam? I'll give you $25 to take that one." Of course, he said "No," followed by, "You must be out of your mind."

The Colonel came into my life as one of my teachers in Education, but he was always fair and I did well in his class, except for one time when we were to do a project in making a beanbag. Of course, I took the easy way out and I asked my Mother to make the beanbag, adding that she shouldn't make it "too good." My only mistake was when I told Mom to make it out of a piece of camouflaged silk parachute material that I had brought home in the bottom of my sea bag. On the final day when we had to produce our bags, the class met on the grass outside the old field house. Every one had turned in their beanbags and waited for the Colonel to pass or fail them. My bag was one of the first ones he examined. "Wellman, I should flunk you," he said. He tossed the bag 20 feet into the grass. "Look out there. You can't even see your bag." Once again, I got a break as he passed on mine and everyone's work of art.

I was really doing very well in classes like Biology and Arts and Crafts. The latter was taught by a young teacher from Romania who had difficulty speaking English. I saw this as an opportunity. My good friend Bob Moore and I offered to do the roll call each day. One day I would take care of the roll call and the next class Bob would do it. The teacher loved her helpers and she never noticed that both of us were only in the class 50% of the time. It worked out for all parties and we both received "A's" in the course.

My life at the Acacia House was okay, but I didn't like being harassed by upperclassmen. I took a dislike to one young pre-dental student. He took a shot at me every chance he got. I spotted my opportunity for revenge on the way back to the house after a basketball game in the old field house.

I had another pledge named "Chigger" Babs in the front seat of my car and two "actives," Jim Cox and Jack Copher, in the back seat. When I saw my "prey" walking on his way home, I went around the block telling the others what I was about to do. I gave them a choice of ducking down or getting out. The two actives both decided to duck down as I pulled along side the pre-dental student.

"Steve, would you like a ride back to the house?" He got in the front seat before he realized he was going on a "road trip." We then put a paper bag over his head in spite of his begging and headed out of town. We drove about seven miles south of Bloomington. I stopped the car and made him take off all of his clothes. He had no idea where he was and it was close to 11 p.m. on a Wednesday evening. I drove "Chigger" Babs and the other two hunched over "actives" back to the Acacia House, leaving my victim to find his way home.

I was wakened at 5:30 a.m. and escorted downstairs where I saw Steve in a pair of bib overalls and the president of the fraternity talking to a uniformed State Trooper. The officer left and the executive branch of the Acacia House asked me to step into the library.

Steve told us he had wondered around naked for a couple of hours and finally woke a farmer who gave him a pair of very large bib overalls and the use of his telephone to call the State Police.

I had my chance to tell my side of the "kidnap" case. I simply said, "This young punk was really giving me a hard time. You can kick me out of the house because I'm not sorry for the road trip, and if he continues to harass me, I'll do it again."

The verdict was a mistrial and they decided I could stay. The pre-dental student never bothered me again. In fact, he left the "Chigger" alone as well. The final chapter of this caper: Steve got a very bad case of the crabs from those baggy bib overalls. Justice will prevail...

At this time in my life I really wasn't dating much until an upper classman, Duke, asked me to go with him and his girlfriend Darlene on a blind date with a pledge from the Theta house. Her name was Joan "Liz" Larsh.

I remember standing in the vestibule of the Theta house waiting for my blind date. She came down the stairs with a half frightened smile on her face and she introduced herself as Liz Larsh. The night was pretty much a lot of talk and a few cokes. Liz was 18 with beautiful long black hair, with a few strands of white hair mixed in. Fifty-six years later I'm still married to my blind date and she now has a few strands of black mixed in with all of the beautiful white hair.

It was a clear spring day. As I walked across the campus, I could hear the crack of a bat hitting the ball and the chatter of the players on the first day of practice. I spent half an hour watching as they finished their workout and then I made the decision to give baseball another chance. I walked into the Athletic Department to introduce myself to the I.U. baseball coach, Pooch Harrel.

The meeting lasted for over an hour because I was asked the same questions about Brother Guy and his war record that

Colonel Shoemaker had asked. Pooch also wanted to know more about Guy's baseball career and where he was headed.

The subject finally turned to me, and what I had in mind for baseball and Indiana University. In my own humble way, I convinced Coach Harrel that I would be worth a "walkon" and a tryout. He agreed and invited me to be at the practice at 3:00 p.m. the next day.

The first question Coach Harrel had asked, was, "Bill, what position are going to try out for?" I answered before I gave it much thought. "Maybe I'll try to follow in Guy's footsteps and put on the 'tools of ignorance' behind home plate." It took me three innings in an intrasquad game to convince both Coach Harrel and myself that I was not going to make it as a catcher. I was moved to second base where I felt very comfortable.

Indiana University Baseball – Freshman year, Coach Harrel

My first year I worked very hard to pick up the experience I missed in high school and the years in the Marine Corps. My second year was under a new coach, Danny Danielson. Danny played on the same team with Brother Guy when they played prior to World War II. I made the team when Danny moved a great second baseman to short stop, Woody Litz. Woody really taught me how to play second base and we turned out to be a pretty good double play combination. I was what you would call: "good field but light when it came to hitting."

Baseball in college was fun and I really enjoyed it. This team was right in the middle of the Big Ten pack during my sophomore year. The one game I will always remember was our last of the season at Minnesota when I took at bad hop from a ground ball to my lower jaw. It reminded me of Dad taking two balls to his face at one time in Kouts. The result was two loose teeth and a big fat lip.

This wild pitch almost took my head off!

During our celebration of both a victory and the end of the season, I drank my beer through a straw. Not a good idea! The party was long and hard, but we knew we had to catch a train to Chicago. I still wish we had a movie of our procession carrying our young, passed out coach to the train station. We made the train and I had just played my last college baseball game.

I was in my second year at Bloomington when I received a telephone call from Dad. It went something like this: "How are you doing with your education?" Of course, I told him that

I thought I had things under control, but I wasn't too excited about becoming a teacher/coach. His next statement threw me a curve when he said, "I have this chance to buy a place called "The Palace." It has a three way license (beer, wine, liquor) that we would move to a new location, but I won't buy it unless you are interested in coming home to run it." I told him I had a definite interest and would call him back.

It didn't take me long to make up my mind. I told Dad, "I'm just not excited about following Guy in becoming a teacher/coach and besides, I would like to make more money and lead a little more exciting life."

The next thing I knew I was on the night shift at "The Palace." It was on the main street in Valparaiso, exactly where the Binders jewelry store is now. If I were looking for instant wealth and excitement, I didn't find it there. My job was working behind the bar and the most exciting thing that happened was when I said to my dad, "Why is the juke box so loud?" His answer was right to the point. "If I turn it down, every one will hear the rats in the basement." Remember, this was before the Orkin Man and pesticides. There were huge rats down there and I thought about them each time I had to go down stairs for supplies. Fortunately for me, we moved to a new location called "The Corral."

Chapter Five

THE CORRAL

In 1948, we moved just down the street to a new location in Valparaiso. We moved from "The Palace," at 23 East Lincolnway and now Binder's Jewelry, to "The Corral," at 66 Lincolnway where The Bon Femme restaurant is located.

The business we replaced was a restaurant called "The American Restaurant", which had been done in red, white and blue, and was operated by a young Greek family. They also operated the bus depot and restaurant on the corner where Kelsey's Steakhouse is now.

The Palace

The American Restaurant had been closed three months. In 1948, if a restaurant closed for three months, the cockroaches became hungry and mean!

I'll never forget the first time I opened the door and walked into the large cooler. I was positive I could hear the scratching of their feet as the little critters ran to safety.

There were only a few pesticide companies, but we picked the biggest in the area. In 24 hours, Mr. Torbeson, owner of our building and the adjacent Torbeson's Drug Store, bolted through the front door screaming, "What are you doing? My cat is dead and I'm being invaded with rats and roaches." We explained our problem, and the imperative for quick action. Mr. Torbeson then hired the same company and pushed the bugs and varmints across the alley to Horn's Meat Market, or further east to the former home of "The Palace."

When The Corral opened in 1948, it was a huge success right from the start. It was located across the main street from the Premier Theater, and the horse bookie called "The Hole."

Premier Theater

To design the interior of The Corral, we hired Bud Miller, who was an interior decorator with Marshall Field in Chicago but lived with his mother in Valparaiso. Hiring an interior decorator, with the reputation of Bud Miller, was unheard of in 1948, but I think the people of Valparaiso were really ready for a quality lounge with great food. Our bartenders came to work for their evening shift in a white shirt with a conservative tie and they wore full-length white aprons. Their uniforms looked good and the customers appreciated the atmosphere. No television or radio, just a jukebox. No air-conditioning, but we had drilled a well and used the cool water with a huge fan, blowing cool air throughout the Corral.

Opening night was a grand event for quiet Valparaiso. Dad, wearing a white ten-gallon Stetson (like Bronco John Sullivan) rode a very calm Pinto (owned by Wilbur Dibkey) down the main street, over the curb and through the front door, not just once but ten times. The only accident occurred when Dad put his shoe through one small pane of glass in the inside door of the front vestibule.

The Corral Opening Night 1948

The bar was filled with more than 200 happy customers throughout the evening. Pictures were taken of people getting on and off the horse until the wee hours of the morning. The horse's fanny was slapped as many times as those of the waitresses with no complaints or casualties, but more important, no liability insurance. The words "liability insurance" were not in our vocabulary in 1948.

Father Guy on his Pinto

This is a real copy of the luncheon menu that we used in 1948. Every time I look at the price points I wonder how we made a living, but Liz and I never seemed to want for too many things. We raised three great kids, all of whom turned out exceptionally well.

The Corral
Wellman's
66 Lincolnway Valparaiso, Ind. Phone 9-1741

My salary in 1948 was $65.00 per week and I worked 6 ½ days a week. Six nights were ten hours per night, but truthfully, a lot of it was fun.

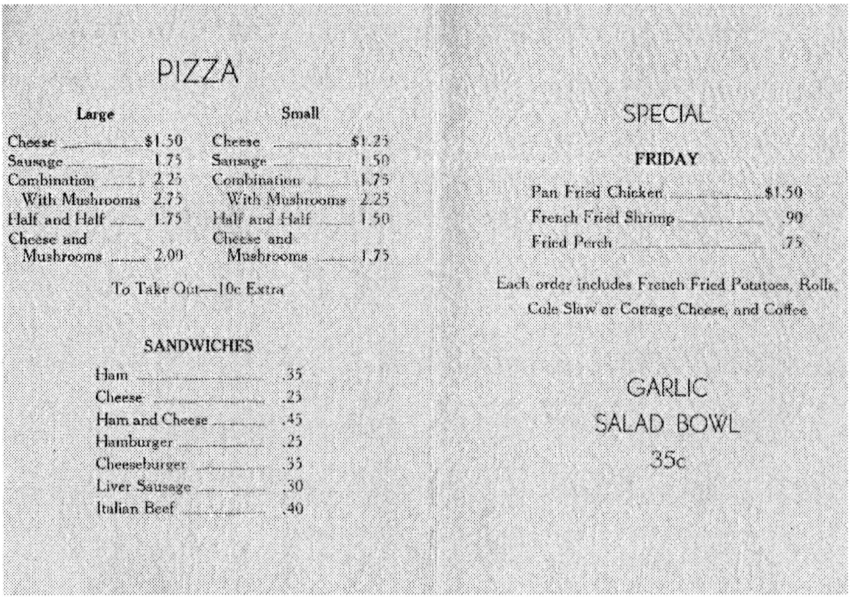

PIZZA

Large		Small	
Cheese	$1.50	Cheese	$1.25
Sausage	1.75	Sausage	1.50
Combination	2.25	Combination	1.75
With Mushrooms	2.75	With Mushrooms	2.25
Half and Half	1.75	Half and Half	1.50
Cheese and Mushrooms	2.00	Cheese and Mushrooms	1.75

To Take Out—10c Extra

SANDWICHES

Ham	.35
Cheese	.25
Ham and Cheese	.45
Hamburger	.25
Cheeseburger	.35
Liver Sausage	.30
Italian Beef	.40

SPECIAL

FRIDAY

Pan Fried Chicken	$1.50
French Fried Shrimp	.90
Fried Perch	.75

Each order includes French Fried Potatoes, Rolls, Cole Slaw or Cottage Cheese, and Coffee

GARLIC
SALAD BOWL
35c

NO T.V. – NO ENTERTAINMENT!

In 1948 operating a bar without entertainment was not as hard as it might seem. These saloons – bars – lounges were gathering places where people could carry on conversations and have a few drinks, and of course a few good laughs along with carrying out a little business every once in a while. A lot like European social clubs!

Ernie Roach and Guy Wellman, Sr.

We had a few real "characters" in Valparaiso, and I think we allowed them a little more freedom to practice their act of being characters. It was our way of offering a different type of show business for our customers.

Ike Norris

Ike Norris was my #1 character. He was interesting as well as way ahead of his time. He always wore a new tan canvas hunting coat (like John Kerry), bracelets, rings on half of his fingers, a thin copper tube around both wrists, and an Indian necklace that had very little value, but just seemed to fit Ike. He had salt and pepper hair that flowed down to his shoulders. He was definitely way ahead of his time.

When I first met Ike I was about 24 years old and I would guess Ike was close to fifty. He hit the door of The Corral about 10:30 a.m. and ordered a Budweiser and a shot of 100 proof Old Grandad.

A young Ike Norris

After his second round he started to double talk to himself – but he did it out loud.

It was interesting that he would double talk until it was time to order his next round, and then the order "a shot of Old Grandad and a Budweiser," came out as clear as a bell.

The next time Ike visited The Corral he unveiled what he thought was his real talent. When he hit the front door, he carried in a music stand and a violin case. The first thing he did was order his Old Grandad and a Budweiser, and then he proceeded to set up his music on the stand. Once he had everything in place he hit the bar stool and started to enjoy his "lubricant." After his first round he reached for his violin and started to perform. It turned out to be terrible! He could not play one note, but he put on the act and continued until he completed what he thought was the entire song.

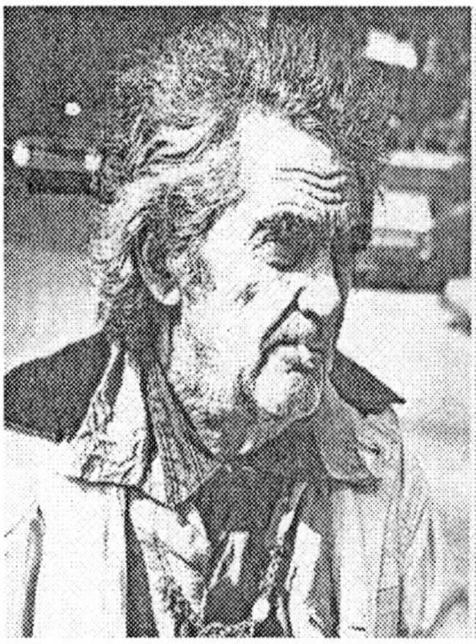

Ike after a few Grandad's

We knew Ike Norris saw himself as a violinist, but he not only couldn't read a note, he had absolutely no idea of how to play a violin. From that first day, we considered Ike as part of our entertainment and we got so used to letting him perform we really didn't pay too much attention to him. It was really interesting to watch the expression of strangers who came into The Corral, as they watched Ike enter, set-up his equipment, and go through his performance. Our reputation as a very unusual bar continued to grow. Who needed high-priced entertainment?!

A young Ray Marrel, Ike's agent

I had heard that Ike's family had setup a trust so that he was financially sound; and there was also the story on the street that the local draft board couldn't convince Ike he was eligible for the draft. He refused to go for the physical, so Ezra Stoner and another member of the draft board took Ike to Chicago to have him take the physical for the Army. On the outskirts of Chicago, Ike asked them to stop at a filling station to use the restroom. Ike walked out the back door and returned to Valpo before the draft board members made it home. After this little fiasco the draft board just took a pass on Ike.

Late one Friday night, after Ike had given our customers one of his better performances, he discovered his violin and case had disappeared. He immediately left The Corral and headed for the local police station, where he filed a report. On the report he listed his violin as a Stradivarius, worth thousands of dollars.

Kelly Gott was the local police chief, under the Mayor John Wiggins, and he immediately started his investigation by coming with Ike to the bar. He began interviewing anyone who had knowledge of the missing violin. The chief was serious because he vaguely knew that a Stradivarius was worth a lot of money and he wanted to hit the trail while the scent was still hot. It only took Kelly one hour. By 1:00 a.m. he was in his squad car and headed east to Plymouth, Indiana to apprehend two key suspects.

Saturday morning the chief called my home and asked me to come down to City Hall. He informed me that the case had been solved with two employees of the Pennsylvania railroad confessing. They admitted they had been doing too much drinking in The Corral that night, and they thought, as a practical joke, they would steal Ike's violin and take off for Plymouth. According to Chief Gott, the two suspects were behind bars and had confessed. By the time they drove home, they thought better of their idea and decided to do away with the evidence by taking it to the backyard of one of their homes and setting fire to the violin and case.

When the Chief arrived at their home, they showed him where they had burned the evidence. It just so happened it had snowed two inches, so when the Chief looked at the crime scene he found the burned ashes in the shape of a violin with the strings waving in the cold Indiana winter wind. He scraped up the ashes, strings, and hardware from the violin case and put the evidence in a cigar box. The Chief brought the evidence and the prisoners back to the jail in Valparaiso.

Before I went to the police station I received a call from the local newspaper in Plymouth asking me about the theft of a very expensive Stradivarius from The Corral. The reporter also asked if I knew if the violin was worth $50,000, as it had been stated in the police report. My answer was, "I have no idea of the dollar value of the instrument, but I did know that there was a lot of sentimental value to the owner."

By this time, what I thought was a very funny caper, had turned into a theft which could send a couple of practical jokers to prison. When I arrived at City Hall the scene looked more serious than even I could imagine. Harry Essler was the Justice of the Peace who was going to hear the case. Harry worked at McGills full-time and he was a duly elected Justice of the Peace from Valparaiso and Center Township. The Chief of Police was there with his two prisoners along with both of their wives and the prisoner's parents. Ike Norris was there with his jewelry, long hair, and his tan hunting jacket. On the table, in front of the Chief was a cigar box that held the vital evidence. The local newspaper reporter was in attendance, along with the reporter from Plymouth who had called me.

The scene was set for a serious trial that could be called "grand larceny." As Harry (the judge) rapped his gavel to call the trial to order, both wives of the accused started to cry, which set off both mothers into a sobbing frenzy. As the judge read the accusations he asked them to plead and they both told the judge they had made a terrible mistake, but that they had too much to drink and they were very sorry for their sins. They both pleaded guilty.

At this point, the Chief of Police looked at Ike and said, "Ike, this caper has gone far enough. Tell the Court the real value of your violin." I thought Ike would give the judge a little of his famous double-talk, but I think it took a little Old Grandad and a Budweiser to set him off! Ike hesitated and looked into the Chief's one eye (I neglected to mention that Kelly Gott had lost one eye in an accident when he was a boy, but I will save more stories about the Chief for later on) – so when Ike looked into the Chief's one eye, the drama was so tense you could cut it with a knife when Ike said, "ten dollars." Harry, the judge, did not hesitate to smack his gravel on the table and say, "The defendants will pay $10.00 and Court costs of $32.50 each and this case is dismissed."

The wives were happy, the mother's were ready to scold their sons, the reporters were disappointed that the violin caper was a bust, and Ike seemed satisfied with his new $10.00 bill! The Chief was happy he had solved another case and Judge Essler went to work on the night shift at McGills. I thought we would miss Ike on our entertainment schedule, but a new character would come along to take his place.

Two weeks later, Henning Tauck presented Ike with a base fiddle he had stolen from Calumet City. The very next Saturday Ike was seen boarding a Greyhound Bus with a rope handle around his new instrument. We later heard that Ike had taken the base fiddle to Lyon and Healy in Chicago for repairs, but when he found out the estimate, he left the instrument in Chicago. Hell, he couldn't play a note anyhow.

One early evening on a busy Thursday, I was the only bartender on duty dressed in the uniform of the day: a white shirt, a very wide tie, dark trousers and a full-length white apron.

The bar was almost filled except for a few single bar stool openings. In walked a very short man (about the size of a jockey) in his early fifties. I recognized him as a dishwasher from Strongbows Restaurant located on U.S. 30 just outside the city limits of the Vale of Paradise.

On spotting this short fellow, it crossed my mind that someone had warned me you should never let this fellow have too many beers because he had the tendency to lose control and would wet his pants.

He also did a lot of smiling, but very little talking. He looked sober so I said, "What would you like to drink?" He didn't hesitate when he said, "A glass of beer." So I drew him his beer and continued to tend the bar and service the two waitresses.

I looked up at the waitress station in the middle of the bar and a customer was waving to me. As I approached, he said,

"Bill, that fellow you just served wet his pants." I'm usually in control of my temper, but just the thought of this little jerk ordering a beer and then immediately soiling his pants raised the hair on the back of my crew cut head.

I walked up to the short smiling man and picked up his half full glass of beer out of his small hand and then I looked him directly in his eyes and said, "Now I want you to leave and I don't want you to come back." He stopped smiling and he said, "Why what did I do?" There was real anger in my voice as I countered: "You know what you did, now leave and don't come back."

He slowly got up and disappeared through the front door. It was some 15 minutes before the second bartender Moon Moser came on duty. I needed to mop up the mess around the bar stool so I got a bucket of soapy water and started to swab the deck in the vicinity where the customer had been seated.

After cleaning up the mess, it took us another 15 minutes to catch up on all of the customers' needs. Then in walked another customer who approached the same bar stool that the Strongbow dishwasher had just left. He said, "Boy someone must have spilled something. The floor is all wet." I immediately came from behind the bar and walked over to the waitress station. Sure enough there was a big puddle in the exact spot that I had just cleaned up.

I went back behind the bar and kneeled on the floor with a flashlight in hand. The beam of light landed on a steady drip of water coming from a leaky water pipe.

I'm sure the "smiling dishwasher" went over to Buck's Bar or Shoemakers on Washington Street and justifiably complained that the bartender at the Corral was "crazy." The description was probably on the mark.

In 1948, our waitresses in the Corral were a little on the rough side, but I think this was an asset in the bar business. Dorothy Jenson, a young lady who worked for my folks at The

Club when she had just turned 17, was an excellent waitress with a small tattoo on her right arm. When asked what the tattoo meant, she always came back with the same answer, "If you can read the tattoo, you are too damn close."

A new waitress in the Corral always had to go through somewhat of a hazing period to toughen her up. One trick that always worked on a new girl was to tell her, "Dot, would you see if Mike Hunt is here. He has a telephone call." Of course, after walking through the bar with 150 to 200 people calling out repeatedly, "Is Mike Hunt here? He has a telephone call," she would soon catch on that the bartenders were pulling her leg!

The bartenders in The Corral also told the waitresses whoever was the lucky guy to have the privilege of taking them home had to help stock the coolers full of bottled beer. It was nothing at 2:00am for a stranger to be on his knees looking up and saying, "Where does the Pabst Blue Ribbon go?"

Of course, there would always be a steady customer who knew exactly where the Blue Ribbon was placed in the cooler. One such customer, who shall be nameless, told me this tale. He had been escorting the same young lady home for several months and while he was riding on some romantic lonely country road, the waitress turned to him and said "Joe (not his real name), if we are going to do anything, let's do it because today is my anniversary and I have to get home!" It was a simple time of life and priorities were priorities!

The best practical joker of the '40s and '50s was Mr. Wilbur "Web" White, the President of the First National Bank of Valparaiso located on the south side of the Court House square. Here's a couple of examples.

Web had made a $10 bet on the Chicago Bears game on Sunday with Bill Take who was a partner with Henning Tauck in a local bar and restaurant, the Old Style Inn.

"Web" lost the bet. So at 8:30 a.m. on Monday he knew that Bill Take was just getting ready to open for the day. Web opened the front door and yelled, "Wilbur, here's your $10" and then proceeded to roll 10 silver dollars into the restaurant. He then headed down the street to open the bank.

With the help of three of his waiters, Bill Take found only eight of the silver dollars. The rest of the day the staff working the lunch shift kept their eyes glued to the floor looking for the two missing silver dollars.

In fact, Mr. White had only rolled in eight silver dollars, knowing the day would be taken up in a hunt for the remaining two dollars. Eventually, Bill figured out that Web had played a joke on him. I never did learn if he finally collected on his bet.

"Web" knew that my Mother was an easy target and she was the victim of a number of his jokes. For instance, The Corral was well known in 1949 for its fresh pan-fried perch and potato salad. So at lunch one day, "Web" called our No. 1 waitress Dorothy Jensen over and said, "Dorothy, there is a raw potato in my potato salad." Dorothy didn't hesitate to hit the swinging doors into the kitchen where at once my Mother and her Number 1 helper Sarah Joyce started to dissect the potato. Mother asked Sarah, "How could one potato be raw when we cooked all of the potatoes at the same time?" After 15 minutes of tasting different portions of the big kettle of potato salad, Mother decided to talk to the customer. But by this time, "Web" was back in his office and I'm sure he had a smile on his face knowing he was playing mind games with Mother.

Who else would have carried a raw potato wrapped in wax paper into the restaurant and placed it in the potato salad? Only Wilbur "Web" White!

It was during my first year tending bar that I learned my first real lesson in inventory and control. I think Dad really trusted people and thought that everyone was honest.

For some uncanny reason, I had a feeling that the young man who was selling and delivering cases of 7-up was cheating us on each delivery. But I wasn't sure how he was doing it until the second time I found a discrepancy involving three cases in our inventory.

He was writing up his receipt at the bar when I informed Dad that I had him cold. So I sat on one side of him and Dad was on the other side. Then I asked, "How long have you been screwing us?" He didn't hesitate to respond: "Only a couple of months." I knew I had him so I told just a little lie when I said, "No, it's been longer than that because I've been checking your count for some time." Again, he didn't hesitate to respond, "It's been about six months." He then broke down and started to cry as he tried to explain that he was hooked on a pinball machine in a tavern in Kouts and he had lost so much money that he had started to steal from us to make up for his gambling problem.

Our next move wasn't the correct way to solve a problem like this, but I think it was another one of Guy Wellman's Laws. Dad said to our young thief: "I want to get free 7-up from you for the next six months to make up for what you have stolen from us." He immediately agreed and he left.

Dad asked me how I uncovered the theft and so I explained that he would bring four cases of quart bottles on a two-wheel cart and take them to the basement. Then he supposedly would take four cases of "empties" out on the same two-wheel cart. But I observed that the two cases on the bottom were always full, and not the "empties." It was a simple case of theft.

I'm sure he picked on another customer to make up for his weakness with that pinball machine in Kouts, but at least our 7-up was free for six months.

The lack of television seemed to help breed characters and The Corral had its share. Sy Thune was one of my favorites.

Sy was a retired railroad worker from the Pennsylvania Railroad who lived on the corner of Jefferson and Campbell Streets. The Corral was only 3 ½ blocks from his home, and he stopped in three or four times a week for various reasons. Shopping for groceries was the usual excuse he gave to his wife so he could drop by in the mornings for a few beers with his friends.

Sy Thune

In the winter, if the grocery trips were not enough, Sy would give his wife the old "Going Hunting" excuse and drop in about 8 a.m. with his 4/10 shotgun in hand. I would take the gun and slide it under the bar for safe keeping while Sy would have a full morning with his friends.

When it was time for him to leave, I would retrieve the gun and he would make his way home. There was never any concern about Sy shooting himself or anyone else because he never brought any shells with him. I often wondered how Mrs. Thune went for the old "Going Hunting" trick.

It was on one of his grocery trips that he brought the groceries into the bar and then spent a full four hours drinking beer. When he made one of his trips to the men's room, I couldn't help myself. I switched his dozen fresh eggs with the same amount of hard-boiled eggs. This practical joke took place on a Friday morning.

At 8 am the following Monday, Sy sat down on one of the bar stools with a huge grin across his skinny face as he said, "I knew it was you when my wife called out while fixing breakfast Sunday morning." She said, "Sy, where did you buy these eggs? They seem to be all hard boiled instead of fresh. I can't fix your breakfast unless you want to eat your eggs this way."

I wasn't the only Wellman to pull a practical joke on this customer. Sy made the mistake of asking Dad, "Guy, when you go out to feed your cattle at your farm and you hit a rabbit with your truck and you don't hit it too hard, would you drop it off at my house so I could show my wife that my hunting is for real?"

I'm sure my Dad's sense of humor runs in the family because the very next day Dad spotted a dead rabbit on old U.S. 30 about 6:00 in the morning. He stopped and used a scoop shovel to scrape up the remains and then delivered the dead critter to the back steps of Sy Thune's home.

The next morning Sy settled on a bar stool with the same grin as he said, "My wife called me while she was fixing breakfast (fresh eggs, not hard boiled) and said, 'Sy, I think a rabbit crawled up on the back steps and died." Still with that grin, he continued, "I knew it was your Dad because the rabbit looked like a steam roller had rolled over it."

Remember, this was in 1948 so life was simple and it didn't take too much have some fun. Sy said he buried the remains in the back yard. My guess is he realized that he had as much chance of getting a slightly hit rabbit from my Dad as he would from his early morning hunting trips to The Corral when I kept his shotgun safely under the bar.

When the Corral opened in 1948, it took Valparaiso by storm. After four years of exceptionally great business, however, the rose started to fade and the business needed a shot in the arm. So, I went to my dad with an idea.

I told him that I had heard about a good product called "pizza." I knew very little about it except that there was a bar in Gary located on Fifth Avenue near Washington Street called The Flamingo Lounge, and they were serving the best tasting pizza in Northwest Indiana. They also were serving a great Italian Beef sandwich on fresh Italian bread that was now very high on Gary's food charts. I told dad that the only negative was, "I have heard that you need to get a pizza permit from the people who own The Flamingo Lounge, before you can operate, and without the permit they might move your oven for you." As I said this I pointed up, and my father did not need a further explanation to understand which direction the oven would go if they moved it.

Dad was always game to try new things, so I took a trip to Gary and found the owners of The Flamingo Lounge. There were three, Tommy Morgano, Chi Chi Paul, and the main operator was a huge Italian called Gus Romeo.

My first visit found the three owners having a business meeting in a very small office behind the main lounge. I introduced myself and told them what my plans were and asked if they could help me get started in the pizza business in Valparaiso.

During the entire meeting, Chi Chi Paul did not say one word. Tommy Morgano and Gus did all of the questioning. Tommy asked, "How far is Valparaiso from Gary?" I answered with short smiling answers "18 miles." Gus Romeo asked, "Do you have an oven?" "No, but I am ready to buy one if you will help me find the right one."

Before the evening was finished, we agreed to a plan. The Flamingo would charge me so much for each pre-baked pizza pie and I was to pay by cash each time I picked up an order. It all sounded good to me; no written contract, just a handshake.

The rumor on the street was that Tommy was the head of the Mafia from Chicago, and Chi Chi Paul was one of his lieutenants, but he was really better known for killing his mother-in-law and getting away with it – just a rumor.

Gus Romeo was the operator of the Flamingo and he was the man I had to deal with for the ordering and the pickup. He was also the man I paid cash to on each pickup. Now, picking up a 150 pre-baked pizza pies, and getting them 18 miles to Valparaiso, was not an easy task. But, whenever I had a problem to be solved I called on "the thinker," Homer Burrus.

I told Homer what I wanted to do and it did not take him long to figure out how to solve the problem. First, I was going to transport the pies in my 1952 Pontiac station wagon by putting the back seat down and placing a solid rod that snapped in where the back seats would snap in. Homer then designed six hardwire carrying racks that would hold 25 pizza pies. Four of the racks were for small pies and two for large pies. When a rack was filled, two straight thin rods were placed down through the eyes that were designed to lock the pizza pies in the racks for that ride from Gary to Valpo.

The pies were pre-baked so the cheese would just start to melt and the dough would start to rise. The cheese was always in small pellets when the pies were being made, so there were times when some of the pellets didn't melt enough to stick to the dough. Therefore, if I had to hit the brakes harshly, some of the cheese would roll off of the pies and find small cracks to roll into. After a few trips to Gary on hot days, the wagon started to have an aroma of its own! Three months of deliveries, three times a week, and my kids were complaining about riding in the "cheese wagon."

I became a very serious customer to the Flamingo Lounge, and after six months of very successful business, I received a visit from Tommy, Chi Chi, and the "always a cigar in the mouth" Gus. I never saw him without the cigar, but I also never saw him smoke the cigar.

The trio looked over the oven; and they seemed to approve of how we were holding the pies in the walk-in covered by clear plastic; and, how we were serving the final product. The unlikely trio spent about two hours in the Corral on the first visit. They were intrigued by the big school bell I had hung (with Homer's help) behind the center of the bar. This bell was used whenever someone would buy the house a drink.

Tommy asked me what was the largest amount we had received when a customer bought the house a drink. I told him, $12.50 was the record. He looked around and then said, "Billy, do you think we can break the record tonight?" It did not take me long to say, "yes" and he followed with, "Let's buy the house and let's ring the bell." The bill was $13.25 and Tommy had the record, but that did not stop him. Before the evening was over, he rang the bell three times.

My pizza was selling and my newfound friends from Gary were known as the Gary Bell Ringers. During the next year, the pizza sold very well, in fact, we decided to sell the pizza on Sundays. Bars were not allowed to be open on Sundays in Indiana, so we went back to "Guy's law." We hid the back bar by covering it with white sheets, and then opened for pizza on Sundays before the Premier Theater started at 7:00 p.m. It was well worth it, and the excise men never stopped us.

Gus Romeo offered to give me his recipe on the almost famous Italian Beef, so I accepted his offer. My mother followed it to the letter, and soon we not only sold the first pizza in Valparaiso, but we had the best Italian beef sandwiches in town.

When we got out of the Corral, my mother gave the recipe to Ray Marrell and he used it for many years at his restaurant called Marrell's.

The trio from The Flamingo never came back to ring the bell, but our business went on for years without a hitch. Gus Romeo called me when there was a beer strike in Lake County, and he wanted to buy 24 cases of bottled beer. It was against the law for us to sell to another owner of a three-way permit, but "Guy's Law" took over. Gus backed his 1953 Cadillac up to the back door of the Corral and I loaded all 24 cases of beer in the "seat-less" back of his caddy. This time the payment was reversed and Gus paid me in cash.

I did not see or hear much of Tommy Morgano during the next few years, but he would appear again later on in my life.

Chapter Six

WELLMAN'S RESTAURANT AND BOWLING ALLEY

In 1958 my Dad was talked into a deal involving way too many doctors. The good physicians were Dr. Eugene DeGracia and Dr. Martin O'Neill. Terms of the deal were that the Wellman family would put up its three-way liquor license from The Corral plus ten years of good will, and the doctors would provide the financial muscle to obtain the needed capital to build a 16-lane bowling alley, a cocktail lounge and a dining room to be located on U.S. 30 in Valparaiso.

I didn't think the deal favored our family, but Dad had the desire to make the move, and he always thought everyone was honest and fair, so we made the decision to move. The bowling lanes and the cocktail lounge worked out very well financially, but the doctors decided to put Dr. Pat Hauff, a retired dentist, in charge of the restaurant. Pat was a great man, but didn't realize how much dedication and long hours were required to operate a restaurant. Within six weeks, Dr. Hauff gave up the job, and the operation of the restaurant was then dropped in my lap.

My experience at the Corral was limited to the bar, so my first move was to order $32.50 worth of restaurant books from a Mr. Wensil from Dallas, Texas. An idea from the first paragraph caught my attention: "If you are having trouble in the restaurant business, try a buffet." We were having big trouble, but I had the desire, and youth was on my side to make Wellman's one of the top restaurants in the area.

I came up with the basic menu idea to call the buffet "Wellman's Chuck Wagon," so I asked Homer Burrus to make it happen. Homer started with two wagon wheels and built what looked like the back end of a cowboy's chuck wagon.

An area was set aside for a chef dressed in white, complete with a chef's cap. He would stand behind the wagon and carve generous slices from a standing, bone-in prime rib roast served with authentic au jus. Heating lamps were added, and to complete the atmosphere, Homer bent a large piece of electricians' conduit to make it look like the canvas cover of a real western chuck wagon .

Wellman's Chuck Wagon – Heinz Henze was in charge

The great one, Homer, then designed and built a stainless steel salad bar with a drain in the middle to catch the water as the crushed ice under the fresh salads slowly dripped away. It was starting to shape up. Now was the time to plan the buffet menu.

Homer's salad bar

The soups, gravies and au jus were always served hot, and were delicious, and whenever my wife, Liz, found a new recipe, she would share it with Karl West, our number-one chef. They always worked well together, and she always made valuable contributions to our menus.

The reputation of Wellman's as a popular restaurant grew slowly, but by the end of the first year we started to see positive results. During our second year, Wellman's was considered among the finer restaurants in Indiana.

To establish this kind of reputation, it takes top people working as a team to produce great food. Hot food is particularly challenging, because you must keep it from drying out. Cold food is another challenge, but restaurants are a lot like a marriage-- you have to work hard at the process, but the rewards are worth it.

Putting the restaurant together reminded me of the success my father had when he told the warden at Michigan City Prison: "If you want to have a great team, you need to build it right up the middle by hiring a good catcher, pitcher, followed by a good shortstop-second base combination and a center-fielder who can hit and catch everything coming his way." He could have been talking about building a great restaurant team too.

The CEO of Wellman's kitchen was our chef, Karl West. Karl served in the German army during World War II for four years, not as a cook, but as a shoemaker. His cooking ability was all self-taught, but his cleanliness came from his German background. No one kept a cleaner kitchen than Chef West, but he had one serious problem: He was very excitable and his strong German temper would sometimes surface. It was easy to spot, because his eyes would be as big as silver dollars when he was having a temper tantrum.

Erna Scheller and Gerta Henze check the salad bar

Nevertheless, he was tops in his creations, and transformed into an artist at work after I explained what we wanted to do with the Chuck Wagon. All of the salads were made in our kitchen. This was before restaurant supply companies learned how to make potato salad and three-bean salad. Our expert salad-maker, Erna Scheller, worked diligently to keep everything in a fresh rotation on all of the salads. Karl's two sons worked on the night shift, along with Leigh Lyle. Werner West was the oldest, and turned out to be one of the most skilled butchers in the area. Dieter West had more desire to work in the steel mills than to follow in his father's footsteps.

Gary Wassman was another dependable young man who learned his kitchen skills from his "wide-eyed" teacher, Karl West. Karl's theory was, "If you made the mess, you clean it up!"

I stuck with the "German tradition" when I hired Heinz and Gerta Henze to fill in on the night shift. They owned their own bakery, and I cooperated with them to produce the popular loaves of homemade bread served at Wellman's. These became our signature bread when each small loaf was served atop a round breadboard along with a serrated knife. This special little loaf sprinkled with flour always came to the table fresh and warm.

Gerta worked in the kitchen while Heinz was in charge of the almost-famous Chuck Wagon. Everyone worked together as a team. Hiring a good waitress staff is just as important as the kitchen personnel. These are the ladies who meet and guide the customer through their entire experience in the restaurant. One of "Guy's Laws" was particularly appropriate when it came to waitress-hiring: "It's just as easy to hire a good-looking waitress as an ugly one, and the good-looking ones will make you more money."

Over my many years of hiring, training and working with waitresses, I have developed a theory about "the wait staff." A large percentage of the lookers were divorced one time and in their second choice of "significant other," they either married again or just lived with the dude. The latter typically was not what I consider a quality breadwinner. Instead, he had a keen interest in the amount of cash she could generate on a good night of business.

Then there was the time in 1969 after we closed for the evening, about 10 of my employees decided to visit my good friend, Dick Batchelor who was running my favorite bar, "The Club." This was the same bar where I learned so many lessons about life from 1933 until 1943. Before the evening was finished, two of my good looking waitresses got into a fist fight outside of the back door of The Club. This reminded me of my childhood when my older brother and I would sit on the back steps to watch the fighters duke it out to solve their problems. This fell under "Guy's Laws: If they can't settle their differences, then take it out back."

The next afternoon Dick Batchelor called me at Wellman's with this message: "Bill, would you please not bring your riffraff waitress crew in my place again unless I have a week's notice to draw a huge crowd. I considered it the best fight of the month."

In 1970, I was managing a waitress staff in Wellman's, Bridgeview VU Theater, and the Portage Holiday Inn. It was also the time I was on the school board in my hometown of Valparaiso.

Two of the girls from the Portage Holiday Inn asked me for directions to get to the nudist colony south of Merrillville where the Miss Nude American Contest was being held on the following Saturday.

I not only gave them directions, but I hooked them up with an engineer from LaPorte who was a member of Dick Droast's Naked City and he offered to get them in free if they would meet him at Wellman's at 9:00 a.m. that Saturday.

The two girls didn't show up on time so my engineer friend left without them. They finally showed up at 10:30 a.m. asking me for directions to Roselawn and Naked City. I gave them directions and they went on their way.

Since I was on the Valparaiso School Board, I was the designated driver to go to LaSalle Peru in Illinois to interview their superintendent of schools, James Risk.

On the way back to Indiana, the other board members – Mann Spitler, Nancy Meyers, and Charlie Bowman – were discussing the interview we had just completed and the three main things that school board members can accomplish. These were: (1) stealing a superintendent; (2) planning a high school; and (3) backing up the superintendent and staying out of his way if we did a good job on number 1.

We were traveling on old U.S. 30 approaching the Pennsylvania railroad crossing when Charlie Bowman (a partner of Orville Redenbacher) said, "Bill, there is someone trying to get your attention in the car behind us by blinking their lights on and off." I pulled off the road as the car pulled up right behind us and two girls got as I watched them in my rear view mirror. They were my two waitresses from Portage, and one of them was wearing a sash that said, "MISS NUDE AMERICA." When they walked up along side of my car, the one with the sash said, "Well, I won it!" After giving them my weak congratulations and a little small talk, I drove my other three shocked school board members to each of their homes.

To this day, Charlie Bowman will never let me forget our trip to hire a superintendent of schools. By the way, we hired Jim Risk and he led the Valparaiso schools for a great number of years and built the foundation for this school system to become one best in the country. In fact, Valparaiso is now rated in the top 30 school systems in America.

PURPLE IS PRETTY

Valparaiso University hired Harry Bellefonte to perform in their new chapel, but evidently forgot to tell him that the entertainment hall was a chapel. He was impressed with the size and the uniqueness of the chapel but after his first rehearsal he made two decisions. One, he asked them to hang drapery along the side walls to improve the acoustics and second, he decided not to perform one of his favorite songs, "Back to Back, Belly to Belly."

The booking was for three days with one performance daily starting at 8:00pm Friday, Saturday and Sunday. He stayed at our Holiday Inn in the Star's Suite designed by Bud Miller from the famous Marshall Field store. It was a very impressive two-room suite featuring a beautiful suede couch with leather chairs and a new large colored T.V.

Mr. Bellefonte would sleep very late each day and would casually wander into Wellman's Restaurant for his one meal a day consisting of a 14 oz. char-broiled strip steak and a very large lobster tail. This menu stayed consistent for the three days he performed at Valparaiso University.

The waitress's comment was short and cute! I happen to walk by two of my finer girls when I heard Bonnie Biggs say to the other waitress as the two of them watched Mr. Bellefonte from behind a wooden screened room divider while he polished off the steak and lobster, "I wouldn't care if he was purple!" There was absolutely no prejudice in her statement and I know Bonnie meant every word she said!

ONE OF THE TOP 10 WAITRESS TALES

One of Wellman's better-looking waitresses was Suzie Daley. She later became a union ironworker and helped build NIPSCO's power plant in Wheatfield located near the straight Kankakee River in south Porter County. No doubt, she turned a few heads on the job.

This tale gives proof that a big percentage of waitresses are sharp and very intelligent, especially on matters of common sense and the business of life. The story goes like this: Suzie had an apartment on the east end of Valparaiso. She was divorced and lived alone.

One late afternoon she had just finished a shower and was in a robe heading for her bedroom when a rather large young man pulled her to the floor to rape her. Her reaction was quick and smart as she said, "Hold it. If we're going to do this, let's do it right? Why don't you take off your clothes and we'll get into my bed. Let's both enjoy this."

They both got up from the floor and the intruder took off his shirt while Suzie took off her robe. As he dropped his pants to the floor, she bolted out of the sliding door and ran buck-naked to her neighbors where they called the police who immediately arrived on the scene.

She was told by the young policeman that she might hear from her attacker again. The officer said, "There are occasions when this type will call back." The officer told Suzie in advance that if it was the attacker, try to keep him on the line as long as possible. Five minutes later the telephone rang. It was the intruder.

The conversation went like this: He asked her, "Why did you run? I thought we had a deal." Suzie made lots of small talk and this ended fortunately with the police catching him in a telephone booth two blocks away.

The morale of this story is simple. "A woman can run faster with no clothes on that a man can with his pants around his ankles." It took courage and smart thinking to outwit this dumb boob. My hat's off to Suzie. An example that shows **"waitresses are made of the right stuff."**

My job as manager of a restaurant team was to get customers in the habit of coming to Wellman's a minimum of twice a week. I needed to make their dining experience pleasurable and worthwhile, and I rewarded them by offering "two-for-one" dinners Mondays through Thursdays. This was accomplished by selling the dinner club cards only to the regular customers.

Our advertisement helped to build the business with the slogan: "Every night is Saturday night except Sundays at Wellman's."

Mondays through Thursdays, the waitress staff made great money, and weekends were a slam-dunk. This kept the waitress staff happy, and we rarely had any turnover on our staff.

This stable of hard-working, great-looking girls was kept under control by our top hostess, Marie Treanor. Marie worked for Wellman's for years, and continued when I left in 1973. I have been kidded about having a "Busboy Hall of Fame at Wellman's." Some of our "stars" included George

Babcocke, who became the general manager of U.S. Steel Gary Works; Jake Wagner, later Northwest Indiana's premiere home-builder and Scott Campbell, who with his wife, Jan, run a very successful outlet factory in Webster, Indiana, and soon will be building their second plant alongside "The Great Wall of China." Scott Wellman was also recently inducted into the "Hall of Fame"--but the vote was not unanimous.

The last-mentioned members of our good restaurant team were the dishwashers. This seems to be the spot to repeat another one of "Guy's Laws:" "Never fire a dishwasher until the night's work is finished." This proved to be a very dependable law.

Ruby Butterfield was known as, "The Queen Of The Machine" and the best dishwasher Wellman's Restaurant ever had but she also was not the sharpest knife in the drawer. A former inmate of the Michigan City Prison took up house keeping in Ruby's apartment. He never had a job and the excuse was, "No one wants to hire an ex-convict." and of course he told everyone his situation, so Ruby was the breadwinner.

During his stay with Ruby, he convinced her need for some type of transportation. He would then be able to take her to work and pick her up when she was finished for the day. The two of them looked around and found a bright red Opel made by Buick. Ruby and her chauffer were getting along fine for four months, when I had a visit from a local car dealer. The conversation went like this, "Mr. Wellman do you have an employee named Ruby Butterfield?" I answered, "Yes, why do you ask?" He hesitated but came up with, "She purchased a new Opel from us four months ago and we haven't had a payment from her." I explained to the gentleman that he might have a little problem but I took him into the kitchen to meet her. "Ruby, this gentleman is from the garage where you purchased your new Opel and he claims you haven't made any payments on the car." She didn't hesitate one second, "Mr. Wellman, they told me when

I bought the car, I need not put any money down and I had three years to pay for it." I looked at the salesman, his face had a priceless puzzled look as he said, "I think I had better take the car back." Ruby agreed. When the shift changed the red Opel pulled up to take Ruby home but this time they decided to walk. The four-month adventure was over but Ruby still had the Scumbag minus the Opel.

Every restaurant has someone who is a workhorse, someone who is willing to work whenever there is a need. Iris Pratt was the girl who filled any spot at any time. If the need was an early-morning breakfast served in Lakes of the Four Seasons or a late-night shift in the dining room, Iris filled the opening—and always with a smile.

During the growing years at Wellman's restaurant, my mother worked in the office, but she always gave me good advice when it came to decisions about the menu or why business was slow. For any slowdown in business, Mom always had an excuse. Some examples of her special analyses: A quick change in weather; It's tax time; School is starting; This is fair-week and business always is slow; McGill's are on vacation; The first heavy snow; Spring and it's the first day of good weather, people are cooking out.

The funny thing about my mother's theories--she was almost always right.

MOTHER'S DAY STORY

One of the busiest days for a good restaurant is Mother's Day. In 1960 I experienced a Mother's Day to remember.

When you are approaching a very busy day, a plan should be in place. We not only weren't ready for the crowds, but some very unusual things happened that Sunday.

Management took turns on the dishwashing machine just to keep up with the volume of business. I had always felt that a good manager should be able to step into any situation and do whatever is necessary to keep things moving. Once the lesson has been learned, it shouldn't happen a second time. That is good management.

By two o'clock in the afternoon, we had almost run out of milk, so I jumped in my station wagon and headed to a store to pick up four one-gallon bottles of milk. As I pulled back into Wellman's parking lot—a bit fast—I turned sharply to take a spot near the kitchen door, when two bottles hit together with a thud. Luckily, I had raised myself up from my seat just enough to avoid being soaked with the cold milk. I opened the door and two gallons poured onto the parking lot.

Needless to say, the station wagon never smelled the same. Whenever the sun hit my car, it reminded me of the many pizza trips to and from the Flamingo in Gary to replenish the huge sales at the Corral.

Finally the day ended--two hours short of our intended closing time. The reason: We ran out of food. But in spite of the low spots, we had served over seven hundred guests, and I considered the day a success...but the day was not over.

If I were a robber, Mother's Day would be the day I would pick, and that's the day Wellman's was hit. This brings up another of Guy's Laws: If you advertise your restaurant is going to be open until 11:00pm, you never close your doors until the advertised hour!

A great lady, Blanche Hermance, worked for me doing cleaning, starting at five o'clock in the morning when no one was in the building. On this Monday, she was ready to start in the cashier-area of the bowling lanes when she heard noise coming from the lower level where my office was located. Blanche called from the top of the stairs: "Bill, is that you?" The answer came back: "Yes, come on down." Blanche did not hesitate, because she was sure it was me asking her to come on down.

It was nine o'clock when I walked into my office and found Blanche on the floor tied hand and foot, with her apron stuffed in her mouth. The safe was lying on its back, and looked like someone had opened it just like a sardine can.

Blanche was OK, but she told me: "Bill, this is my last day, I'm retiring." I couldn't blame her; the experience must have scared her to death.

The total loss was $4,800. In 1960 that was a lot of money, but I thought that we were covered by insurance, so I was not too worried - until I had a conversation with the insurance man. "Bill, don't you know the difference between a robbery and a burglary?" I had to admit I didn't know, but I thought we were covered either way.

It took two weeks for the insurance company to come back and tell us we were covered, but only because Blanche Hermance had come down the stairs and had been tied up, which changed it from a burglary to a robbery. Thanks to Blanche, we were paid our $4,800 and we continued on our way. The moral of this whole story is to check that small print in your policy and listen when your insurance man explains it. Above all, ask questions.

Wellman's restaurant was building a solid reputation, and we were steadily improving our financial position, so the decision was made in 1960 to add on to the dining room and include a banquet area as part of the new addition. This addition brought our seating capacity of 100 to 250 in our dining room, and an additional 300 seats in a lower level banquet room.

New addition to Wellman's - 1960

This addition also meant we had to be busy so we could pay back the hundred-percent financing the good doctors arranged for us using their financial muscle. No infusion of cash, just muscle.

In 1962 our investors decided to buy a Holiday Inn franchise, so we built a 60-room Holiday Inn. The idea was great, but the doctors made a wrong decision when they decided to lease out the motel instead of operating it. Running a restaurant is hard, operating a 60-room Holiday Inn was a piece of cake.

The success of the complex continued, and the money pressure started to ease, so the decision was made to put ourselves back in the financial pressure-cooker by adding to our Holiday Inn with fifty-four additional rooms.

It was at this time that I decided we needed a grand opening. I had in mind not just a weekend event, but also an entire month of celebration.

We started with what I called "Purveyor's Night." This meant we sold very expensive tickets to all the purveyors who sold or rented their products to Wellman's. No supplier turned us down. In fact, tickets were at a premium, so we limited the number of tickets that a company could buy.

This event was popular because of the great food and the quality of the entertainment. The Glenn Miller Orchestra was the headliner, and Homer and Jethro were the second act. The only problem occurred when Jethro failed to show up because of illness, but Homer, the musician, amazed all of the audience as a "duo minus one."

In the Empire Room another 250 people enjoyed the now almost-famous Chuck Wagon buffet, followed by top-notch entertainment, the Ike Cole Trio. Ike looked a lot like his famous brother, Nat King Cole, except that he was six-foot-three and tipped the scales at 250 pounds. Ike and his trio played the Empire Room twice a year. He also had another brother, Freddy Cole, who came to Valparaiso and entertained along with his trio once a year.

The Ike Cole Trio

Playing in the cocktail lounge called "The Wellhouse" on Purveyor's Night was Allan D. Blasio with his inimitable antics, billed as "The World's Lousiest Piano-Player."

Over the years "The Wellhouse" was the home of some of our best lounge acts, including J.R. Waters, Jack Rowland, George Graves, George Green, The Martin Brothers and Tim and Tom. The most famous lounge act was Tom Dreeson of Tim and Tom. He was originally from Harvey, Illinois, and ended up as the opening act for Frank Sinatra for years.

Tom Dreeson from Harvey, IL

"Purveyors Night" was a great success, and continued for many years. The price was steep, but as long as the quality of food and entertainment was there, the tickets were always a hot item.

In 1968 I was approached by Ted Hrycak and his family to join them in purchasing a franchise for a Holiday Inn located at the right corner of State Road 249 and I-94 in Portage, Indiana. The term "right corner" came from Kemmons Wilson, the president and CEO of Holiday Inn of America. His theory was when you exit off of a major highway; you should make two right turns to enter the "right" property for developing a Holiday Inn. If you are across the street from this, theory has it that you will do 15 % less occupancy. His theory was right, or should I say right-right.

I felt that my main partner, Dr. Martin O'Neill, should be offered a chance to have the same opportunity to be involved with this new venture, so I gave him the chance to join this new investment.

The two Hrycaks, Ted, Sr. and Ted, J.R., along with Dr. O'Neill and myself, each put up $1,000 to purchase the franchise to build a 150-room Holiday Inn in Portage.

PLAN SECOND MOTEL – Dr. Martin O'Neil and W.F. Wellman, first and second left, executives of local corporation, and Ted Hrycak, innkeeper, consult plans at site for Wellman's second Holiday Inn in Porter County at northwest corner of U.S. 20 and Crisman Road (Ind. 249) in Portage. Corporation's first Holiday Inn is at U.S. 30

It took less than one month for me to realize that the doctor would never be able to get along with the Hrycak family. This was hard for me to understand, because I had never worked with people who were more dedicated and as honest as this family.

I realized that we had a crisis of sorts. The decision to send in the final papers on the franchise came down to the last few days. I finally told Dr. O'Neill: "Since the four of us are not able to get along, one of us has to give in and I can't afford to lose $1,000." He bowed out, so the two Hrycaks and I paid the good doctor his $1,000. Now there were three in the new Holiday Inn in Portage, Indiana.

In 1969 the Golden Nugget dining room and lounge opened with great reviews from my favorite writer and champion, Blaine "On The Go" Marz, known for his newspaper column, "Dining Out." It took one week of business for us to realize that we had picked the right name for the dining/cocktail lounge.

The month before we opened the doors, we booked Mayor Art Olson's birthday party in our new banquet room -- minus carpet. The party was a huge success; we took in $800. This was deposited in the Gary National Bank as our opening account.

MYSTERY OF MISSING MANHOLE COVERS

We had just finished Mayor Art Olsen's birthday party and we were close to officially opening the Portage Holiday Inn. The head of the Holiday Inn construction out of Memphis Tennessee informed both Ted Hrycak, J.R. and me someone had stolen four of our manhole covers from our parking lot surrounding the motel/restaurant.

This theft really puzzled the construction people, Ted, and me, but I didn't hesitate to hand it over to the Portage police. By this time I knew exactly where to go and who to see. As I was giving the information to Lieutenant Herb Olsen, I noticed a small smile start at one corner of his mouth and quickly spread to his entire face. I asked, "Herb, what's with the smile?" With no hesitation, he responded, "Bill, give me a couple of days and I will solve this case, but I would suggest you cover the holes before someone falls into one of them."

Two days later Herb called and told the construction manager to send someone over to the station with a pick-up. He had the culprits in hand, along with the four missing manholes covers.

Once we had the covers back over their holes in the parking lot, I couldn't wait to hear why they were stolen, so I made another trip to the station. In the two years I spent in Portage I would make this trip many times.

My personal theory, young people were stealing the covers for scrap resale, wasn't even close to the true reason. The young people part was right, but apparently they were cutting circles in the floors of their new apartments and placing the covers so they were flush with the finished floor -- strictly to add to the décor of their apartments. That's right; they were conversation pieces. Of course, each one had PORTAGE, INDIANA forged in big letters.

TV THIEVES

Things were going exceptionally well in both the Holiday Inn occupancy and the food and beverage sales, in the Golden Nugget dining room in Portage.

I heard on the news that some TV's were stolen from a Holiday Inn in St. Joseph, Michigan. The article discussed how three color TV's were taken Saturday night from three different rooms. The reporter gave his theory three men checked into the Holiday Inn Saturday in St. Joe and used three separate rooms. When the maids checked the rooms on Sunday, they discovered the new color TV's were missing in all three rooms. The police report theorized the thieves carried the TV's to their car in some type of very large baggage.

This news report was very much on my mind as I was helping my partner, Ted, work the front desk for the six o'clock guaranteed reservation list on Monday night. Ted had just finished checking in three single men into three separate rooms for an over-night stay. I wondered, "Could these three fellows be the three from the most recent news story out of St. Joe?"

It was forty-five minutes after the check-in when one of the three men stopped back at the reservation desk. He said, "We are going to have dinner in the dining room and I would like to charge all three meals to my room. I would also like to buy a bottle of Johnnie Walker Red Label Scotch and add it to my bill." During his little speech, this fellow kept dabbing his eye with a handkerchief like it was watering.

When they entered the Golden Nugget, I turned to Ted and said, "Didn't you think that fellow acted a little strange?"

Ted didn't think he was acting strange. I told him about the TV heist in St. Joe Holiday Inn last Saturday.

By this time, it was really starting to bother me, so I looked up their license plate number and model of their registered car and headed for the parking lot. There was no matching plate in the entire parking lot. It didn't take me long to tell Ted, "I have never done this before, but I'm going upstairs and check out all three of their rooms." Ted agreed with me and I took off. As I entered the room the first thing to catch my eye was a very large black zippered bag, which I discovered, was full of four pillows and two blankets. It looked ready to be carried to their car. Once they made the trip to their car with the pillows and blankets, they would always look like this heavy luggage was full. Down with a TV and back with pillows and blankets.

There was no luggage in any of their rooms. I was completely convinced we had the same robbers from St. Joe, ready to hit us for three brand new colored TV's. In addition, they would stick us with a very expensive dinner for three, with dessert, cigars and of course, a quart of Johnnie Walker Red Label Scotch. I convinced Ted to call the Portage Police and told him to ask for two squad cars with no lights or sirens. I met Lieutenant Herb Olsen (brother of Mayor Olsen), along with three other plain-clothes officers at the back door of the Portage Holiday Inn and explained the situation.

Lieutenant Olsen immediately came up with a plan of putting a police officer in two rooms adjacent to the three suspect's rooms. The plan included a police officer in each of the outside rooms, waiting for any of the three suspect's doors to open. His hope was to catch the thieves in the act of carrying the oversized zippered bag to their car. I had just opened the second door to allow the second policeman to enter the room when one of the three interior doors opened. The man with his handkerchief held to his eye, came out directly in front where I was standing. My first instinct was shock, but I recovered enough to say, "Hi, how are you doing?" He answered immediately with "Fine thanks." The next statement just seemed to jump out of my mouth and I almost shouted, "By the way, the man in the room with the open door would like to talk to you." I was surprised when he walked into the room and the Portage Police officer immediately put him against the wall, searched him and put him in handcuffs.

We had just changed the original plan and went to Plan B. The problem was we hadn't talked about any other plan. The police officer asked me to get the other two officers to come upstairs. I did as asked and the two officers responded. As we were coming up the stairs, I noticed the second suspect was being put in handcuffs by the second policeman. With one to go, the Lieutenant asked me to use the old, "knock on the door trick", followed with "room service". I could feel a little nervousness when the door opened, but I was almost knocked out of the way by the two rushing officers. They put him against the wall and searched him.

There were no rights read to any of the three. The final "dude" was told to put his clenched hands on the top of his head, because they didn't have enough handcuffs.

The sun was just about to set in Portage as this unusual parade marched down the second story hallway to the back stairwell. We passed several incoming, surprised guests, who stepped out of the way when they saw two handcuffed men, and one clutching the top of his head, followed by three policemen with drawn forty-fives, and the fourth wielding a sawed-off shot gun, followed by "yours truly," who was about to wet his pants.

The culprits were loaded into the back seat of the squad car with the cuffless one in the center. As they started to pull away, I noticed the police officer with the sawed-off shot gun was on his knees facing the back seat, with the end of the barrel about six inches from the head of the man in the middle.

It occurred to me that if the driver were to hit a pothole on the way to the lock-up, they could have a headless prisoner. Things started to settle down as Lieutenant Olsen opened the trunk of the suspect's car, which contained a very complete set of burglar tools. What really brought a chuckle to the three of us though, were the three sets of baby blue sneakers, lined up neatly in row, next to the tools.

The next day I made a trip to the Portage Police Station to read the final report on the TV thieves. It didn't surprise me to find out that they were the same men guilty of the St. Joe, Michigan heist, along with 32 other color TV's taken from a host of Ohio and Michigan Holiday Inns. I was surprised to learn one of the three was wanted for murder in upstate New York.

I gained a great respect for the Portage Police Department that day for the way they handled the entire situation. Their reputation of being the toughest police department in Northwest Indiana was growing every year.

THE HEALTH INSPECTOR

It was about 8:00 pm on a very busy Saturday night. There were about twenty-five people waiting in line to get tables in the dining room when my partner, Ted, came up to me and said, "There is a Portage Health Officer in the kitchen giving us an inspection." The two of us headed to the very busy kitchen and sure enough there was this fellow with a pad. He seemed to be writing notes as he was checking the hood over the range and french fryer units.

I walked up to him and very sternly said, "Sir, how would you like to spend the night in the Portage Jail?" He looked at me shocked as he said; "I was just doing it on a dare and a joke." I followed with, "I want you to leave our kitchen and I suggest you leave the building before I change my mind and call the police." He immediately left the kitchen. I followed him back to his two friends in the cocktail lounge, there was a short conversation, and the three comedians left the building.

I went into the kitchen to explain to the chef that we had just asked a not-so-funny comedian to vacate the building. It didn't take too long to get the kitchen back to normal but my partner was still very confused. How did I know that the clown in the kitchen wasn't a bone' fide health officer?

The explanation is very simple, I said, "Ted, Portage doesn't have a Health Officer. The only Health Department is in the County, so I knew immediately when he said he was from the Portage Health Department that he was a phony."

Even though we started out on a shoestring, we really did well. It didn't take long to build a reputation as a fine restaurant and a great entertainment lounge.

During our first year in Portage I hired a handwriting expert to work the dining rooms on weekends. He was exceptionally good, and only charged $2.00 for a short session. The customers seemed to enjoy it because he was good, and his background, working with industry, gave him the experience to do a very accurate job.

Ted Hrycak and I were having a closing up drink about one-thirty in the morning after a very busy Saturday night, when I suggested to the handwriting expert that he give Ted a free analysis of his handwriting. Ted wrote the required number of words, followed with a short report that hit Ted right between the eyes.

After the expert gave his report, Ted looked at me and said: "You told him!" I answered immediately: "I told him nothing!" Ted was hooked as he turned his attention back to the expert.

"Are you able to give me a report by just seeing someone's handwriting?"

The answer was a strong: "Yes I can. I do this for a living by working with industry."

Ted made an appointment to meet on Monday afternoon, and brought several sheets of handwritten material with him. After one hour, the report was ready, and Ted was told that this person should never be put in any position of trust.

The report was on Ted's night manager from the Holiday Inn on Route 421 in Michigan City. Ted was leasing this motel from Dr. Kessling, who was involved with a large dental clinic in Westville.

It didn't take Ted long to follow up on the report. He went over to Michigan City three nights in a row, unannounced. He sat in the parking lot from eight in the evening until seven in the morning.

He got the shock of his life when his night manager unloaded a two-wheeled cart that held the identical National Cash Register the Holiday Inn was using strapped to it. The scheme went like this: The manager was working with a head housekeeper, and all the business that came into the front door after nine o'clock in the evening was validated on the manager's cash register, so nothing went through Ted's register.

Ted was still in a state of shock when he set up a meeting at his manager's house on a Sunday evening.

The meeting went something like this: The manager and his wife were told early on in the meeting that they had to make a choice: First, if he didn't pay Ted back everything he had stolen from him--in cash--the second option would kick in: Ted would prosecute him to the limit, and see to it that he spent the next ten years in prison.

Ted had him cold, so the very next day his night-manager called a family meeting with his parents and his wife's parents. They were told the two choices, and the young man came up with a figure of $58,000, which included the used NCR hotel cash register.

It took the rest of the week for the parents to come up with Ted's money. The young manager lost his job, and the young couple moved to Indianapolis for a new job and a new life. None of this story would have happened if Ted had not taken the free test offered to him at one-thirty in the morning on that Saturday night in the Golden Nugget in Portage, Indiana.

OLD BELL RINGER RETURNS

Valparaiso was also doing great business, but it was with my pizza connection from the Flamingo Lounge on Fifth Avenue in Gary, Indiana, that re-acquainted me with my old friend, "The Bell-Ringer," Tommy Morgano. He became a good customer at Wellman's. He seemed to appear about eleven o'clock, four nights a week, and he usually stayed until we locked the doors for the night. He would sometimes go for breakfast before he headed back to Gary.

He was not a heavy drinker, but he did spend a lot of money buying drinks. I'm sorry we didn't bring the bell from the Corral so that the "Bell-Ringer" from Gary could buy the house a drink whenever he felt the urge.

Tommy told me that he wanted me to introduce him to people in Valparaiso, because he was planning opening a pizza parlor near the old campus of Valparaiso University, and would like to become acquainted with as many people as possible. He even asked me how well I knew Mayor Wiggins, and, of course, I told him that the mayor was my old football coach, and that an introduction would be a piece of cake.

About a week after this request, I followed through with the introduction after Lou, Mrs. and Mayor John Wiggins had finished their dinner in Wellman's dining room. Tommy was friendly and always a gentleman, so the mayor asked him to have a seat. Tommy bought them an after-dinner drink. Before the evening was over, Tommy promised Lou that he would bring her some of his "almost famous" spaghetti sauce. He followed through with his promise three days later, when he dropped off two jars of sauce at Wellman's, along with a nice note to the mayor's wife. It was obvious that Tommy was trying to get to know people.

Not long after Tommy's meeting with the mayor, the Vidette Messenger came out with the story that a Mr. Tommy Morgano was accused of trying to bribe Porter County Deputy Sheriff Harold Rayder. The story went on to say that Deputy Sheriff Harold Rayder had worn a wire when Mr. Morgano allegedly asked Deputy Rayder to accept a bribe to help him bring prostitution and drugs into Porter County. It seemed that Tommy got to know too many people too quickly.

Three months after the news release on Tommy Morgano, Liz woke me up about nine on a Saturday morning saying: "Bill, there are two FBI men in our living room, and they want to talk to you." Saturday morning at nine is too early to talk to two strangers, but the three letters "FBI" caught my attention, and I was awake when I introduced myself to the two young FBI agents.

My wife made coffee, and we were having a good conversation until I made a young, smart-ass remark: "It seems to me that you fellows entrapped Mr. Morgano." The tone in their voices changed completely, and the whole conversation was cut short when one of them said: "Mr. Wellman, why don't you come downtown to the upper floor of the post office this afternoon to listen to some tapes of telephone conversations that we have of your new-found friend, Mr. Morgano? I think that you will find out he is not the kind of old Sicilian gentleman you think he is."

I said that I would be there at one o'clock that afternoon, and I was looking forward to being convinced I was wrong. After thinking over my conversation, I realized that I would like to have a chance to change my smart-ass remarks to these fellows, but it was too late, so I headed to the U.S. Post Office.

The upstairs of the post office was always a mystery, but here I was, getting a chance to look things over first-hand. The design of this building wouldn't pass today's laws. Someone would file a lawsuit on violating the rights of someone. The architect had designed secret peepholes, so that the postal workers could be observed from this upper level, unbeknownst to anyone involved.

While I was sitting at a table wearing a headset, listening to the taped conversations, I am sure that my mouth was wide-open in AWE of what I was hearing. After ten minutes of listening, I was convinced that my newfound friend and customer was not just the kind, generous Sicilian who made a great spaghetti sauce.

While I was still listening to the tapes, I noticed that my friend, "Bud" Schuler Miller, had just finished carrying a huge box of records up the stairs, which put him on the same level with me. Bud had a shocked look on his face when he saw me with headphones, and I gave him only half of a weak smile and a very small wave of welcome to the FBI's special room.

Bud Miller was an interior decorator with a great reputation, who lived in Valparaiso, but worked in Chicago at the prestigious Marshall Field's store. Bud was a bar customer of mine for many years, and I always tried to do some business with him at both my home and my restaurant. I was willing to scratch his back if he was willing to scratch mine.

Bud's reputation went in two directions. First, his ability as a decorator was tops in Valparaiso; and then his reputation as being "a little light in his moccasins" was also well-known in the bar circles of the "Vale of Paradise," as Valparaiso was called. This latter knowledge of Bud didn't surface until he had a few drinks, and then it became very obvious that he was on the prowl for the company of a man.

During these years, the word "gay" simply meant that someone was "exceptionally happy." Back then, I think that all homosexuals were "in the closet," and there was very little conversation about people who were interested in someone of the same sex. Bud was in his early sixties and lived with his widowed mother at her home on Lafayette Street, and no one questioned it.

On Friday evening when Bud returned home from work in Chicago, his mother got her alphabet confused when she gave him the message that "the IRS was here and they want to see you at one o'clock on the second floor of the post office tomorrow."

When he went to his appointment, Bud brought his box of income tax records with him. Later he told me that when he spotted me, his thoughts went something like this: "Oh my God, they have Bill Wellman, and he paid me cash for the work I did for him at Wellman's Restaurant and at his home last year, and I did not declare it on my taxes!" After he reached the top of the stairs and saw me, he said that he almost had "the big one."

It turned out that the FBI, not the IRS, was interested in talking to Bud, because he was a frequent bar customer at Wellman's, and they were questioning several people to find out if Tommy Morgano was a big spender and a big tipper when he frequented these "dens of iniquity." Taxes and Bud's records had nothing to do with Bud Miller's appointment.

After this lesson about "when to smart-off and when not to smart-off" to aggressive young FBI agents, I received my subpoena to appear in Kentland, Indiana, as a witness for the prosecution in the deportation trial of one Tommy Morgano.

Kentland is a small close-knit community, and it seemed to me that some jury members looked like they could be related. In fact, one man looked like he could be the judge's son.

The first trial started on August 1, 1960. Tommy Morgano was an alleged underworld figure who was charged with attempting to set up a vice operation in Valparaiso by offering a bribe to a Porter County Deputy Sheriff, Harold Rayder. It started very slowly.

During those years, it always seemed the trials in Lake and Porter Counties in Indiana were very predictable. But whenever there was a change of venue to Knox, Plymouth or Kentland, it was a different ballgame.

During the questioning of prospective jurors, Tommy's attorney strongly objected that the press was condemning Morgano before the trial had even got underway. After two full weeks of questioning by opposing attorneys, a jury of six men and six women was finally selected. But throughout the trial, the prosecutor defended the media.

On the second day, several witnesses were well known to me. First came Mrs. Joyce Findling Brownell, a former fashion model listed as living in Chicago, along with Mrs. Phyllis

McNamara, a very reliable waitress who worked at Wellman's Restaurant.

Phyllis testified that Morgano was in Wellman's bar when Joyce Brownell asked Tommy to take her to the Valparaiso Elks Club, where they talked to Harold Rayder. Phyllis also testified Morgano insisted she and Joyce accompany him to this nightspot, where the bribe offer was allegedly made.

Mrs. Brownell was expected to take the stand the next day to corroborate this testimony. The defense attorneys maintained that Harold Rayder and Richard Sinclair, a former investigator for the Senate Rackets Committee, deliberately laid a trap for Morgano in an effort to frame him. This sounded very familiar. In fact, this was almost word for word what I had told the two young FBI agents when they woke me up on that early Saturday morning in Valparaiso.

Several unusual events happened during these trials. First, Prosecutor Barce charged that his office was broken into over the first weekend of the trial, in an apparent effort to obtain evidence. Then, Harold Rayder collapsed in court and was taken to the hospital, where the attending physician advised him to rest a few days before returning to court as a key witness. Moreover, Tommy spotted me in the hallway of the courthouse and yelled: "Billy, come have lunch with me at the New Joy Café."

I accepted, not thinking about how unusual it was that a witness for the prosecution was planning to have lunch with the accused. We had lunch several times, and Tommy always picked up the tab. Actually, this is the only time that I received anything for all the trips I made to Kentland. I was supposed to be paid a per diem and mileage, but it never happened.

As the trial proceeded, Bud Brownell, the ex-husband of Joyce Brownell, also testified that Harold Rayder and Tommy Morgano met at the Elks Club. Mayor John Wiggins also testified as a character witness, since he was considered a good friend of Tommy Morgano. When I heard this testimony, I had a flashback to the time when I introduced Tommy to

Lou and John Wiggins at Wellman's, and Tommy gave me two jars of his "almost-famous" spaghetti sauce to pass on to Mayor Wiggins and his wife.

The last event made the first trial a complete "sideshow." It happened on August 27, 1960, when Morgano's lead attorney, Robert Salek from LaPorte, was making a fiery plea for acquittal during the closing arguments in the six-week trial. He grabbed his chest and fell to the floor in a heap, dying of a massive heart attack. Making it worse, his thirteen-year old daughter was in the courtroom observing the proceedings when her father died.

The next day, the jury reported that it was unable to agree on a verdict, and Special Judge Russell Gordon of Monticello dismissed the jury. The state denied that Harold Rayder instigated the idea of entrapping Tommy Morgano. "If we turn this man loose, you might as well go home and kiss your flag good-bye," said Special Prosecutor Robert Moore, a 74-year-old official from Gary. He added: "It could not float over a land contaminated with man's evil, vice and corruption."

Tommy Morgano

I was surprised to learn that Tommy Morgano was not an American citizen.

The second trial started on May 8, 1961, and once again, it was held in Kentland. For the second time, it ended without a verdict, after the jurors reported that they were hopelessly deadlocked.

Al Pivarnik, Valparaiso High School Class of 1943, was the prosecutor in Porter County, and he made the statement that if Morgano was going to be charged again on bribery, it would not be in Newton County. He also indicated that he would not wait for possible action by the U.S. Immigration authorities, because Morgano was appealing a deportation order to be sent back to Sicily.

On November 16, 1962, after a week of attempting to select a third jury, Tommy Morgano pleaded guilty to a $100,000 bribery charge.

The last time I saw Tommy Morgano, he told me: "Billy, save your vacations and come to see me in Sicily -- I am going to be a king."

I heard about Tommy two more times. First, the rumor around Valparaiso was that he tried to come back into the country through Mexico and was captured. Second, I heard that he had one final "curtain call" when he had a heart attack and died.

The next time I heard the name Morgano mentioned was in 1988, when I was buying my grandson, Guy Wellman, a baseball bat at Blythe's Sporting Goods store in Valparaiso. As I paid for the bat with my credit card, the next customer in line heard my name, and he introduced himself as Tommy Morgano's son. He was also buying his son a new bat.

The conversation went like this: "Mr. Wellman, I am Tommy Morgano's son, and this is my son, and I just want to thank you for being a friend to my dad. You are a person who always had something good to say about my father, and I just want to thank you for that."

I really did not know how to respond, so I just shook his hand and left it at that. It was not long after that meeting in 1988 that the name Morgano hit the newspapers. It seemed that Tommy's son had been arrested for bookmaking in Gary. He was found guilty and sent to prison.

Lessons were learned: Don't smart-off to the FBI and pick your friends carefully.

VIETNAM VETERANS PARTY

Wellman's Restaurant was in need of good public relations, and my two best sources were columnist Blaine Marz from The Gary Post-Tribune and radio-king, Wally Phillips, of WGN radio in Chicago

While listening to the radio, I heard Wally Phillips talking about the plans he had for a trip to a Saturday afternoon football game at Notre Dame for a busload of thirty wounded, valiant Vietnam veterans from Great Lakes Naval Hospital. He had made arrangements for wristwatches, blankets, jackets, gloves, hats, boots, cushions and lunch in South Bend before the game. It occurred to me that the only thing missing from this special outing was dinner on the way home at Wellman's Restaurant in Valparaiso.

So I gave Mr. Phillips a phone call, along with an offer to have the bus stop in Valparaiso. He accepted, and I received more publicity, not only from WGN, but also through the Blaine Marz column in The Post-Tribune. He wrote: "There have been many fine moments at Wellman's, but Saturday, September 23, 1967 has to be the shining hour. It was hoped that the wounded men could be convinced, although in a small way, that a heck of a lot of home-folks do care."

The busload of happy, laughing Vietnam vets who had seen some bad times, virtually became "Kings for a Day." Steaks, beverages from the bar, premium tables, sparkling-eyed waitresses and professional entertainment all combined to give these American heroes a night on the town.

A genuine "good-time-had-by-all" atmosphere prevailed. As one waitress commented: "I was afraid that I would cry, but in a little while they had me laughing -- because they were laughing."

When a brilliant birthday cake was delivered to a table elsewhere in the restaurant, "Happy Birthday" sung with more gusto and sincerity by this gathering than ever before. This same "birthday" spirit was apparent in everyone by the end of this gala evening.

But soon after their departure, when solitude returned and the party spirit wore off, the whole spectrum of the Vietnam mess -- and all the people bound by it -- suddenly returned. All at once the realization hit home: The party was over, but the war would go on.

The great public relations continued, as Wally Phillips continued to talk about it, and Blaine Marz continued to write about the event at Wellman's. Blaine told my number-one hostess, Marie Treanor, that after this night, he wanted to know about everything that happened at Wellman's. He didn't even care if it was about a waitress having a baby, he just wanted to be notified. This kind of attention might even have pleased Bill Veeck (my P.R. hero and guru.)

It was nearing the end of November when Wally Phillips arranged for two busloads of veterans from the Great Lakes Naval Hospital to take another trip to a football game at Notre Dame. My salesman from WGN asked me if I would like to be involved. I told him that I would get a sponsor for the dinner, because I had received so much great public relations that I was almost embarrassed to do it again. My first call went to the Valparaiso Chamber of Commerce, telling them that this was a public-relations "dream," and that the city could really get some good publicity if the chamber picked up the cost of dinner for the sixty veterans.

The Chamber called back to tell me that it would take the approval of the Chamber board, and that the earliest that a meeting could be held was in two weeks. I explained that that would be too late.

My next move was to go back to my roots and call the Chamber in Kouts, Indiana. I left a message for President Pete Hudson. He returned my call within one-half hour, and he said that the Chamber already had the money and it was a "go."

Besides providing the guys a great dinner party, this event turned out to exceed our wildest expectations. A headline appeared in The Chicago Tribune: **"Little Kouts a Town with a Big Heart—Hoosiers Foot Bill for Wounded Vets."**

The headline was followed by a wonderful story:

Most folks probably don't know that Kouts, Indiana, is in southern Porter County in Northwest, Indiana, and contains 1,300 people—boastfully-speaking. But sixty wounded war veterans know all about Kouts after last night—and to them it's the biggest place in the state on their maps."

Last week lots of Kouts folks who listen to Wally Phillips WGN Radio heard him talk about a special trip for 60 veterans from Great Lakes Naval Hospital to the Notre Dame versus Navy football game in South Bend. Wally had sponsored a similar trip and all the veterans were treated to a dinner by Bill Wellman in his restaurant in Valparaiso.

The Tribune story continued:

"H. P. "Pete" Hudson and a few businessmen in Kouts decided last week to ask Wellman if Kouts could treat the veterans in his restaurant. Wellman agreed, so the folks in Kouts took up a collection for the dinner. Then Hudson called the high school to see if the band wanted to be involved and play a welcome to the 60 veterans. The band agreed.

So last night, when the two buses full of veterans pulled off the toll road, they were met by a Valparaiso Police squad car with flashing lights to direct them down to U.S. 30. The buses pulled into Wellman's parking lot, where they found the "Heart of Kouts" waiting for them.

Four hundred people from Kouts cheered and the band played lustily. The buses even had three airline stewardesses on each bus to brighten-up their great day.

The first veteran off the bus tripped as he got off the bus and fell to his knees. There were people crying as the band played and two of the stewardesses helped him to his feet.

Little did they know the fall was from a little too much lubricant and not his wounds!

Arriving one-half hour late was sailor Dave Estadt from Zanesville, Ohio, who missed the bus completely, but a bus service and a state police escort gave him a ride to catch up to the caravan. The only thing he missed was the Kouts band and their warm welcome.

It has always amazed me how patriotism comes and goes in our country. Just when it seems to nearly go away, it comes back strong just when we need it most.

THE ABC's OF INDIANA

The ABC's of Indiana are a little different than the American Bowling Congress. In Indiana, ABC means Alcoholic Beverage Commission, and under their restrictions, they had an enforcement organization called the Excise Department.

In 1938 I remember hearing my parents talking about the "excise men" for whom my father refused to open the front door of the Club at four in the morning when the place was still packed. Dad followed "Guy's Laws" and wouldn't open the door, even when they showed their badges.

Dad also believed that a good customer could be under twenty-one years of age, as long as he could control his emotions and not cause a problem. The ABC frowned upon this type of logic, so they passed their feelings on to the excise officers.

Dad said that he had never been told off more than when he had to appear in front of the judge in Indianapolis in 1938. The Excise Department did not try to give bar owners a hard time unless they received complaints. They didn't have enough officers to patrol all the bars in the state, so they just answered complaints.

My first experience with the Excise Department came at Wellman's Restaurant, but before the incident, I became good friends with the Commissioner of the Alcohol Beverage Commission in Indiana, Joe Harris, a fine gentleman. I relied on his friendship to solve a problem with one of his investigating officers.

Some of Indiana's laws were out-dated, and one such law gave us at Wellman's a real fit. The law stated that you must have a railing around a dance floor. In our dining room, we had a small stage in front of the dance floor. The stage was used for comedians, singers and trios.

A pipe rail would just kill the entertainment atmosphere we had created in the Empire Room. So I used "Guy's Laws" and didn't put up the railing as required by the ABC.

It was unusual for me to be at home on a Friday night, but I was there when the telephone rang. Havie Deck called from the cashier's desk in our dining room to tell me that an excise patrolman was giving us an inspection prior to our upcoming annual hearing on our three-way liquor license. The officer wanted to talk to me.

The conversation went something like this: "Mr. Wellman, I'm Officer McDougal, and I'm giving your restaurant an inspection prior to your hearing next Tuesday. I find that you do not comply with our regulation requiring a railing around your dance floor." He was standing in our reception area while he was looking directly at our dance floor-entertainment area. So I was able to answer him with a terrific comeback: "Yes, that's right." He then followed with: "Mr. Wellman, you will have to comply by next Tuesday's hearing or you will have to stop serving alcohol until you have it corrected."

By this time, my answers were really on a roll, as I answered: "Yes, I'll take care of that." He thanked me and hung up.

On Saturday morning, I called Commissioner Joe Harris of the ABC state office and explained my problem. I told Joe I would do whatever he told me to do. There was a long pause as he mulled over my situation, and then he came back with the answer I had hoped to hear: "Bill, a railing around your dance floor in front of your entertainment stage will kill that atmosphere in your room. Don't do anything, but make sure that you show up at your Tuesday meeting."

Of course, I thanked him and could feel the weight removed from my shoulders.

On Tuesday morning I appeared for my nine o'clock meeting, and by ten o'clock Wellman's Restaurant was approved for another year. Yet another year later, the same situation arose, and I received a call from Havie Deck to inform me that it was "déjà vu all over again."

Wellman's was being inspected again for their annual inspection, and the senior officer would like to speak to me. The law calling for a railing around the dance floor had not changed.

"Mr. Wellman, this is Officer McDougal, and I am giving your restaurant its annual inspection, and I just wanted you to know your dance floor and entertainment room is okay this year. "

I thanked him and the conversation ended. I enjoyed Officer McDougal's way of letting me know that he knew that I knew someone in authority above him who had already explained the situation to him.

My next lesson in ABC's came when we built Bridge VU Theater. The law was very specific: A three-way liquor permit must be used under the same continuous roof. My problem was that the Salt Creek separated Wellman's Restaurant from the new theater, so there was no way we could comply.

Once again, though, I got help—not only from Joe Harris, ABC chief, but from my good friend, Warren Spangle, head of the Indiana Restaurant Association. I was told to attend the upcoming ABC local hearing, and was to bring along my roll of plans for the theater—but at no time was I to unroll them.

I sat through the meeting, and no one mentioned Wellman's or Bridge VU Theater. Near the end of the meeting, the official representing the State of Indiana made this statement: "This is my last day on the board, so I would like to invite all the members to meet me at Wellman's Restaurant on U.S. 30. I would like to have coffee and cake at my final meeting."

With my plans in hand, I followed along as they gathered at a large round table in the Empire Room. The state official started the conversation with, "I hope you noticed that I didn't close out my final meeting, because after we finish our coffee and cake we are going to walk over "The Kissing Bridge" and we are going to inspect the new dinner theater.

During the inspection, the state official explained that since Wellman's was willing to give up its regular three-way license, it would qualify for liquor sales under a hotel designation. In other words, the State of Indiana was going to allow for the license in spite of the lack of a continuous roof separating the restaurant from the theater.

Looking back on this experience, I realize that it took friendship and lots of horse sense to make Bridge VU and Wellman's Restaurant legal under the outdated ABC regulations of the state of Indiana.

It was during my thirteen years developing Wellman's and Bridge VU Theater that I also developed a friendship with a true friend, Junior Waters.

The Great Junior Waters

When I first ran into Junior Waters and his trio on the east side of Indianapolis, Indiana, he seemed relaxed and had a noticeably-good rapport with the audience. During Junior's break, I sent him a drink, and instructed the waitress to ask him to drop over to my table when he had time.

I wanted to talk with him about performing, and I could tell that Junior was used to customers referring to different clubs that might be potential spots for his performance. However, when I told him that I would like to have him perform at Wellman's Restaurant in Valparaiso, the look on his face was priceless. Years later, he told me that when he received his contract from his agent, "Honest Hal" Monroe, informing him that he was booked in Valparaiso, Indiana, he immediately went out to buy an Atlas to look up where he was headed.

When he arrived on a Monday, the hostess in the dining room told him that his trio was to be entertaining in the Empire Room of Wellman's Restaurant. I am not exactly sure why I decided to steal that classy name from a hotel in Chicago, but it sounded like it was a fit. In those days, stealing names and ideas was a lot easier than now. So it was called "The Empire Room."

While Junior Waters and his trio was setting up the drums and adjusting the sounds and lights, he went into the lobby to ask a short, gray-haired gentleman where he could find the Sand Man Motel. The answer was very short: "Hell, I have no idea, I am just the janitor here." This was Junior's first meeting with my father. As he found out over the years, my Dad had a great sense of humor, and he loved to "get" Junior.

Valparaiso has always been a conservative small town, so when Junior came to town, people tended to be over-friendly. You could feel that they were not accustomed to having a black man in their community. Junior and I took advantage of this feeling on many occasions, like the time we took a fifty-foot tape measure and a couple of pieces of chalk to the corner of Washington Street and Lincolnway, right on the town square, where we measured and chalked, then measured and chalked again.

It is amazing what this practical joke did to germinate rumors that would continue for weeks: "Bill Wellman and Junior Waters are planning to build a sidewalk café at the corner of Washington Street and Lincolnway." Or: "I think that they are going to buy the Old Style Inn." And: "This will be the first black businessman in Valparaiso." Just the thought of that gave the typical Valparaiso citizen the chills.

My dad thought that it would be a great idea to test out the unwritten rules of the Valparaiso Country Club by inviting Junior to fill out his foursome on a Saturday morning.

The tee time was 9:12 a.m. and we were ready to go: my father, George Mackaluck, a salesman from General Store Fixtures, Junior Waters and yours truly. Junior had purchased a pair of new white sneakers from Fetla's Bargain Center, along with white socks and a Chicago Cubs baseball cap. He looked nothing like a golfer, and we soon found out that his "get-up" fit his game: He was bad.

It was a hot, sunny day, and after fifteen holes, Junior took off his cap. George Mackaluck was surprised to see that Junior had a sun-line on his forehead. George was really shocked and said: "Junior, you look like you got a sunburn." Junior immediately came back with: "Hell yes, we get burns. What the hell do you think, we have alligator skin?"

After eighteen holes, my dad was thinking of pushing this to the next level when he announced: "Let's go into the clubhouse to get a drink and a sandwich." This was the first time that a black man had played at the country club, and it was also the first for their food and beverage operation. If my father was looking for someone to be upset, it did not take long. Jim Trump, owner of Trump Steel in Crown Point, Indiana, made a remark that raised the hair on my father's neck: "Who has the balls to bring a black nigger into a private country club?"

Of course, Dad popped right up from our table with: "I am the one with the balls, and what would you like to do about it?"

It took a few cooler heads, but we settled this one without my cocky father stirring up a ruckus with Jim Trump. I am sure that Jim took those hard feelings to his grave, and I know that Dad could have cleaned his clock.

I don't think that Junior ever came back to the Country Club to play golf, but he did participate in a Chamber golf outing. At this one, I continued with the Bill Veeck promotion idea: I gave out Wellman's golf caps to all participants on the second hole, except that I did not actually hand out the caps. Instead, I had Junior Waters drive the 1938 Packard Limo to the second hole, where two Greek belly dancers took over. First they placed, and then adjusted the caps on all the golfers. It was considered a huge success, and many thought it was really a good move.

MAYOR HATCHER

Mayor Richard Hatcher was elected mayor of Gary, Indiana in 1967. After moving to Gary, Indiana, Hatcher began practicing law in East Chicago in 1961. He moved from being a deputy prosecutor to the City Council where he was the first and only freshman elected president in Gary's history.

I had no idea the election in Gary would effect Wellman's Restaurant and our Holiday Inn until I received a phone call from Governor Roger Branigan informing me they need to take over our Holiday Inn to house two hundred state troopers for one week to insure peace and safety during and after the upcoming mayoral election! This meant they would take over one hundred of our one hundred and fourteen rooms. It also meant we were to feed two hundred troopers three meals a day for an undetermined number of days.

Wellman's – November 10, 1967
No place for J.R. Waters and his hog (Cadillac)

"Would you stay at this Holiday Inn-with two hundred Indiana State Trooper squads in the parking lot?"

I must admit it was very impressive to see the troopers go through inspections in our parking lot before they departed for the night shift in Gary. They were issued ammunition and gas masks as part of their equipment. Eight cars would head west down US 30 after each inspection in ten-minute intervals. The National Guard was also on alert and on stand by at the National Guard Armory on US 30 in Valparaiso. There were also "tractor type" vehicles designated as personnel carriers stationed at the fairgrounds in Crown Point two days prior to the election.

Lake County Fairgrounds – Friday, November 10, 1967

It was during this exciting time J.R. Waters was performing in the Well House Lounge at Wellman's as a single piano player and he was also staying at the Holiday Inn. This scenario was a perfect set up for my dad! We all were friends with a state trooper named Al Smidt and Dad knew there was a daily poker game going on in his room. Dad goes to J.R. Waters room and knocks on the door. J.R. opened the door and the conversation went like this: "J.R., come on with me. I want you to meet your neighbors." J.R. follows Dad to the "poker" room and knocks on the door. Al opens the door with "Hi Guy, come on in. There's a seat open." Dad explains he can't stay but says, "I just wanted you fellows to see what "they" look like," as he turned to J.R. Waters. Dad wasn't finished: "Tell them they are parking in your spot in front of your room and they should respect who you are as the star in the Well House!" It was taken in fun and so was J.R. Waters thirty dollars he lost in the poker game!

The riots in Gary didn't happen because Mayor Hatcher won the election. If he had lost there was no doubt in my mind the riots would have been huge. The pictures show what our Holiday Inn looked like on November 10, 1967. All of the cars were State Police squad cars except one "Hog", J.R. Waters 1965 Cady! I wouldn't recommend this type of "PR" for improving business, but it was part of history!

AIR RIGHTS FOR RESTAURANT

If you ever want to attend a very dull meeting, try to make it to the next Porter County Drainage Board, which meets once a month in the Court House.

On Wednesday, March 22, 1972 I appeared before the board and I could see the excitement in the board members eyes as I told them, "I would like to get air rights over Salt Creek to build a restaurant." This was the most exciting request the board had ever received and it was obvious from the start they wanted to hear my story.

"I plan on building a wharf-type seafood eatery spanning Salt Creek, which runs through the property separating Bridge

Vu Theatre from the Holiday Inn, bowling lanes, billiard parlor, two cocktail lounge/night clubs and meeting rooms. Because the ground is so bad I have to sink pilings to hold the restaurant up, I may as well use the pilings as décor. What do you think?" The excitement was overwhelming as the entire board moved to approve the request.

The headline in the Indianapolis News was **"Porter County Okays Air Rights for Restaurant."** I had Doug Pierce from Design Organizations build a model but that was as far as I got. Not all of the ideas work out but the Drainage Board will never be the same!

FETLA'S

When it comes to characters of the time, (1948) I have to talk about my good friend Walter Fetla. Walter was a Polish boy who left school in the sixth grade to help support the family. At the age of 28 he opened Fetla's Bargain Center out of a two-car garage, which grew into a rambling huge store located on State Road 2 on the south side of Valparaiso. Walter would buy or sell almost anything to make a dollar. One of his sayings to me was "Bill, when you spend pennies you make pennies, but when you spend dollars you will make dollars."

One of my favorite items at Fetla's Bargain Center was a barrel of false teeth that Walter had placed at the front door with an appropriate sign: "Take your pick, $5.00 per set." It always amazed me to see customers checking out the inventory and actually depleting the inventory.

Walter was a very good bowler and I had the privilege of bowling with him in five of the American Bowling Congress tournaments in different locations throughout the country. We were attending a tournament in Columbus, Ohio and decided to have dinner in a Chinese restaurant, but first we consumed a few beers.

George Walsh, Frank Filwalk, Walt Fetla, Jack Gray and Larry Dahl

We were just finishing our meal when I noticed Walter in a heated discussion with the owner near the cash register. Of course, I went to his aid with "Walter, what's the problem?" He turned to me with his big smile and said, "No problem. We just settled it. He tried to charge me the Ohio State sales tax, but I convinced him that since we were from Indiana we didn't have to pay it." A typical Walter story.

I had the pleasure of going on a local hunting trip with Walter and his two brothers, Eddie and John. Before we started, Walter told everyone the rules for the day: "If anyone shoots a cock pheasant, the other three will pay him five dollars. If you shoot a hen, we know this is illegal, so that's ten dollars, but if the one who shoots a hen gets arrested the other three will pay his fine. Rabbits are two dollars and crows are three." This set the tone for the day.

After hunting for an hour the slate was still clean on who owes whom so Walter decided that we should sit down in the middle of a cornfield and play buck euchre for over an hour. Playing cards in a cornfield in November will give you a chill, so once again our leader suggested we split up and hunt the area. About twenty minutes later I heard someone's shotgun go off five times. I ran over a small hill where I saw Walter running after a cock pheasant and there were two more birds on the ground. This meant John, Eddie and yours truly owed

Walter (the hunter) fifteen dollars each. It was hard to believe but the three birds were proof enough.

It took about a month, and a few beers, one night after league bowling when Walter confessed that he had made a deal with Chuck Black, the local game warden, to plant a cage with three cock pheasants, in a certain location, near a certain corn field, on a certain day. For a few laughs and forty-five dollars Walter would go to any extreme.

One day I received a telephone call from Walt and it went something like this, "Bill, I have a chance to buy a truck load of liquor at a great price, do you want to go in with me?" After I caught my breath, I answered, "I'm just shaking talking to you about it, Walt, that is a federal law and you could go to prison for a long time if you are caught!"

He didn't buy that truckload, but one month later he and a friend were caught by the FBI with a truckload of electric shavers and cooling fans. Walter hired Max Cohen to defend him in the case. Max got a lot of business people in Valparaiso to write letters, explaining that Mr. Fetla was a good citizen and that he had done a lot for the community. Luckily, the judge was very lenient, and Walter got a pass.

Before the judge made his decision, I walked into Fetla's and was greeted with a display of fans and electric shavers with a sign that read "HOT SHAVERS AND COOL FANS FOR SALE" I explained, if the judge heard you were making fun of your case, I think it might upset him. Evidently Walter took me serious enough, because the sign disappeared before I left the building.

My last Fetla story comes after another American Bowling Congress tournament. This time we were in St. Louis, Missouri. We had just finished bowling in team event, doubles and singles and we were on our way home. In the team event, four out of the five members bowled great, but one member, George Walsh, had bowled terribly. I was driving my station wagon and as we were crossing the Mississippi River George said, "For two cents I'd toss this damn ball in the Mississippi River." I looked at Walter at the same time he looked at me, "Walter, what do you think?" There was no hesitation as he said, "Turn around and lets find a camera." We pulled up to the St. Louis Dispatch newspaper office and Walter and I took only ten minutes to hire a photographer to take this historical picture.

What every bowler always wanted to do!

The picture turned out great and Walter gave the photo man a nice tip. Unbeknownst to our group, the photographer worked for the United Press. He presented the picture to all of their newspapers throughout the country. We were really surprised when we found our picture on the sports page of the Chicago Tribune on Monday morning.

George Walsh made a complete scrapbook out of letters and newspaper clippings from all over the country. The best one though, came from the Centliver Brewing Company, who offered George the services of a deep-sea diver to retrieve his ball from the river if he desired.

The PR from the bowling ball toss would make Bill Veeck smile. It has given me many opportunities to add to my tales from speeches at Rotary Club luncheons, to late night bar stories.

BETHLEHEM COMES TO PORTER COUNTY

I consider myself somewhat of a dreamer when it comes to ideas.

The bowling lanes were doing well, when I approached Dr. O'Neill with the idea of adding a simple building addition to the north wall of the bowling lanes. We could add twelve new Brunswick pool tables in a long narrow carpeted room. He agreed, and we finished the block building in record time. The Brunswick Tables arrived by Landgrebe Transport, but I told them to put everything into storage. A Mr. Harry Wood from Bethlehem Steel had made me an offer I couldn't refuse.

When I first met Harry Wood, he impressed me with his knowledge of the restaurant and hotel business. He was very friendly and easy to work with. Though, it did take me a while to get used to the aggressiveness of Harry and the steel executives. He suggested that we knock down two walls in our Holiday Inn in order to give them three open rooms. These would be made into one large real estate office to handle the large number of employees who would be moving to Northwest Indiana from the Pennsylvania area.

I tried to tell Harry that our motel would cave in if we took out any of the supporting walls but he explained that the walls would be supported with huge steel beams. The space was needed for their real estate offices and -- they would replace everything when the move was completed.

The next request went something like this. "Bill, I would like to have you put your billiard tables in storage for one year so that we can use your room as a private dining room called the Bethlehem Room. Figure out the profit you would have made on the pool room for one year and add it to all of the food and beverage charges from the people we will be bringing to Valparaiso within the next year. It didn't take me long to agree with Harry Wood's proposal.

Harry's boss, James Daig, was the plant general manager who supervised the construction and operation of Bethlehem Steel Corporation's new 400 million dollar Burns Harbor Plant. C. William Rittenhoff was the assistant general manager. Harry invited me to attend a meeting with the plant manager to discuss a spring dinner dance. The meeting was completely controlled by the manager, as he explained to Harry and me what he expected. "Harry, this will be the first spring dinner dance and it will become a yearly event. I want it to be so good that everyone will be looking forward to receiving the invitation. Let Bill handle getting the orchestra and he will also handle the food and beverages, but there is one thing that I don't want to see -- a bill on anything."

The event was set up to be catered in a hall north of US20 called Johanis Hall. Everything turned out exceptionally well. I'm not sure how Harry handled his end of the billing, but we were paid and I started to be called "the fair-haired boy of Bethlehem Steel." I was asked to be involved in a three-day party to celebrate the grand opening of the Burns Harbor Plant in September 1965.

My part of this celebration was to furnish the wine and liquor for the party and my only obligation was to come up with a refrigerated semi to keep the produce and the wine in. Wellman's Restaurant was dealing with Borden's Dairy so I asked my good friend Art Young, the District Manager for Borden's Dairy, for the use of a refrigerated semi and he agreed, at no cost to Wellman's. It was exciting to be involved in the planning of a huge three-day event.

One week before the grand opening, Harry Wood planned to hold a press conference dinner in Wellman's lower level banquet room for one hundred invited media guests. Thirty days before the event Harry asked me, "Bill, do you have a tuxedo?" I said, "No, but I can rent one." He immediately followed with, "I want you to go to Marshall Fields and buy a good one and just add it to the bill because I want you to pour the wine at the head table where the Chairman and Chief Executive Officer, Edmond F. Martin, will be seated." By this time I didn't question Harry, I just followed his instructions.

The press dinner went off without a hitch. Life Magazine, and the New York Times were included in the guest list. When the evening was finished, I gave Harry one of my young smart-ass remarks; "Harry, Mr. Martin stopped me right in the middle of pouring his wine to compliment me on doing a fine job and he really liked my tux!"

Feeding 2,500 people at one time took some major advance planning. The mill turned the tin mill shipping building into a carpeted dining room; (7000 yards) with 58 bars, 116 bartenders. The meal was catered by a company out of Chicago. They had a total of 2500 guests at 250 round tables serving ten people per table. When you arrived, you parked your car in the new parking lot (a week prior it was all grass). You walked to the edge of the lot where a bus picked you up for a tour of Burns Harbor. Goggles and hard hats were issued to all guests. After the tour we were dropped off at the tin mill shipping building where Bethlehem employees took our goggles and hardhat and directed us to the fifty-eight bars for the cocktail hour. As we entered the bar area we were told to draw our dinner table number from various large fish bowls. I thought that this was a very neat way to distribute 2500 guests at tables. I stood in the cocktail area with a gin and tonic in hand, looking at the 250 tables with crisp white linen and beautiful fresh cut flower centerpieces. There were 20 eight-foot chandeliers and 60 shaded drum lights to completely eliminate the warehouse look.

The wine served with dinner for 2500 people for three nights had a story of its own. One month before the grand opening, three chosen employees were sent to New York with the sole purpose of selecting the wine to be served. Now you can see why these people got my attention the day they asked me to tear down a couple of walls. Money didn't seem to matter when it came to this three-day party.

Another interesting thing came up in the early planning session. What do you do for toilet facilities for 2500 guests and 600 catering employees? This was solved by using stainless steel train cars designed especially for large expensive parties. They even included porters with whiskbrooms to hand out towels and brush off the dandruff from your blue serge suit.

I forgot to mention my other task -- furnishing the entertainment. The executives of Bethlehem were interested in having Julie London as the star, backed up by the famous Woody Herman Orchestra. I called my favorite agent, "Honest" Hal Monroe from Associated Booking Corporation and settled on the date and the price.

Julie London stayed in our Holiday Inn in Valparaiso for four days. It was during the early hours after the second night of festivities, that a bridge game was going on in Wellman's dining room. Julie London was playing a serious game of bridge with Bethlehem Steel's Chairman and chief Executive Officer, Edmund F. Martin. It was about three thirty in the morning when one of the four card players was asked what he wanted. His comment was, "I'd like a little of Julie." After that comment Julie London politely said, "Boys, I think it's time to go to bed." The card game was over.

The first night of the celebration was strictly for Bethlehem's customers who included 48 corporation chairmen, 803 presidents, 535 vice presidents, and 1114 other steel customers. Over six hundred people traveled from Chicago on a special train.

The following week Bethlehem cut up the practically new carpet and sold it at a discounted price to their employees. The chandeliers were rented, but the new parking lot was torn up and returned to grass within days. The reason for the urgency on the grass was that blowing sand would cause havoc to steel mills and their making of steel.

The opening of burns Harbor caused lots of rumors about landscaping and driveways being put in private homes at no cost to special employees. There was also a rumor that certain employees were picking out the color of their new Cadillac. It was not a rumor that Harry Ward took a fall.

I really never heard the full story of why Harry was incarcerated or for how long, but I know he was a fall guy for several executives. I always wondered why, if Harry Wood was a bad guy, he hadn't asked me for some type of a kickback with all of the money that Bethlehem Steel paid Wellman's during those fun years. I was young and very impressed with the big business I was doing with this huge steel mill. I'm not really sure what I would have done if Harry had asked for a kickback, but the point is -- he didn't ask.

I really think he went to prison following orders from his bosses. When Harry was released from prison he went to work for my partner, Ted Hrycak, at the Portage Holiday Inn. He also ran Ted's Holiday Inn, located in Logansport, Indiana, for several years. Eventually, Harry had the same urge that a lot of people get; wanting to run his own restaurant. He purchased a classy restaurant that had just recently shuttered its doors in Arizona.

Harry called me two to three times a week seeking advice. Restaurants can eat a financial hole, especially if your cash reserve is not capable of standing up through the first six months. My mother used this wise saying about restaurants. "If you want to make a million dollars in the restaurant business, start with two million dollars and volume will cover a multitude of sins." Harry Wood died a young man several years after he closed the doors on his Phoenix restaurant.

Chapter Seven

BRIDGE VU THEATER

The idea to get into entertainment was always there, but the seed really germinated in 1967 when I attended the yearly franchisee conference of Holiday Inns of America in Memphis, TN.

My first chore was to deliver a one-gallon pail of gourmet popcorn seed to the president of Holiday Inns, Kemmons Wilson, who was known as a popcorn freak and absolutely loved good popcorn. I placed the pail on Kemmons very full desk and told him, "Kemmons, I have a very good friend in Valparaiso, Indiana who asked me to deliver this to you in hope you would try it and want to place it in all of your Holiday Inns through out the country." He thanked me and promised to give it the "Wilson Test" before the conference ended.

The event during the conference that really hooked me was the opening night of Holiday Inns first Dinner Theater. The musical was The Music Man and it was well done.

Kemmon's idea was to build dinner theaters where the population was large enough and his Holiday Inn had enough extra property to build a theater. The actors and the play would travel from one Holiday Inn to another. It sounded great and I was hooked!

The conference was in its last day when Kemmons looked me up to praise the sample gallon of popcorn. "Bill, that is by far the best popcorn I have ever tasted and you can tell the fellow from Valparaiso if he could figure out a way to drop ship to my Holiday Inns I will buy his corn exclusively. By the way, what is his name?" At the time I didn't know how to spell Redenbacher, but I did my best when I wrote "ORVILLE REDENBACHER" on the back of my card.

In 1967 Orville was not the famous hawker of gourmet popcorn, he was the fellow who spent three hours aerating my lawn and explaining exactly how I should maintain it!

When I returned home after the Holiday Inn Franchisee Conference I was full of "show biz" enthusiasm. I was sure if I could produce good quality entertainment, great food and a good, clean well run Holiday Inn for some of the customers to stay overnight, it would some how work out financially. There was very little thought about demographics or a feasibility study.

This is how a dreamer's logic works! "Build it and they will come." The money was not there to build a theater, but my desire was so great I forged ahead by convincing my main partner, Doctor Martin O'Neill we needed to test the water by trying theater in a tent for one summer. He agreed and I started my plan.

IN-TENTS

The first move was to contact the President of Valparaiso University, Dr. O.P. Kretzmann, and tell him my idea; hoping that I could work with the drama department and offer their top students summer jobs and part-time work when school was in process.

The meeting went great. I think he had completely forgotten our last meeting in 1946. In fact, the President came up with the idea for the name Bridge VU Theater, using the play on words VU, and the connection of using students from the university as actors and actresses. He thought my idea of buying the "Kissing Bridge" from the Pennsylvania railroad was a way to keep some of the nostalgic history alive. With the presidents blessing, I introduced myself to Dr. Fred Sitton, who had been a professor since 1961. He had established the VU (Valparaiso University) Summer Repertory Theater in the Pocono's in Pennsylvania in 1962, and for the five summers since then he had produced over 25 plays there.

Convincing Dr. Sitton to move the group from the Pocono's to the Vale of Paradise was easy because the move would allow him to increase the number of participating students from 10 to 15. He also could see, if I was a success and could build a permanent theater, his program would grow by leaps and bounds. It was evident that the students had the chance of receiving more than just experience, when financial help was on the horizon.

Dr. Sitton was an excellent director. He came from a small town in west Texas called Pyote, earned his Bachelor's degree at Texas Western in El Paso in 1943, and was awarded his Ph.D. from Northwestern University in 1962. Once Dr. Sitton was in the fold, it did not take long to convince his No. 1 assistant, Richard Pick, to join the team. He was a graduate of Valparaiso University in 1957 and had a Master's degree from Northwestern in 1963.

Dr. Fred Sitton

We now had the permission from the top man at VU, a set builder and a top-notch director that could match anyone in the Midwest. The team not only brought 15 young actors and actresses with it, but it introduced me to a young sound and light genius named David Thon. With very little capital, David put together a very professional lighting and sound system that fit the needs of the upcoming first season.

David Thon graduated from Valparaiso Technical School and then put himself through Valparaiso University. One thing that made David unique was his hairstyle. He had the best Afro for a white boy that I had ever seen. It even impressed J.R. Waters!

David Thon and his Afro!

With the team in place, we needed a theater to perform in, so I ordered this huge green and white striped tent from a tent company in Indianapolis. The stripes were three foot wide and hard to miss. I was completely confidant and convinced that if we had a good product on the stage and a comfortable place to perform we would draw people.

When it comes to using a tent as a theater, I developed into an expert rather quickly. The idea to put the tent on the black top parking lot seemed very logical to me, especially using the parking lot that had a slight 10-degree slope toward the stage. It made great sight lines for the upcoming audiences.

One bit of advice: if you ever put a tent on a parking lot, make sure the end opposite the stage is on bare ground at the edge of the lot. If you have ever seen the amount of water that comes off of a tent during a typical Indiana downpour you will understand how important the placement of the tent is. You guessed it – the water came off the tent and hit the parking lot with a 10-degree slope towards the stage and a river formed evenly throughout the entire theater. There were times when customers had to keep their feet up whenever it rained or take a terrific chance of being washed away during the performance. I can just imagine the headline in the local newspaper: "Theater-goers drown at first showing of 'Today is a Good Day to Die'."

After our first mistake we moved the tent to solve the river problem, but as we moved it I brought up another fear that kept me awake at night. That was the fear of the tent collapsing from a windstorm. To solve this one, I put the Homer Burrus logic to work. Homer seemed to be able to solve any problem if you gave him all of the facts and then enough time. His logic was simple: he placed a 25' telephone pole on each side of the tent and stretched a cable from one pole to the other, along with the center loops of the tent. If the wind blew all of the tent poles down, the cable would still hold up the main part of the tent. Good thinking Homer!

I wrote an article in our "Wellman's Review and Forecast" describing our outdoor theater and the Homer Burrus safety factor that would prevent the tent from falling on the customers. I explained that this beautiful tent and the 56 poles holding it up would seat 350 people. One week later a Mr. Kropockie wrote me a letter complaining that I was picking on the Poles and I should be ashamed of myself for having the Poles do such dangerous work in bad weather, and why didn't I hire some Irishman or Blacks to do this type of dangerous work. I think the people had a better sense of humor in the sixties than they do now!

A tent of this size is usually too cold or too hot. It was never just right. We did have sides on the tent and vents at the top to regulate the temperature, but it always seemed to be a guessing game. Heat, cold, and potential water on the customer's feet was not the end of the discomfort. Mosquito's attacked without too much warning and 1967 was a banner year. The truck and automobile noise from nearby U.S. Hwy. 30 were other problems that seemed to escape our (nonexistent) feasibility study.

I thought I had the noise problem licked when I bought several wagonloads of bales of straw from my friendly farmer, Carl Halberg, and formed an eight-foot wall on the south side of the tent. Everything worked well until the Fire Marshal decided that I would have trouble spraying the straw with a non-flammable substance. Once the Fire Marshal explained the danger to me, I had to agree that the wall would have to come down.

To solve the dressing room problem, we had purchased a small hotel called the Quonset Motel and included in the inventory was a prefabricated 6-room motel that we put in place by using the Homer Burrus logic of moving it about a city block. We actually put it on skids and pulled it across a field. These 6-rooms reminded me of cabins on a ship. They really worked well for dressing rooms and Homer's theory saved the day once again.

Everything seemed in place and we were ready to test the tent and my idea that "if you build it they will come." It was time to have a free night with over 250 handpicked invited guests.

Free cocktails started at 7:00 p.m. at Wellman's Restaurant banquet room. Dr. O.P. Kretzmann always called cocktail hours, "preliminary adjustment periods." The hors d'oeuvres were great and the free lubricant started the conversation to roll. At 7:30 p.m. the clouds opened and the rains came and continued to come. At this point I made an executive decision and extended the cocktail hour for another thirty minutes. After the extension to the "preliminary adjustment period," the rains let up enough to allow about 180 brave souls to wade across Wellman's parking lot, over the bridge and into the new-tented theater. The 70 other guests either were smashed, smart, or just did not want to be a part of Valparaiso's history in the making.

The performances started at 9:15p.m. but to make matters worse, the tent leaked. It didn't just leak in one or two spots, it leaked on every other seam. The stripes were about three feet wide and one side of the seam was heat treated (glued) and the other side was sewn with a very heavy thread. The tent maker from Indianapolis had told me when I had complained earlier about possible leaks, "the thread would swell up to fill the needle holes after one good rain." This rain on opening night was too good! We discovered later (through Homer Burrus' school of logic) the material in our beautiful tent was a new plastic material and wherever the sewing needle made the holes, the thread continued to make those holes larger as time went on. It was definitely a fair weather tent!

Near the end of the play I counted 52 brave guests. Most of them were very close friends, smashed, or family members of the actors. Some of the 52 actually had umbrellas up and their feet on empty chairs in the row in front of them.

The president of Valparaiso University, O.P. Kretzmann, stayed until the end. No umbrella, and his feet (wet) were firmly on the parking lot and he had not moved one "stripe" forward. He really enjoyed the play in spite of the fact that his black clerical coat was completely soaked.

I discovered that the people who were wider than one tent stripe and participated in the extra forty-five minutes of cocktails did not care about the water problems.

The rest of the summer proved to be a lot dryer than usual, so the tent worked. I found out we could draw people to the theater, and the spin off to our restaurant and our Holiday Inn seemed to make it economically feasible. At the end of the summer I hired my tent attorney and we sued the tent company from Indianapolis. Jim Sullivan was the barrister and we won the case. I did not have to pay for the tent and they took it back to Indianapolis. I heard they heat-treated and glued both sides of the stripes to make it a useable tent for the next dreamer.

It was a long summer, but I proved that theater would work in Valparaiso if we would give quality entertainment, good food, and a fair ticket price. I realized a dry theater would also help!

My next venture was to come up with the plans and money to move into a permanent building. I talked to Dr. O'Neill about how we could build a permanent building to house our fledgling theatrical group. Between the doctor's financial muscle and my dreaming mind, the plan was hatched. With the help of a team of thinkers like Dr. Fred Sitton, Richard Pick, David Thon, and the ever-steady Homer Burrus, we worked with Charlie Bowman and his all metal building crew to come up with the plans to build Bridge VU Theater for a grand opening slated for June 27, 1968.

The copy from "Wellman's Review and Forecast" went something like this:"

NEW DINNER THEATER WILL BE PROSCENIUM TYPE AND SEAT 500. IT WILL ALSO BE USED FOR CONCERTS AND CONVENTIONS.

Bill Wellman, general manager, has announced plans for a unique 13,000 square foot dinner theater and entertainment center adjacent to Wellman's Restaurant.

Construction is scheduled to start immediately and the theater is to open June 27, 1968 when the Valparaiso University Summer Repertory Theater will present "The Fantastiks," the first of five different plays scheduled at Bridge Vu Theater this summer.

The 170 foot long building is to be placed in a park-like setting along U.S. 30 between Salt Creek and Horse Prairie Ave., just east of Wellman's as a part of the Wellman's Magnificent Mile entertainment and recreation complex. The new center will differ from other theaters around the country. Many dinner theaters in the past have been built for theater "in the round." The Bridge VU Theater is the proscenium type with a revolving stage, wings for the sets and complete dressing rooms and other facilities back stage. Dinner theater patrons will be seated at tables on three different levels above the stage with excellent visibility and acoustics.

In addition to being used for summer stock, the building will be used for concerts, conventions, banquets, private parties, and receptions.

To get things started, I hired a local firm called Peller, Tanck and Gertsmeir to put together all of the plans and ideas from our think tank theater group consisting of Doctor Fred Sitton, Richard Pick, David Thon, and naturally Homer Burrus and myself.

The local architects handled the plans for the building but our group made all of the decisions on the interior plans. The idea was to build a box 145' long by 90' wide and decorate the box. There were three different levels in Bridge Vu, which gave the customers excellent sight lines.

Homer Burrus checked the architects' preliminary plan and immediately came up with an idea that eventually saved the theater from becoming a flood plain. "Bill, I think the lowest part of the floor plan in front of the stage could really be a wet problem. The water table is very high and when Salt Creek rises every spring, water will seep through the concrete and cause mold problems with your new carpet. I suggest we dig the pit four feet deeper, fill it with field tile and gravel and run the tile back to Salt Creek. When the water table comes up our systems will take the water back to the creek and keep our carpet dry." The whole thing made sense to me so I ran it by Paul Tanck, the architect. He didn't hesitate when he answered, "Sounds like a good idea."

Once again, Homer and his logic saved the day! If you check out the area where the Kissing Bridge was located, you will still see water coming out of field tiles engineered by

Homer Burrus. For years I had a sign at the base of the field tile:

FOR DRINKING – NO
FOR FISH – YES

The idea of using the old student bridge (Kissing Bridge) from Valparaiso University came to me one night when I was waiting to fall asleep. I could picture patrons casually strolling from Wellman's Dining Room or the new 114-room Holiday Inn, over the bridge to attend a performance at Bridge VU. I even pictured weddings performed on the nostalgic Kissing Bridge.

Path to Kissing Bridge from old campus

Picture of wooden section of Kissing Bridge in 1928

I bought the "old student bridge" through a famous contractor and friend, Jack Spencer. When we started to put the bridge up, I received a letter from a very famous Valparaiso alumnus, the late Lowell Thomas. The letter was short and to the point. He asked me to do him one favor, "Please do not to paint the bridge gold."

Kissing Bridge post card

I followed through with his request by choosing black. We exchanged several letters and during the exchange I asked him if he would consider dedicating the bridge and the theater and to my complete surprise he said yes.

Kissing Bridge in place over the blue waters of Salt Creek - 1968

"Dreamer" during construction

Judge Jack Allen in charge of the first ceremony

I thought I had really pulled off a winner by having such a celebrity to speak at our opening night. My dream ended two weeks before the opening when Lowell Thomas was suddenly transferred to New Guinea and I had to hustle up a substitute. I came up with two substitutes – Wally Phillips, well-known WGN radio star, and my old college friend Abe Gibron, former coach of the Chicago Bears.

I want to tell you more about the "Kissing Bridge" before I get to opening the theater and the best way is to give you the copy from our "Wellman's Review and Forecast," and it went like this:

When Jack Spencer, well known local contractor, personally lifted out the first shovel full of dirt last week, construction had officially begun for the abutments to the relocated romantic "Old Student Bridge" which is being memorialized as part of Wellman's Magnificent Mile entertainment complex in Valparaiso. Dedicated to the preservation of this romantic symbol, Mr. Spencer is progressing well ahead of schedule and pledges completion of the project to the extent that the bridge will be passable by June 27, the scheduled date for the opening of Bridge VU Theater.

Upon completion of the erection by Spencer (who incidentally is involved with other projects in Muncie and Ft. Lauderdale), it will be gilded and dedicated to the generations of VU students who hold fond memories of what was perhaps their first kiss. It has always been a tradition to kiss your sweetheart on the footbridge over the Pennsylvania railroad tracks.

What could be more appropriate than to have the "Kissing Bridge" erected high over Salt Creek and lead directly to the new Bridge VU Center, where the Valparaiso University Summer Repertory Theater will open on June 27, 1968 with "The Fantasticks."

Even now, with the old bridge not even repaired, we see sentimentalists strolling and kissing along the bridge as it just rests there in an empty field. Photographs accompanying this article show the bridge and construction progress, but out of courtesy we have not photographed the many people who have come from miles away to once again feel the excitement and adventure of romance on the student bridge.

"If this bridge could talk it could tell plenty," said Mr. Sharp in 1936, and he should know because as long as he could remember the bridge had always been there over the Pennsylvania tracks.

The bridge has been repaired time and time again during the century of its existence. Lois Brauer, while a student in 1936, was reported by the "Torch" (campus newspaper) as commenting, "I am glad the bridge is repaired again – one always feels so much better after being out there."

It was the custom for a young woman to be kissed on the bridge after the stroke of midnight and now this wonderful custom can live on – and live on it would – thanks to great romantics like Spencer and Wellman. Perhaps as you walk across the bridge, your pulse, too, will beat faster and your breath will quicken as the person you love holds you tightly in the middle of the bridge, high over the rushing waters of Salt Creek.

I am sure this article from our almost famous newsletter somehow fell into the hands of the great commentator Lowell Thomas, and because of the key word "gilded" he wrote to me about not painting the bridge gold.

OPENING NIGHT

Opening night was a big success. The news that Lowell Thomas was transferred to New Guinea didn't slow me down but I reached into my friendship bank and came up with two for one. Wally Phillips of WGN radio and my old friend Abe Gibron, the Chicago Bears Coach, agreed to be co-hosts for opening night on June 26, 1969.

Wally and Abe

My first chore was to dedicate the Kissing Bridge. Along with 100 people, we watched Wally take hold of a bottle of champagne tied to a short rope from the bridge. My instructions to Wally were simple, "Wally, if you will swing the rope and bottle into the side of the bridge, we will take the picture and head into Bridge VU for dinner." The only problem was, Wally didn't let go of the bottle and a small trickle of blood ran through his fingers as he turned to the small crowd and said, "I would like to invite all of you back next week because instead of Bridge VU it will be known as Wally's Place!"

In the sixties lawsuits were few and far between for small instances like a little cut on the hand. I told Wally, "The show must go on!" The dinner was great and the play LUV staring Jim Lampl as Harry was outstanding. Dorothy Eagen from the local newspaper, The Vidette Messenger, wrote, "Lampl in his portrayal of Harry, the gifted, talented, yet gutless failure, was teriffic! You could almost see in yourself how easy it could be to become a Harry."

Jim Lampl was one of the talents in the group who could have made it as an actor but decided to become a drama teacher and has headed the Drama Department of LaPorte High School for the past thirty years. I'm still amazed at the success of the original group of young people who worked so hard to make our theater the place to go in Northwest Indiana.

In July of 2004 I e-mailed my good friend JoBe Cerny and asked him to give me an update on what happened with the careers of some of the original cast. His answer came back immediately, "Hi Bill, Katie Hanley got off to a great start after Bridge VU. She created the role of Marty in the original Broadway cast of Grease and she was on the original cast album. She got off to a great start in movies, too! She was in the feature film of Godspell and then danced with Gene Kelly in his last movie, Xanadu. David Rupprecht has had a very good career. He lives in California and hosted Supermarket Sweepstakes on TV for a number of years. He has done a lot of national theater tours and I know one of his favorite credits is appearing with Donald O'Conner in "How to Succeed in Business Without Really Trying." He also has done television and a lot of Improvisational Theater in Los Angeles. When Gloria English first left the company she appeared with Ethel Waters in "Member of the Wedding" at Chicago's presentation at the Ivanho Theater Company." (Ethel Waters was J.R. Waters famous Aunt Ethel, but as J.R. always said, "That didn't put any bread on my table." J.R. also said that he would see Aunt Ethel once a year when she dropped off a turkey for Thanksgiving, but no money! Ethel Waters died penniless because she gave all of her money to the church and a fast-talking minister.)

JoBe continued, "Rusty Stieger had a number of great years acting in Chicago Theater and produced several very successful puppet shows. His production of The Hobbit played 48 states during a seven-year period. He has been an executive with Live Marketing, one of the largest companies producing industrial theater for major corporations. John Szostech has been an innovator in an ancient form of theater known as Mask Theater, and he taught at Governor's State University for a time and of course Jim Lampl has headed up the drama department at LaPorte Indiana High School for over 30 years."

JoBe Cerny

JoBe Cerny, the author of the e-mail that updated me on the original cast from the "Theater in the Tents" through the first two years, is by far the most interesting and most successful of the entire group.

JoBe has been a professional actor for the past thirty-six years. He has consistently been in the top 2% of wage earners in the Screen Actors Guild for the past two decades. JoBe is best known as the voice of the Pillsbury Doughboy and on camera as Proctor and Gamble's silent-spokesman for cheer Detergent. His work has won nearly every major award in advertising including the Golden Lion at the Cannes International Film Festival for the best commercial in the world. Ad Age, entertainment Weekly, TV Guide, and Nickelodeon have rated his work among the fifty greatest commercials of all time. On stage, he has performed in thirty-five plays and worked extensively in improvisational theater. He toured nationally for The Second City and has also appeared in many feature films and numerous television shows. Additionally, he has performed in hundreds of videos, most notably in staring roles for John Cleese's Video Arts. JoBe is also a well-respected member of AFTRA, SAG and Actors Equity and is involved with developing union contracts for new technology.

In addition to his acting work, JoBe has had a twenty-five year career as a writer, director, and producer. His Chicago production company, Cerny/American Creative, is nationally recognized for excellence in sound design. JoBe designed and built the first digitally networked recording studios in the United States. His company currently produces 400 projects annually covering a range of work from commercials, music and industrial videos to feature films. His company recently produced its 5500th consecutive project without going over budget. JoBe is a recommended speaker of the American Advertising Federation on the subject of creativity. He also is a regular speaker on the college circuit on the business of acting.

In June of 1971 I became "star struck," so Fred Sitton directed Imogene Coca and her husband King Donovan in Plaza Suite. Richard Pick designed the set and received the best compliment a designer can get when Imogene said, "Mr. Pick, I have worked on a lot of stages but the scenery you have designed is the best I have ever worked with. The glass in the windows is real and when it rains outside the windows, it's really wet!"

It was evident to this couple I was new to the theater business and really needed some help so, after the first day of rehearsal King Donavan asked me to come to their suite that evening to have a drink. They wanted to talk to me. I arrived at 8:00 p.m. and it was obvious that they had had several martinis, and of course I tried to catch up by downing two in record time.

The T.V. was on, but I do not remember what the program was. It didn't really matter, though, because they seemed to argue about everything that appeared on the screen. They acted like they were on stage at all times, but there was no script – just plenty of ad-libs.

The reason for my invitation was to give me as much help as needed to pull off this almost impossible feat of making my theater successful in Valparaiso, Indiana. I soaked in all of their suggestions like a sponge, but the big mistake of the evening was forgetting my father's #1 rule, "It's made to sell, not to drink."

I had four very strong martinis and when I left their suite I was smart enough to knock on the door of the room next to their suite. When there was no answer, I opened it with my master key, called the reservation desk and told them not to sell this room, and then called my wife to apprise her of the situation. I couldn't drive and I shouldn't drive. I was as drunk as I could, or should be, but oh how much smarter I was!

I remember waking up at five a.m. and being half sick, but also very hungry. I found breakfast at the diner, and then I found my way home about 6:30 a.m. To this day I can't remember the advice Imogene and the King passed on to me that night!

Plaza Suite was an excellent show and it lasted 14 performances. King Donavan was the surprise; he was an excellent actor and he carried his wife almost every show. The two of them together was an absolute riot!

Once again, we received great reviews. Financially we were still not making a lot of money, but our reputation was growing by leaps and bounds!

After the last performance, it was part of my job and responsibility to take the stars to the airport. J.R. Waters and I helped load Imogene and King's luggage, along with her cat in his traveling cage. They were to leave at different times and they were going in different directions. Imogene's flight was one hour before her husband's. We were rushing to check in her luggage and the cat when she gave a goodbye kiss to J.R. and me and started to board the plane. Suddenly, King Donavan let out a yell like he had been shot; "Everyone gets a goodbye kiss except your husband! We are not going together and we won't see each other for two weeks!" Imogene gave a big laugh and finally gave the King a goodbye kiss before they both went their separate ways.

Plaza Suite was my first taste of working with real stars and I knew immediately that I was hooked.

The next star to take over Bridge VU was a beautiful lady and a great actress, Joan Bennett, in the comedy by Noel Coward, "Fallen Angels."

Bill Wellman, Joan Bennett and the director of Pheasant Run

I took Ms. Bennett to Chicago for her interview in booth #1 in the famous Pump Room. This was all new to me but I had to admit I was eating it up like chocolate candy. On the trip to Chicago I tried to keep a conversation going by asking about her husband and her married life, just making small talk. All at once she stopped me in my tracks with, "Mr. Wellman, I know what you would like to ask me so just blurt it out and I'll tell you the story." It set me back but I decided I wanted to know the truth so I forged ahead. "Is it true your husband shot another man?" There was no hesitation when she told the story. "My husband caught the two of us in the back seat of a car in the studio parking lot and yes, he shot him directly in the crotch. The man lived and our marriage went down the tubes. Does that story satisfy your curiosity?" I felt a little embarrassed, but I really enjoyed how honest and frank she was. The interview in the famous Pump Room, in booth #1, was a great experience and I vowed I would return more than once!

During Joan Bennett's three weeks she struck up an acquaintance with our bartender, Bob Gratton. Bob was a good-looking man and it was great fun to see him driving this elegant lady around Valparaiso in his 1950 Ford. He was a volunteer chauffer/companion, taking her to the beauty shop, drugstore, and many trips to the grocery store. I felt no obligation to warn him about parking in the parking lot and of course I didn't pass the story on about her ex-husband!

I struck up a relationship with my next star, Robert Horton, which has lasted over the years. Robert Horton played Scout Flint McCullough, a real hero on TV's Wagon Train, for five years. In Horton's capable hands, Flint McCullough

Robert Horton – Grand Opening at Admirals Health Club, Merrillville, IN

spoken and thoughtful without Horton's ever sacrificing the toughness expected of a wagon train scout.

To prepare for the role, Bob got in his car and drove the route the wagon train actually traveled to get a feel for the terrain. After five seasons of riding the trail, Robert Horton left Wagon Train in 1962 to pursue his career in the musical theater. The producers offered huge sums of money for him to stay on, but his heart belonged to Broadway!

Bob and his lovely wife, Marilynn, appeared in several great plays at Bridge VU: "There's a Girl in my Soup" and "The Owl and the Pussycat." Some of the same actors and actresses from the original group were also involved, Jim Lampl, Gail Wahlenfeld and David Rupprecht.

In May of 1972, Robert Horton came to see me with the idea of doing "The Odd Couple" in living black and white. The idea was to have Bob Horton direct and play Oscar, the loud, exuberant, boisterous, sloppy, messy and uncultured. The real shocker was Bob hand picked Junior Waters to play Felix, the quiet, refined, controlled, meticulous, in fact the very picture of neatness. It didn't take me long to jump on the band wagon of doing a real ODD COUPLE, but it soon hit me Junior Waters had never acted in a play. He had all the stage presence but could he remember his lines and would he accept the challenge? Robert Horton convinced Junior he could do the job and promised to help him over the hard spots.

The night before The Odd Couple had its grand opening, I watched the dress rehearsal and halfway through the first act, Bob Horton came down on Junior heavy. He chewed his fanny out in front of everyone. After the yelling was finished, Junior spotted me and screamed, "Don't you ever get me involved in anything like this again." I wouldn't have been surprised if he had not shown up for opening night, but he did and he really did well as the review in the Post Tribune relates:

Poker Players plus Waters and Horton

AREA "ODD COUPLE" is theaters best by Jean Isaacs, Drama Critic

Divorce may be what you make it, however, Neil Simon's play on the subject, "The Odd Couple," as now being staged at Wellman's Bridge Vu Theater, is consistent and by far the best theatrical production that has been given at Wellman's.

Part of this can be attributed to Simon's play, but most of the credit goes to Robert Horton, who both directs and takes the role of Oscar Madison in the production.

The set is good. The four poker-playing buddies who gather every Friday night are great. Outstanding in the group is Vinnie, played by Larry Maraviglia, who managed to make his final bow funny.

Junior Waters plays the part of Felix Unger. It was not until the middle of the first act that he seemed to relax and enjoy his role. The scene, which can almost be pinpointed, came while Horton was rubbing his stiff neck. From there on Waters was the picture of cooking, cleaning, crying half of the de-wed duo.

The roles of the two English sisters are not big ones, but they were well played by Gloria Lynn and Donna Henslee.

Horton was superb. He was messy without working at it, except in the defiance scene with Felix, when he is supposed to be.

Acting is not limited to just saying the words in the right way or even making the proper stage movements. There must be the correct facial expressions as well. Horton wisely uses every professional trick.

This is a funny, funny play about two men who find themselves divorced. It is only after a period of sharing an apartment together that you have the feeling that they understand themselves better and even something of the reasons their respective marriages fell apart.

A GEM P.R. JOB

BRIDGE VU THEATRE was still not on solid financial ground, and I needed to come up with some publicity that did not cost a lot of money, but would get me into the Chicago market. To this day, I remember going to a marketing and advertising workshop at McCormick Place in Chicago, and listening to one of my heroes, and the best promoter in the business, Mr. Bill Veeck (rhymes with wreck).

Most people think of Bill Veeck as a sportsman, but I knew him first and foremost as a promoter. I always used a quote from Bill Veeck whenever I talked to groups, or when I wanted to sell a show. This quote seemed to inspire me and I often thought about it when I tried to reach for a little more than was possible: "A strange thing happens when you don't promote. Nothing. Promotion and advertising are two different things," said Veeck. "Advertising costs money. Promotion is entirely different. Most people are not good promoters, because they are not poor enough," continued Veeck. "They can spend their money and buy advertising. Promotion takes more ingenuity. You have to find a way to get your message across for free. This means do something different – something that attracts attention and makes everybody talk about it," said Veeck. "Promotion is creative and it is accidental and it is luck – a lot of times, it's when you run into something that just clicks."

Promotion and advertising do go hand in hand. Many times a promotion will grow out of an advertising theme. "You will double the effectiveness of the dollars you have to spend for advertising, because your promotions will outdo your advertising," said Mr. Veeck.

Illustrating his point that advertising and promotion should continue strong in good times as well as bad, Veeck related an anecdote involving Mr. Wrigley, the chewing gum magnate. Mr. Wrigley was riding the train, going to the West Coast. He was sitting in the dining car and people at the table with him looked out the window and saw a billboard (I am sure it was a Whiteco/Dean White owned board!) that was advertising "Wrigley Chewing Gum." One of his companions said, "Mr. Wrigley is it true that you are selling all the chewing gum that you can make?" Wrigley responded, "Yes, we sell all we can make." "Then why do you spend your money on billboards, when you are already selling all you can make?" Mr. Wrigley answered, "This train is going 70 miles an hour, right? And it has been going 70 miles an hour for quite some time right? Well, they aren't going to take the engine off."

Let's go back with a little history on one of my great heroes. William Louis Veeck Jr. was born in Chicago in 1914, and died in Chicago in 1986. A self-proclaimed "hustler," Veeck was the greatest public relations man and promotional genus the game of baseball has ever seen. The son of former Chicago Cubs president, Bill Veeck Sr., he got his start in the baseball business by selling peanuts and hotdogs at Wrigley Field. He was fond of saying that he was "the only human being ever raised in a ball park." Over the course of a fifty-year love affair with baseball, Veeck owned three major league teams, and would establish himself as the game's most incorrigible maverick.

My hero and I had several things in common. First, I was always considered a maverick; whether I was on the Valparaiso School Board, or doing promotions on the public. Second, both Mr. Veeck and I served in the United States Marine Corps. Sadly, when Bill Veeck returned from duty in World War II, he had received a severe leg injury that would require amputation.

He bought his first major league team, the Cleveland Indians, in 1946 at the ripe old age of 32. After selling the Indians, Veeck took on his greatest challenge in 1951: ownership of what he called "a collection of old rags and tags known to baseball historians at the St. Louis Browns." Veeck operated under the premise that fans should have a good time at the ballpark, even if the home team lost (and the St. Louis Browns finished dead last in the American League in 1951 with a 52 – 102 record, 46 games out of first place). It was during this year that Bill Veeck pulled off one of the greatest promotions of all times. He signed a legal baseball contract with Eddie Gaedal, a 3'7" midget. He was placed in the line-up as a pinch hitter only one time. He walked, and he was immediately replaced with a pinch runner, but this promotion was short (play on words) and simple, and Mr. Veeck received all the publicity that a "hustler" could get from one great P.R. job.

After saying all of that – what I needed was a good old fashion show business P.R. job done on my theatre. I knew what I was doing in Valparaiso, Indiana was out in front of my times, and I did not have the capital to put a lot of money into advertisement, so I hatched a promotion gem.

Will Leonard worked for the Chicago Tribune, and he was the "in" theatre critic in Chicago. His newspaper articles were like gold to directors, producers, and theatre owners. But, I could not convince Leonard that Valparaiso was in the Chicago land market. He, along with a lot of Chicago customers, thought that traveling to Valparaiso, Indiana was like driving to Indianapolis. It was my goal to change his mind, and let him convince Chicago customers that we were just a short trip away.

After many telephone calls that were not returned, along with two letters not answered, I finally talked to Leonard on the phone at the Tribune office. The short conversation went something like this: "Mr. Leonard, I am Bill Wellman, and I run a dinner theatre in Valparaiso, Indiana that is called Bridge VU; and I would like to invite you to a dinner show to see Albert Salmi in *Last of the Red Hot Lovers.* There was a silence on the phone, so I said, "Mr. Leonard are you still there?" He was very short as he said, "Yes, I am here and you are too far outside of Chicago." He then hung up on me. I was devastated – I had him and let him go.

That night I didn't fall asleep early; I tossed and turned and tried to figure out how to convince Mr. Leonard that we were in the suburbs of Chicago, just like Downers Grove or Arlington Heights. In the middle of the night, I got out of bed and wrote my next plan of attack on Mr. Leonard.

The next day I sent Mr. Will Leonard the following Western Union over-night telegram that went like this:

"Mr. Leonard: I realize you are a busy man, but I need to convince you that my theatre is worthwhile and that we are in the Chicago market. If I can have you in my dining room in 28

minutes from downtown Chicago, will you come? Please call me. Sincerely, Bill Wellman."

The hook was baited and I cast it out. The next day I received this call from the Chicago Tribune: "OK Wellman. I must say you have my Irish curiosity aroused. How the hell are you going to pull this stunt off?" I am sure my voice was a little high, and I talked a little too fast when I unveiled my plans. "I have a captain friend who flies for American Airlines and he owns a brand new twin engine Cessna. He is willing to moonlight for me. We will meet you at Meigs Field at 5:00 p.m. on Thursday, July 6, 1972, and I will have you in Wellman's Dining Room in 28 minutes."

There was that awful silence on the other end of the phone, but I remembered he had had enough interest to call me. The next thing I heard was "OK Wellman. I will be at Meigs at 5:00p.m. on Thursday and I expect you to be on time."

Mr. Longnecker, the captain who lived two blocks from my house on Park Avenue, and I landed at Meigs at 4:30 P.M. and I walked into the main building to wait for the famous Will Leonard. At five minutes of 5:00 a checkered cab pulled up and Mr. Leonard stepped out. He was wearing a shiny blue serge (well worn) suit. His tie was loose and the top button on his shirt was open. He had white wavy hair, with a slight tint of yellow, and wore thick glasses and he looked like a typical newspaperman.

I introduced him to Mr. Longnecker and we prepared for our 28-minute flight over the top of the U.S. Steel plant and into Porter County Airport. I noticed that Mr. Leonard checked his watch as we reached the end of the runway at Meigs Field, but I was convinced I would fulfill my 28-minute promise. What could he do to me if it took 36 minutes? I had him!

As we taxied up to the small main terminal at Porter County Airport, I spotted my 1938 Packard limo on the tarmac headed right for us. The plan was that my faithful piano player / actor / songwriter / and good friend J.R. Waters was also doubling as my chauffer. J.R. looked the part with his black suit, white shirt, red tie, and the black visor chauffer cap; standing with the back door open and ready to finish off the two and a half mile trip to Wellman's Dining Room.

The next thing that happened sucked the wind right out of me. As Will Leonard stepped out of my shiny Packard limo in front of Wellman's, J.R. noticed that Will Leonard had a terrible dandruff problem and his shiny blue serge suit showed it off. Without a word, J.R. reached over and with the palm of his hand he whisked Mr. Leonard's left shoulder clean. Leonard said nothing, but immediately looked at his right shoulder and followed J.R.'s idea and brushed another load of dandruff off of his other shoulder. No words were spoken.

I had previous inside information from a good friend, that my newfound buddy "The Critic" liked good Irish whiskey, so I proceeded to have a bottle at our table when we arrived at Wellman's Dining Room. Oh, by the way, we pulled up to the front door with about ½ minute to go on the 28-minute time schedule. I was feeling good!

After several jolts of Irish whiskey, Mr. Leonard ordered pan fried perch and a creamy garlic salad. He also ate the entire loaf of fresh warm bread. During his meal he took time to belt down another shot of Irish whiskey. After dinner we started to take the short trip over Salt Creek to Bridge VU Theatre, and I could tell by the conversation that the Irish whiskey was starting to work when Mr. Leonard spoke these words of wisdom to me as we approached the *Kissing Bridge:* "Wellman, what the hell is this Kissing Bridge shit?" I gave him the history of the bridge and told him that Lowell Thomas attended Valparaiso University, and a picture of the bridge was in his last book, and that a coed was not considered a real coed until she was kissed on the bridge when a train was going by and the kiss was to last as long as the train.

After my definition I wasn't too surprised when he said, "I am going to walk over this bridge and if you touch me during the process I will write that you are a fagot queen." The Irish whiskey had done its job. It was working.

I had also received a bit of advice regarding Will Leonard from Jerry Kaufman, owner of Mill Run Theatre in Niles, Illinois. He told me not to push Leonard on what I wanted him to write in his review. He was considered to be very opinionated and bull-headed so my next move was brilliant when I ordered another Irish whiskey as we set down at our table in Bridge VU.

It was just about curtain time when Mr. Leonard said, "I have seen this play so many times that I could cue all of the people in the play if they forgot their lines, so please don't ask me to review it. Wellman, you are a nice young man, and I will write a story about you, but please don't ask for a review. No Review!" After the first act Will Leonard knew that he was watching a great actor in Albert Salmi, and a top quality play, *Last of the Red Hot Lovers*, in Valparaiso, Indiana.

Marilynn Horton and Albert Salmi in *"Last of the Red Hot Lovers"*

Albert Salmi was the type of actor who, when you saw his picture, you immediately knew him from some movie. He usually played the bad guy, and he guest-starred on almost every series on TV, including Bonanza, Gunsmoke, Rawhide, Ironside, and The F.B.I. He was very proud of an award he received from the National Cowboy Hall of Fame.

Albert was a quiet man and was somewhat of a loner. When he did stray into the bar at Wellman's, his order to the bartender was always, "bourbon neat." This term was very unusual for Valparaiso, but the bartenders caught on because it was so simple. It meant a shot of bourbon and nothing else including conversation. Albert had a hobby of buying antique walking sticks and his stay in our community added two sticks to his collection.

In my opinion, he was by far the best actor to appear at Bridge VU Theater. He died tragically in a murder-suicide on April 23, 1990 in Spokane, Washington at age 62.

The next move by my good old friend, "The Critic," surprised me. He said, "Wellman, are your plans to get me back to Chicago the same way and the same time that you got me here?" My answer was short; "Yes sir that was the plan." Will (only his close friends call him this) then asked, "Do you have a telephone I could use before the second act starts?" "Yes sir, follow me upstairs."

I took him up to my office where he called the Tribune and told them to pull his story for Friday and he would be back in Chicago 28 minutes after midnight to write a review on the play Last of the Red Hot Lovers. He had changed his mind. I really had him!

It is hard to get a review in a major city like Chicago, but to get one like this was amazing. My personal thanks to Bill Veeck for his help and inspiration in this promotion.

On the following page is the three-column review the Bridge VU received in the Chicago Tribune. What do you think it was worth in dollars!? When this review hit the theater page of the Chicago Tribune on Friday, it was as if someone had switched a light on.

Our volume started to pick up and we paid our bills a little faster. Our reputation was headed in the right direction, due to a very good P.R. Gem.

Theater

A crackling winner in Porter County

Valparaiso, Ind.

● NEIL SIMON, already successful on the stages of Broadway and the Loop, is cutting a swath in Porter County, Indiana. Bridge-Vu-Theater, on Route 30 just outside Valparaiso, just concluded an engagement of the first racially integrated staging of "The Odd Couple," and now has a crackling production of his "Last of the Red Hot Lovers," which may run well into the summer.

Albert Salmi, as the middle-aged, would-be lecher who seeks just one extramarital fling, and strikes out three times with three different females in three comic acts, is a tall, slender hero, whereas his predecessors in the role have been short and plump. But Salmi is one of those actors who can do comedy and quiet tragedy at the same time, and he makes the poor misfit as lamentable as laughable, in a hilarious but touching portrayal.

Each of the three ladies who cross his path without touching him are well cast and played with verve—Marilynn Horton as the hard-boiled nymphomaniac of the first act, Mary McTigue as the kooky young unemployed nightclub singer who turns him onto pot, and Aviva Crane as his wife's gloomy friend who so depresses him that he gives up all thought of seduction forever.

Bridge -Vu is a dinner-theater with a thrust stage, directed with liveliness by Robert Horton, and with an attractive set by Richard Pick.

Bill Wellman, who started with a restaurant on Route 30 some 14 years ago, and now has the cafe, a motel, the theater, pool tables, 16 bowling lanes, ice skating, and several entertainment rooms on his hands, is a man who'll try anything. After "Last of the Red Hot Lovers" closes, the comedy team of Bob Hudson and Ron Landry will play his theater in August, to be followed by Woody Woodbury in September, and Phyllis Diller [in a return engagement] in November.

Once Wellman tried "black tie" wrestling in his playhouse. But, after the Beast of Berlin versus Dick the Bruiser thrilled him but didn't sell any tickets, he retired from that area of show biz.

This is the third year of theater in a modern structure, hard by the restaurant and motel buildings, after two years in a tent that used to leak. Wellman has produced a lot of light comedies of the "Last of the Red Hot Lovers" genre, but he also put on "Jesus Christ, Superstar," and the world premiere of a rock opera, "Today Is a Good Day to Die," about the present plight of the American Indian. That is a long way from "black tie" wrestling.

Why did he call his theater the Bridge-Vu? Because it has a view of a bridge, of course.

The span is a foot bridge, about 15 or 20 feet in length, that once crossed the Pennsylvania Railroad right of way on the campus of Valparaiso University, and there's a plaque which reads, in part: "Legend has it that a Valparaiso University woman was not officially a coed until she had been kissed on Student Bridge while a train was passing underneath."

"Legend, of course," Wellman told us, "is something that can be believed in whole or in part. But it's now called 'the kissing bridge,' and kissing is not forbidden."

Albert Salmi: Hilarious, touching portrayal.

Bill Wellman doesn't miss a trick.

The food is his Wellman's restaurant, which adjoins the motel, is excellent. Harvi Griffin plays a dulcet harp in the main dining room. Junior Waters [who played the neat and fussy guy in "The Odd Couple" at Bridge-Vu last month] now is playing piano and singing in the lounge.

Valparaiso is about 50 miles east by southeast of Chicago.

William Leonard

Mr. Leonard gave us three columns of great "free" publicity

This review in the Chicago Tribune got me another invitation to the Ambassador East Hotel and I was starting to enjoy the interviews from booth #1 at the famous Pump Room in Chicago, but the Albert Salmi interview was exceptional.

Porter County 'stars'

It was Porter County Day at the Pump Room in the Ambassador East Hotel when unbeknownst to each other, Bill Wellman and his star at Bridge-Vu Theater Albert Salmi, right picture, were seated next to Mrs. Neil Fry; her daughter, Mrs. Frank Vackar, now of Wheeling, Ill.; her son, DeWitt Fry of Chesterton, and Mrs. Phoebe Leeds of Valparaiso. Bill was seated in famous Booth No. 1, while the others were in Booth No. 2. "There were some other celebrities in the room," laughed Mrs. Fry. "Irv Kupcinet and columnist Jack Anderson were in Booth No. 4!" The photographer took Mrs. Fry's picture just as she answered the phone and heard her grandchildren from Fort Hood, Tex., singing "Happy Birthday." They are the children of Leonard and Susie Harsel. Bill no doubt will be back in Booth 1 at the end of the month when his star will be Frank Sinatra Jr. Frank will give two performances Sept. 1—at 8:30 and 11 p.m. The comedy team of Hudson and Landray open Tuesday for a 5-day run, and guess who is coming back "home" in November? . . . Porter County's queen, Phyllis Diller.

It didn't appear in the newspaper, but my conversation with Mrs. Fry while Albert Salmi was in the rest room went like this: "Bill Wellman, I'm celebrating my 75th birthday waiting for a telephone call from my grandkids from Texas, anticipating seeing a super star in booth #1 and who the hell am I looking at, YOU!" Albert Salmi showed up in the nick of time, so I introduced him to my good friend from Valparaiso, Mrs. Neil Fry, her daughter and son.

They asked for his autograph and Mrs. Fry seemed to start to enjoy being in booth #2 next to a couple of super stars!

Albert Salmi and yours truly!

PHYLLIS DILLER

Phyllis Diller by Ken Fallin

The success of "The Odd Couple" and "The Last of the Red Hot Lovers" gave me the courage to try other stars and one of my favorites was Phyllis Diller.

Her personality was "fun and games" even when she was not on stage. My first booking with her was just after she had her first face lift; and it was also the time in her married life when she was with Ward Donavan, a want-to-be actor who would take the microphone back stage and introduce Phyllis each show, and then did nothing but drink champagne (starting in the morning.)

I heard a rumor later on they got a divorce after Ward was interviewed by a national newspaper person and this question came up: "Mr. Donavan what do you do?" and his (alleged) answer was, "I introduce her every show and I screw her a lot." This was a rumor, but we heard he was no longer on the tour after the interview. Ward was not the original FANG that Phyllis spoke about.

Each night I would drive my Pontiac station wagon over the Holiday Inn and pick my star up and deliver her to the back door of Bridge Vu Theater. My first glimpse of Phyllis was a little shocking because her head was completely shaved for the face-lift, but she was wearing what looked like a skullcap make out of a nylon stocking. Her hair was less than a quarter of an inch in length, but of course the audience would never see this because she always wore a "fright" wig.

To Bill Wellman
Fabulous Entrepreneur
Gentleman & Scholar
& a terrific guy to
work for!
Best Always
Phyllis Diller

At the same time she got the first face-lift she also had work done on her teeth, so she was wearing a rubber mold on both her upper and lower teeth when she was not on stage. This was quite a sight to see, but it did not affect her ability to make people feel comfortable and laugh.

Her opening show turned out to be one of her best and funniest shows she ever put on. This is not my statement, but this is what she told me after the first show.

J.R. Waters was the opening act, but he did not use his comedy routine. He played the piano and sang about a half dozen familiar songs; but every show he would also work in one or two of his own original songs like, "Boone Grove Woman," or "There Ain't Nothing Like a Northern Indiana Girl."

Phyllis was introduced and brought on to the stage by her husband, Ward Donavan, and she knew immediately that she had the 500 people in the palm of her hand. After five minutes she noticed that she had blown out one of her temporary front teeth and stepped on it. The only people who noticed it were a few people at the front tables, but when she looked down and saw the pulverized white powder it completely broke her up to the point where she threw her head back and gave out one of her best laughs. At the same time she flipped her "fright" wig completely off her nylon covered head. The audience gave the loudest single laugh she had ever received. It sounded like a shotgun going off.

She never lost her composure as she leaned down to the first table and borrowed a napkin from a tearful customer and put it on her head like a babushka, and then returned to the grand piano and played twenty minutes of concert piano.

On the way back to her suite in the Holiday Inn she told me that was the loudest single laugh she had ever received. She tried to duplicate the flipping off of the wig during the second show, but she couldn't quite pull it off.

David Thon was our very talented lighting and sound guy who always tried to give Phyllis something to laugh about by placing something in her piano seat that would make her smile. The best one came one evening when she went for her music by lifting the lid. She broke up as she tried to explain to the audience that she had gold fish swimming in her bench, but she couldn't tip the bench to show them so she gave them a graphic description. David had made a plastic liner for the bench and placed three small gold fish in it. He had even given the inside pool a blue paint job to make it realistic.

Several months after this performance I received a call from Phyllis requesting that I sell her my piano bench. I told her I would not sell it but I would make her a gift of it; so, I got David Thon to take it apart, he crated it up and we mailed it to her in Chicago. Her reasoning for wanting that particular bench was somewhat explained to me when I asked. It seems that she just liked the way the latch worked and the lid stayed open while she was sorting through her music.

It was on her second trip to Bridge VU Theater that I received a telephone call from Phyllis telling me that she needed to have her back adjusted, so she would need a chiropractor or a doctor. It happened on a Thursday and in Valparaiso that is the day that all the doctors are out of their office. Never have an emergency on Thursdays in a small town. You just might die!

I told Phyllis the problem, but I also said I knew this Dr. Ogle in Lacrosse, Indiana and I would give him a call. He immediately said, "Bring her down and I will give her an adjustment." I picked her up in my faithful Pontiac station wagon and we took off for the 18-mile trip to Lacrosse.

On the way down I told Phyllis this story about the chiropractor she was going to see. Dr. Ogle and his wife were great customers of mine, both in the dining room and the theater. Whenever you saw them, however, they were always with another couple from Wanatah who owned the Wanatah Stone Company. If there was a dinner reservation or 'will-call' tickets at the theater you could count on the two couples being together.

Dr. Ogle's wife was not what you would call attractive, although not ugly; she definitely was not good looking. Now the other lady, married to the stone quarry man, was exceptionally good looking. The two couples always took a couple of trips each year to Las Vegas. It was during one of these trips when Dr. Ogle's wife suddenly, and unexpectedly, "cashed in her chips." She had not been ill so it shocked everyone when we read in the paper that 42-year-old wife of Dr. Ogle died in Las Vegas.

Six months after her death, Dr. Ogle married the stone quarry queen after she suddenly divorces her husband! This was almost as shocking as the death of Mrs. Ogle.

Phyllis had been listening to my story with intense interest all during the 18-mile trip. I was just finishing my story when we pulled up in front of the doctor's office on road 421 in Lacrosse, Indiana.

I helped Phyllis out of my wagon and into the office where Dr. Ogle was waiting for us. After introductions Dr. Ogle said, "Come on in Ms. Diller and let me see if I can straighten out your problem."

I waited in the lobby and started to read one of the outdated magazines, when all at once I heard that famous cackle of a laugh from the inner office. It seemed like every few minutes a new burst of laughter would come from the office. Forty-five minutes later the new Phyllis bounced out of the doctor's office, proclaiming that Dr. Ogle was the best and he had saved her life. She wanted the doctor and his wife to be her guests at either show on Friday or Saturday night. I tried to pay the bill, but the good doctor would have none of that. It was his pleasure and all he was asking was an autographed picture for his lobby. I followed through with that request.

On the way home Phyllis told me the rest of the story. She had asked Dr. Ogle about his wife's sudden death and his quick marriage to what everyone thought was his best friend. Her story was that the stone quarry magnet was too busy making tons of money and working too many hours in the quarry and not paying enough attention to his wife.

Now, on the other hand, the doctor always had his eye on the good-looking friend and when the opportunity suddenly arrived, after the death of his wife, the doctor used his strength to convince her to leave her husband and marry him.

Phyllis told me that it was the strength of the doctor's hands that convinced this good looking one to make the big move. Her husband was two tired and just didn't give her enough attention. If it weren't for Phyllis, I would have never heard "the rest of the story."

If you happen to run into Phyllis Diller today and ask her about the good doctor in LaCrosse, Indiana, I am sure she would tell you that Dr. Ogle is the best and he does have strong hands.

The next Phyllis Diller story came close to popping my ever-present ulcer.

I was pleased I had her booked in my theater in November of 1971 for six "sold out" shows. The warm and lively lady could sell tickets and in a short time all six shows were sold out and half of the money was already spent when I received a telephone call from Ms. Diller's agent informing me my "sold out" week was canceled. This meant I could be asked to refund 2700 pre-sold tickets. I needed to come up with something fast! The next paragraph is a copy from the Gary Post Tribune, "On The Go" written by my good friend Blaine Marz.

WELL THAT'S SHOW BIZ DEPT

After canceling a scheduled November engagement at Bill Wellman's Bridge VU Dinner Theater, Valparaiso, and then canceling out again on the resulting January of next year's engagement, zany Phyllis Diller, electrified hair and all, has a confirmed week, opening Tuesday, February 27 at the house that Wellman built.

Who is to blame for the cancellation? Why President Nixon (if you stretch things a bit), who else? Isn't he to blame for everything? It happened like this:

Sammy Davis J.R. was working at some small club or other in Las Vegas, The Sands, at the time of the Republican National Convention in Miami. He wanted to be on the platform when President Nixon accepted the nomination – which he was. There were some who thought for just a minute that Sammy had received the nomination, as they watched the proceedings on television.

To be in Miami for the convention's main event, Davis asked Phyllis to substitute for him at The Sands for that one night – which she did. In fact she did so well the management begged, pleaded, cajoled and offered money (they pay slightly better at The Sands than Bill Wellman does at Bridge VU Theater) to return for a four-week tour – which she did! And there went the earlier scheduled Bridge VU appearances, right down nearby Salt Creek! We became victims of massive re-scheduling.

Don't go away – This story of why theater entrepreneurs, such as W.F. Wellman, also known as Bill, gray early, has another twist!

After Phyllis succumbed to all that blandishment – and money – from The Sands management, Wellman obtained Gordon MacRae as her replacement for the November show. A little later MacRae canceled to work in the same Las Vegas show with that dilly Diller!

Entertainers are as human as the rest of us when it comes to pursuing the almighty dollar, which Wellman and others in the entertainment business both know and understand. Phyllis Diller may be more human than some of them in other ways. The following letter from her to Wellman tells its own story along that line.

"Dear Bill,

I must apologize personally to you for two postponements of my engagements at your beautiful dinner theater. I'm sure you know how much I look forward to and enjoy working for you. I hope that your patrons know these postponements were absolutely necessary.

As you know, I never go out of my way to inconvenience people who have been so kind to me over the years. I guarantee you that when I do play Wellman's it will be a smashing show! In the meantime I would like to extend my sincere wishes for a Happy Chanukah, Merry Christmas and a very Happy New Year, or whatever! See you next year!"

"Tickets previously sold for the scheduled Diller shows in November and January will be honored for the same nights of the week for her engagement opening February 27," said Wellman.

By the way, does anyone know if Caesar's Palace, The Sands, etc. are solidly set for the week of February 27, 1973 with CONFIRMED bookings of named stars? I just recalled my mother insisting everything happens in "threes."

To end my Diller story, no one asked for a refund on all six shows. I did, however, spend a lot of money on TUMS during this stretch of show business. I also received a letter from the White House thanking me for sending the president our newsletter. It is amazing how well our "hot line" worked in 1972.

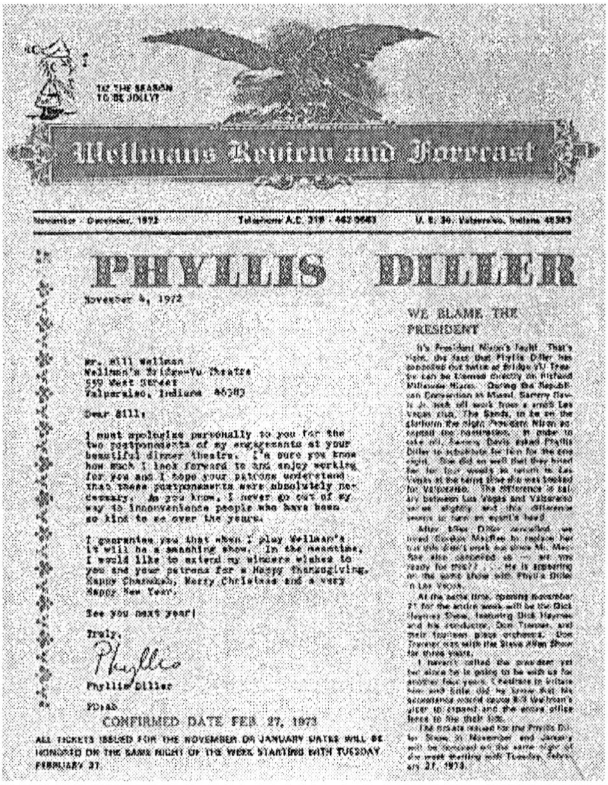

'TIS THE SEASON TO BE JOLLY!

Wellmans Review and Forecast

November - December, 1972 — Telephone A.C. 219 - 462-9683 — U. S. 30, Valparaiso, Indiana 46383

PHYLLIS DILLER

November 4, 1972

Mr. Bill Wellman
Wellman's Bridge-Vu Theatre
559 West Street
Valparaiso, Indiana 46383

Dear Bill:

I must apologize personally to you for the two postponements of my engagements at your beautiful dinner theatre. I'm sure you know how much I look forward to and enjoy working for you and I hope your patrons understand that these postponements were absolutely necessary. As you know, I never go out of my way to inconvenience people who have been so kind to me over the years.

I guarantee you that when I play Wellman's it will be a smashing show. In the meantime, I would like to extend my sincere wishes to you and your patrons for a Happy Thanksgiving, Happy Chanukah, Merry Christmas and a very Happy New Year.

See you next year!

Truly,

Phyllis

Phyllis Diller

PD:ab

CONFIRMED DATE FEB. 27, 1973

ALL TICKETS ISSUED FOR THE NOVEMBER OR JANUARY DATES WILL BE HONORED ON THE SAME NIGHT OF THE WEEK STARTING WITH TUESDAY FEBRUARY 27.

WE BLAME THE PRESIDENT

OUR HOT LINE WORKS

Someone misplaced our red (hot line) phone to Dick so we sent him our last Review and Forecast just to let him know of the problems caused by his accepting the nomination and the Phyllis Diller cancellation. We thought you might like to see the answer from the White House.

THE WHITE HOUSE

WASHINGTON

December 20, 1972

Dear Mr. Wellman:

On behalf of the President, I want to thank you for your letter and for sending him the newsletter. He appreciates your thoughtfulness in writing.

With the President's best wishes,

Sincerely,

Roland L. Elliott
Deputy Special Assistant
to the President

8-foot toy-filled Christmas stocking winner - Greg Emig. Girl's winner - Gwen Sartain.

COMING IN 1973

APRIL 12---DUKE ELLINGTON
APRIL 13—DOUG OLDHAM
MAY 9 & 10---WAYNE KING
MAY 19---CARMON CAVALARO
MAY 23 & 24—HARRY JAMES
JUNE 8 & 9---VICTOR BORGE
AUGUST 20-25---FATS DOMINO

WELLHOUSE ENTERTAINMENT

Now Playing - ME & MY BROTHERS

G. GRAVES

THE EVER POPULAR GEORGE GRAVES IS RETURNING TO THE WELLHOUSE DECEMBER 30 and WILL APPEAR thru JANUARY 13.

CARLIN HAS POWER!

Norm "Grinny" Carlin has added Tyrone Power to his act. "Grinny" is famous for his saxophone playing and Power is a top notch organ player. Besides the ever present comedy, Carlin and Power team up and play dance sets. They'll be in the Wellhouse Lounge March 19 thru 31.

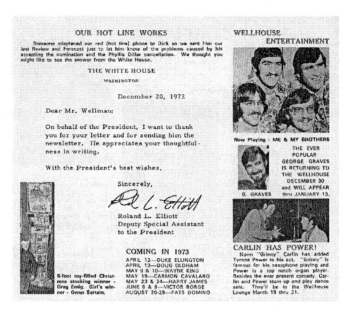

Letter from Roland L. Elliot, Deputy Assistant to the President

UNION LESSON

Two weeks in front of my first sold out "Big Band" night starring the great Count Basie, I received a telephone call from the head of the Motion Picture Operators and Stage Hand Union informing me, "If you don't hire one full-time stagehand for Bridge VU Theater we will bring a picket line to your theater the night Count Basie is to appear and the Basie Band will not cross a picket line. We will close you down!"

I had never heard from the union before but it did give me a scare, so against my logic I gave in and hired one union stagehand. Enter from stage left one Russel Casey, who just happened to be the president of the Porter County Union.

Mr. Casey came to work two weeks before the Count arrived but it only took one week to catch my only union employee cheating on his time card. It was my mother who pointed out the discrepancy to me and I in turn collared my union stagehand. He denied it but we had him cold, so it was my real pleasure to say, "You're fired."

The next day I had a call from the president of the union in Lake County informing me I would have to hire another stagehand or the picket line would be set up on the opening night of the sold out Count Basie show.

Catching the prior stagehand cheating gave me the courage I needed to say, "Bring on your picket line, but if you do I will have a story ready to go in the paper the next day telling the story about the cheating president of the union and why we fired him."

The Basie night went on without a hitch and I never heard from the union again while I operated Bridge VU Theater, but they would reappear again later in my life!

THE BIG BAND SOUND

I decided in 1971 that the Big Bands would be good for business and our stage was deep enough to put the band on platforms to the rear of the stage and use the front of the stage for dancing.

Burrus' safe dance floor

I gave Homer Burrus the job of how to safely keep everyone from falling off of the three-foot stage. He designed a double stairway and pipe railings wrapped around the huge proscenium stage.

Yours truly and the King

I started with Clyde McCoy, the Sugar Blues Man and his six musicians and singers playing in the "Wellhouse" Monday through Friday and then they moved to Bridge VU Theater for Saturday nights. This gave us two great weeks.

Wayne King, the Waltz King took over for a weekend and pleased hundreds of dancing couples with this sweet music. The day he arrived, he asked me if I had some young person he could hire to sell his records and of course I introduced him to my oldest daughter, Dawn, who was 22 at the time.

Dawn was as shocked as I was when she told me after two nights of selling records, for a total sale of $560.00, Mr. King split with her 50/50, giving Dawn $280.00. In 1971 that was a lot of money.

Junior, Count Basie and Bill

Royalty appeared twice a year in 1971 starting with "The Count", Count Basie who was considered by the late Louis Armstrong as the "Greatest Ever." He has been in the Encyclopedia Yearbook of Jazz since 1956.

The Count was followed by the "Duke." Duke Ellington and his full orchestra also took over Bridge VU in 1971 and played to a packed house of lovers of Duke Ellington...Love You Madly.

"Where's the Duke playing?"

"Well, tonight he's doing a concert in Grant Park. Tomorrow he's playing a testimonial dinner for W. Clement Stone at the Hilton and Saturday night the band will be in Holland."

Duke Ellington and 2 other guys!

"Michigan?"

"No Amsterdam."

"Concerts, dinners, proms, night clubs, sacred concerts in houses of worship are all strung together in a series of one nighters (with periodic engagements in one place) for Duke Ellington's orchestra as it travels around the world. The Duke is currently taking a five week tour of Russia for the state department, followed by 14 weeks abroad before he returns home to Bridge VU Theater in Valparaiso, Indiana."

I remember the night I introduced the Duke to my eldest daughter. He gently kissed her hand and sweet-talked her. After the meeting, Dawn looked at me with stars in her eyes as she said, "I can see why he has the name Duke. He is ROYALTY!"

JERRY VAN DYKE

If you are operating on a "shoestring" the general manager has many tasks. It was on a Saturday night I drove my new Pontiac station wagon to meet a 1:00am plane at O'Hare airport. The "star" for the upcoming week was Jerry Van Dyke, the actor, comic, and occasional banjo picker. He had a casual style that is not only refreshing, but also very entertaining!

Jerry has been active in all medias of entertainment. His lists of television appearances are countless (Ed Sullivan, Andy Griffith, Tonight Show, Dick Van Dyke, etc.); and he had starred in several successful television shows ("My Mother the Car," "Accidental Family," "Headmaster," etc). He also played a major role in "Coach" along with being a headliner at Caesars Palace, Harrah's Club, etc.

"Bill, can I get my $20.00 back?"

The plane was 45 minutes late and the airport was not too busy at 1:45am in 1973. I waited for my pick-up near the luggage turn styles and suddenly I heard loud singing off in the distance. As the jovial group headed my way I had the feeling the singers were led by Mr. Jerry Van Dyke. He was smashed, but in a great mood! It took him ten minutes in the front seat of my wagon to completely fall into a very sound sleep for the trip to the beautiful Holiday Inn located on US 30 and the west banks of Salt Creek, Valparaiso, Indiana.

I helped Jerry and his group of three, unload their luggage at the Holiday Inn and to my surprise Jerry gave me a $20 tip. It was just after lunch on a Monday when Jerry came into Bridge VU to give out instructions to the great David Thon on lighting and sound for the upcoming five performances. After a sound check Jerry dropped into my office and asked, "Is there any chance I could get my twenty back?" I didn't hesitate when I gave him a "No, but thanks for asking." Somewhere Jerry found out that the same fellow who picked him up and handled the luggage was the same man who would sign his paycheck after the last show. Jerry gave Bridge VU Theater five great successful shows.

I saw Jerry Van Dyke one more time in 1994. Liz and I were standing in line to check into the Conrad Hilton where the Indiana Society was having their annual banquet and the advertised entertainer was Rich Little, but because of a shot at Las Vegas, Jerry Van Dyke was the substitute. When Liz said, "There's Jerry Van Dyke," I immediately walked over to say hello and he spotted me and came up first with "Valparaiso, Indiana, and you still owe me $20." I still hadn't given him back the twenty!

The Indiana Society of Chicago is where 1800 (mostly men) Hoosiers dress like Penguins and come to Chicago once a year for a bad dinner!

MICKEY ROONEY

I booked Mickey Rooney for a two-night dinner show on May 15 and 16, 1973 for $1,650, which included a five piece musical back up including a female singer. The article in Wellman's Review and Forecast read:

MICKEY ROONEY

The 40's sound, the Old Glen Miller, Larry Clinton, Artie Shaw, Lawrence Welk stuff will be presented by Mickey Rooney and his orchestra May 15, and 16. If you're a patron of the old standards, if you like to reminisce over the sweet and jumpy music of the 40's, plan on spending an evening with the Mickey Rooney Show.

Mickey Rooney, star of the screen and television, conducts the orchestra, but sings, plays several instruments and does imitations. Backed by Michelle Scott with her renditions of familiar melodies, and accompanied by an orchestra comprised of first rate musicians guarantees you an evening of top notch entertainment.

The price of the ticket was $6.50 per person. Mickey was fun to work with and his price was just right for Bridge Vu. We definitely made money on Mickey!

I made arrangements for Mickey to play 18 holes of golf with my old friend Abe Gibron at the Valparaiso Country Club. Watching the two of them driving down the number one fairway in a golf cart was worth the price of admission! Abe weighed in at 395 lbs. and he was the driver. Mickey tipped the scales at 141 lbs. The golf cart was on a 45-degree angle and Mickey looked to be joined at the hip of the "Abester."

Mickey and friend

When I booked Joe Yule Jr. (Mickey Rooney), he had been married six times. After 1973, he tried it two more times for a grand total of eight. If you have interest in seeing whom and when, pull the Mick up on the Web and look up "Confessions of a Much Married Man." His first wife was a babe of World War II – Ava Gardner.

HENNY YOUNGMAN AND MORIE AMSTERDAM

In 1972 I booked two of the old time comedians in the same month, but two weeks apart. Henny Youngman came first and played a weekend of three shows, one on Friday and two performances on Saturday. The shows were not well attended, but I didn't lose any money.

"Henning – Stop!"

Two weeks later, Morrie Amsterdam took over for a weekend stint at Bridge VU. I was giving him a tour of the theater when he asked, "I understand my good friend Henning was here a few weeks ago. How did he do?" I answered, "I really was disappointed with the turn out." Morrie quickly turned to me with, "Let's go to your office and give my old friend a call."

It only took ten minutes to get the two of them on the telephone and the conversation went like this, "Henning, I'm standing in the lobby of Bridge VU Theater and it's still here, it's HUGE." I'm sure Henning was puzzled and must have asked, "What is huge, what are you talking about?" Morrie had a wide grin on his face as he laughed and almost giggled as he said, "The EGG – the huge EGG you laid in Indiana. It's still here in the lobby of this theater, but I'll get around it and try to save our reputations as BIG TIME comedians!"

They finished their conversation and I must say I really enjoyed how fast and sincere Morrie was in setting up his good friend Henny Youngman.

I arranged a golf game for Saturday at the Valparaiso Country Club with our in house pro, Guy Wellman Sr., and Morrie Amsterdam. They had a great game but for years my dad complained about the short little comedian who stiffed him out of $1.75 in golf bets.

TALL FISH STORY

This next story reminds me of an old saying (OK, I am repeating this story), that one of the great promoters of all times said at a trade show that was held at McCormick Place in Chicago back in the early sixties. Bill Veeck was the promoter. He was explaining the difference between advertisement and P.R. Advertisement costs too much money, while P.R. takes a lot of time and, once in a while, requires some luck. Another statement of Bill's that has stuck with me all of these years was, "A funny thing happens when you don't promote. NOTHING."

This will segue me into my Tall Fish Story. In 1969, I booked a weekend with the Harmonicat Rascals; their leader was a midget named Johnny Puleo who was well known by his costume. It was a cowboy outfit with chaps that were covered with curly lambskins.

The Harmonicat Rascals consisted of five people who were excellent on Harmonicas and they were very entertaining. Because they had added a lot of good clean humor to their performance, it was considered a "family show" and we always made money with the Harmonicat Rascals.

One night, during their weekend performance, a young 12-year-old fisherman caught a 28-pound Coho salmon off of the Kissing Bridge adjacent to Bridge UV Theatre.

J.R. Waters and 28-pound Coho

Once I saw this fish still flopping around, my promoting mind shifted into high gear as I thought of how I could turn this into some great P.R. gem. I had J.R. Waters, with fish in hand, go from stage right and hand this 28-pound monster (still flopping) to the great Johnny Peuleo. Immediately, and at the same time, I had our blond, good-looking photographer snap a picture of Johnny trying to hold this fish. The picture turned out great and I had it hand delivered to the Gary Post

Tribune office with the following information for Mr. Blaine Marz and the following column appeared the next day:

THE POST-TRIBUNE

ON the GO

WITH BLAINE MARZ

Extended periods of lousy, blah! weather can do strange things to people. A case in point is a picture delivered to my desk from BILL WELLMAN, the Valparaiso fun complex operator, along with the following note:

"I'm sure you will remember this great former Valparaiso University basketball player, Johnny Puleo. He is 6 ft. 7 inches tall so you can see that the fish he caught off our 'Kissing Bridge' (which leads to Wellman's Bridge-VU dinner-theater) must be a world record.

"We measured it twice and came up with 4 feet, 11 inches and weighing in at 92½ pounds. We weighed the fish on our meat scale and we are assured by the Salt Creek Coho Association that our scale is accurate to 1/16th of a pound. Would you check with your sports department and see if we could be considered for a world record?"

Sure, Bill, I'll check with 'em about the first of next April.

Now for the facts, still a little startling if you're familiar with Salt Creek, which the 'Kissing Bridge' spans and which is a long way from being a mighty, rushing stream, via a P.S. to the note:

"The kids in the neighborhood pulled out ten fish like the one in the picture from Salt Creek near the bridge. We even took this one out on the stage last night and showed it to 500 people. They could hardly believe it came out of that little creek, but it's true."

That's Johnny Puleo holding the fish in the picture for the edification of a Bridge-VU audience, all right. But he's 4 feet 6 inches tall and is an entertainer, the leader of the Harmonica Gang, formerly the Harmonica Rascals of movie fame, not a former Valpo U basketball star.

Puleo, whose show continues through Saturday night at Bridge-VU, has a reputation as one of the few remaining masters of the art of pantomime. If you don't believe that reputation is valid, take another look at the picture — and try to keep from smiling.

* ★ *

On Saturday night, after locking up the doors of Wellman's, I was headed to my station wagon when I noticed a convertible parked near the bowling alley entrance. I saw that the motor was running and the headlights were on, but the real thing that caught my attention was little Johnny's brown and white saddle shoes. His legs were crossed as he leaned on the open window talking to a very recognizable lady, Joyce Brownell (or in another life, Joyce Findling).

Although I didn't spend any time in conversation as I got into my car, I could not help thinking, "What an odd couple." Joyce was a very attractive young lady who looked thirty when she was sixteen. Her most famous stunt was when she appeared in the Corral in a very attractive fur coat with nothing on under the fur. The lack of television did not hurt entertainment in 1948!

The next day there were rumors around Bridge VU Theater that Johnny Peuleo had lost his diamond ring. When I heard this, I approached Johnny and said, "Johnny, I know Joyce very well and if you want me to get your ring back, I can." His answer was right to the point, "I think I enjoyed myself and I gave her the ring without pressure, so let her keep it." It took a very "big" man to come to that conclusion.

BLACK TIE WRESTLING

In 1971 I was willing to try almost anything to once again work the magic of good P.R. Thus came the idea of Black Tie Wrestling. The following article, written by Blaine Marz gave me the advertisement (free) that I needed to kick off the show.

I looked around for a ring announcer who looked great in a tux, had stage presence and could speak well through the microphone. It didn't take me long to convince my piano player, entertainer, star actor (from the Odd Couple) and chauffeur to take over as the #1 ring announcer for my first Black Tie Wrestling show.

Junior did an excellent job but when he announced the main event he was standing on the front of the stage directly in front of the ring, which was three feet higher than the stage. As he gave the final statistics he received a tap on his shoulder and he turned looking up at 395 pounds of Moose Cholak glaring down and screaming, "Don't you ever announce my name last. I'm always to be first, do you understand?" Junior didn't know exactly how or what to say, so he released the over-head microphone and immediately headed off the stage.

The first person he ran into was yours truly and he yelled, "Don't ever ask me to do anything like that again! You know those guys are really crazy!"

THE POST-TRIBUNE

ON the GO

WITH BLAINE MARZ

Bill Wellman may just have the answer to those who bemoan the passing of elegance from the American scene.

Black tie wrestling, no less!

This first on the local scene kind of entertainment (hmm . . .) will unfold (hmmm . . .) on Thursday, March 25, at Wellman's Bridge VU Dinner Theater on U.S. 30, Valparaiso.

I can see it now, Mom and Pop, or maybe Jack and his date Jill, sitting at the table with the romantic flickering candle and the gentle sound of glasses clinking all around. And perhaps a discreet burp or two from those who have dined too well while awaiting the opening of the gladiatorial proceedings.

And then a hush falls as 8:30 p.m. is at hand and Kenny Dillenger (meaner than John, even though the spelling is not the same) shuffles forward to do combat with Tom Lynch, who is none other than that nice Mr. Indiana, from South Bend.

And then follows Mad Niccoli Volkoff (it says right here on the program) vs. Prince Pullinn, a properly regal type.

And those two matches are only a delightful tuneup for the real taste of genteel elegance to come, the team match!

Featuring (are you ready for this?) Moose Cholak and Wilbur (Snorter) Snyder vs. the Fabulous Kangaroos.

Wellman

Inasmuch as this novel offering is in the Bridge VU Theater, and wrestling being what it is, perhaps the night could be billed "The Triumph of Good Over Evil." The playbill doesn't list the good guys or the bad guys but odds are Mr. Indiana will wear light trunks, symbolic of you-know-what, along with sweet Prince Pullinn. And mean looking guys like Moose and Wilbur (Wilbur is mean?) likely will be in the dark trunks.

Entrepreneur Wellman, a man of imagination as well as business acumen, said he decided to put on the wrestling show to see if women are interested in one of the oldest sports. He says there must be a women's lib angle, too, but isn't quite sure just where it lies. In any event advance reservations indicate Northwest Indiana's first black tie wrestling event is meeting with favorable public reception. Better hurry if you want to get in on this being entertained by mayhem—on an intimate, candlelit scale.

What's that you say? You don't have the right kind of elegant attire for this kind of elegant affair?

Fret not. We've persuaded Wellman to put the black ties on the "rasslers," thus black tie wrestling.

I wouldn't miss it for anything! Besides, the food is good at Wellman's.

I only had two nights of this type of entertainment and the value of the advertisement was hard to measure, but once again Bill Veeck would have been proud of my effort.

COUNTRY – WESTERN

I staged a country and western show, and had Ernest Tubb as my star, but I still needed a warm-up act besides the music. So where would I get a country comic on very short notice? Junior Waters was approached, and before he had a chance to think about it, I put a black Stetson on his head and handed him a big black guitar. I knew he couldn't play it, but it would help him look the part as he did his routine.

Ernest Tubb

On opening night, Mr. Tubb was standing alongside of me as Junior was doing his country comedy routine. Ernest asked me: "How long has he been doing country?" I looked at him and answered: "About ten minutes. This is a first, what do you think?" Mr. Tubb responded: "He should consider doing it full-time; there is a need for a black comedian in country. Can he play that guitar?" Naturally, I lied and said, "Oh, yes."

That was the first, but not the last time that Junior would doff the Stetson.

HONEST HAL

Over the years of booking everybody from J.R. Waters to Duke Ellington, I still dealt with one agent 90% of the time. He was Hal Munro. I gave him the nickname of "Honest Hal" early on in our relationship. He was vice president of Associated Booking Company in charge of the Chicago office.

The following article from the Chicago Tribune comparing Honest Hal to Woody Allen's comedy movie "Broadway Danny Rose" seems to be appropriate and explains what an agent's life is all about:

4 Section 2 Chicago Tribune, Sunday, February 12, 1984

Chicago's own Danny Rose stars on River Road

By Paul Galloway

HAL MUNRO is talking on the phone. "Don, a horn would screw up the whole act. Dennis, I don't come on strong very often. I'm not a power salesman like you. You know me. Self-effacing, modest. Good, honest, sincere Hal, but. . . ."

Munro has been interrupted. Reluctantly, he waits. After a few seconds he gets his chance to speak. "Don, you're jealous. You're jealous because I'm a young, up-and-coming agent, and you're afraid I'm going to ruin your career."

Munro is kidding. He looks over and smiles. He wants to make sure his visitor is getting the joke.

Hal Munro is not a young, up-and-coming agent. He has been in business here in Chicago for 35 years. His wavy hair is white, and as time has passed, his waistline and the lenses in his glasses have thickened.

But the years also have girded him with know-how. Hal Munro is savvy; he's experienced. He can smell a rotten deal, and he can spot a winner. He knows the score.

WE ALL HAVE a mental picture of agents, and, at least in some areas, Munro already has measured up. He has a great gift of gab. He is bombastic and overbearing. He plays the phone like a Stradivarius.

"Look, *Dennis*, book 'em. You'll thank me. They're not neurotic, there's nothing wrong with them. . . ."

Munro is forced to pause again. He is exasperated. This time *he* interrupts.

"*Dennis*. You know the name of the act; you've got material on them, okay? Goodbye, Don."

He hangs up, and the phone rings almost immediately. It's a client with problems. Munro listens, almost patiently.

He is a vice president of Associated Booking Corp., a national outfit with offices in

Tempo

Chicago's Danny Rose stars on River Road

Continued from first Tempo page

Chicago, New York, Beverly Hills, Dallas, Las Vegas and London; it handles big concert acts, mostly black performers such as B.B. King, Melba Moore, Phyllis Hyman, Anita Baker and Pieces of a Dream.

Munro is in charge of the Chicago office. In fact, he is the Chicago office, which is a one-man show these days.

The reason for being in Hal Munro's office, other than to kill a Thursday afternoon, is to seek the truth.

THERE IS a new Woody Allen movie out. It is a comedy entitled "Broadway Danny Rose," and in it Allen plays Danny Rose, a struggling theatrical agent with a heart of gold, who fights for the most motley collection of terrible acts in the history of show business.

He has a ventriloquist who stutters, a tap dancer with one leg, a xylophonist who is blind, an overweight crooner with a drinking problem.

The idea is to find out how close to reality the movie is and to learn something about an agent's life.

Agents, after all, are part of the culture and as old as history. When Adam and Eve were thrown out of the Garden of Eden, the world's first agent, whose name has been lost in the mists of time, was waiting with a book contract, an option for a made-for-TV movie and a guest shot on Donahue.

Munro, by the way, is still on the phone. "Well, if you want to quit, quit. I can live without your three nights a week commission. I'll call New York, but first tell me you want to go. It pays $1,000 a week. . . ."

It's odd, in a way, to hear all this show business talk, considering where we are. Not only is Munro not on Broadway or in Hollywood, he isn't even in Chicago.

ASSOCIATED MOVED from the Playboy Building eight years ago. It's now in Des Plaines, in an office building on River Road near the Kennedy Expressway, hardly the heart of our entertainment district. Also, River Road doesn't have much of a ring to it. *River Road Hal Munro?*

There is more. Except for a stack of Varietys and Billboard magazines, you wouldn't know what kind of business was conducted here.

In a loud, dramatic voice, Munro is urging his caller to buy an addition to his sound system. "It's a capital investment, and it's tax deductible. Do you have $100? I'll loan you $100. Go get the bleep-bleep thing. I'm lending you the money. I've never done this for anybody else. I hate all entertainers and all musicians!"

Once more, Munro smiles at his visitor. "I'll send you a check for $100. I want you to be happy. I need some decent talent for a change. All right? Goodbye."

At last, Munro turns off the phone and concentrates on an interview.

Right off the bat, we discover that the Woody Allen picture distorts things a bit. Danny Rose, for example, is never seen in his office, but in discussing what makes a good agent, Munro addresses the essential nature of the desk and telephone.

"AGENTS ARE born," he says with deep solemnity. "The intrinsic talent has to be within. I know I've tried to train five or six people. To no avail. There is a fantastic mortality rate in this business.

"Learning to be an agent is like learning to be a doctor. You've got to go to school, and your school is right in the office."

There are other, obvious differences. Danny Rose dresses with all the panache of a coat tree in a greasy spoon. Munro, on the other hand, is as dapper as a torts lawyer.

There are similarities. Danny and Hal began on the other side of the footlights. Rose was a failed Catskills comic, and Munro had a dance band that played the Midwest before and after World War II.

His real name is Harry Berkover, and he is the son of an orthodox rabbi who moved here when young Harry was 17. After leaving the University of Chicago after one year, he changed his named to Hal Munro (for band leader Hal Kemp and Monroe Street) and at 22 had his own band.

"I WAS WHAT you might call a semi-name. I knew I was never going to be a big star," he says. "I was always booking my own band, and it dawns on me, what do I need an agent for? I could be one myself."

Among the criteria we have for agents are:

1. He must smoke a cigar.
2. He must reminisce about when times were tough and, at one point, say with a sigh, "You can't believe

Woody Allen as Danny Rose; and Hal Munro: Taking care of business

how the business has changed."

3. He must philosophize and offer sage advice.

4. He must have a story about an unknown who made it big.

Close your eyes when Munro talks, and you'd swear he has a cigar in his mouth. He sounds that way for a reason. For all but the last 10 years he chewed enough panatellas to fill the Rosemont Horizon.

He also passes the test for point No. 2.

"The first check I got was for $1.25," he says. "I put a piano player, a guy named Jimmy Bowman, in a lounge on a Monday night for $25; $2.50 was the commission, of which my half was $1.25."

And: "The agency business has changed. We used to have 10 people in our Chicago office; that's when we had Louis Armstrong and Brubeck. . . ."

FOR A LONG TIME he booked hundreds of lounges; now he does a lot of everything.

"I book at the Palmer House, the Ritz-Carlton, the O'Hare Hilton, Rick's Cafe Americain. I'm the concert booker, the one-night booker, the packager, the guy who books off-night piano players, private parties, you name it."

He has a philosophy.

"I have my version of the Miranda rule—you know, the rights the cops read to a criminal. When a guy who wants to promote a concert comes to see me, I give him my Munro Doctrine. I tell him, 'I myself wouldn't promote a concert for a million bucks. Now, you want to promote? God bless you.'

"That absolves me from all guilt. People think it's easy money and all they have to do is count seats in a hall and multiply by $10 and they have what they're going to take in. Wrong. You've got to have the right act, the right time, the right town, you have to sell the tickets. There are a million things you have to know."

He offers some wisdom about honesty and the perfidy of performers.

"Agents have a two-fold function. You've got to take care of your acts, and you've got to take care of your promoters or you're not going to stay in business. And you must be honest. My reputation in the trade is that I'm a son of a bitch to deal with, but I'm honest.

"You have to be rough, or these kids will step all over you. Musicians and entertainers have no conscience. You can beat your brains out and get 'em to a certain place in the business, and they'll leave you."

And, finally, some show biz stories. He gave Ann-Margret her first job as a singer with his band. He booked Barry Manilow for $150 a week as a nonsinging piano act in a Merchandise Mart restaurant and then put him and a young female singer into Mister Kelly's nightclub as an intermission act for $275 a week. The singer's name was Bette Midler.

"I TELL A CLASSIC Streisand story," Munro says, "and I'm sorry every time I think about it. How did I know she was going to be a big star?

"I was booking a room up in Canada called the Town and Country Restaurant. It paid a fast $300 a week if the owner didn't know the act and $350 if they'd played there before and done wonderfully well.

"We had a man in our New York office who had a great knack for sensing talent, and he says, 'There's a girl in Brooklyn by the name of Barbra Streisand. I want you to put her in that room in Canada you're booking.'

"She pays her own way from Brooklyn to Winnipeg and pays her own room and board, and the owner calls me and says, 'That chick you got here, she's crazy, she bombed bad, but she's going to be great. She's different.' She bombs, and the guy still knows she's great.

"She forgets to pay my commission and so I write her a letter, a nice, polite little note: 'You still haven't paid me the $60.' The joint paid $300, and it must have cost her $400 to $450 to play the damn thing. She writes me back, one paragraph—I wish I'd saved it, it'd be worth a fortune today: 'I'm sorry, Mr. Munro, I forgot to pay you. Here's my check for $60. Thank you very much. Barbra.' "

The phone is ringing. Hal Munro goes back to work.

Hal called me and we made arrangements to take his old Mercedes and drive to Grand Rapids, Michigan to see a group of entertainers doing "Jesus Christ Superstar" in a large banquet hall in the Mr. President Motor Inn.

Mr. Munro knew I would fall in love with this group and the show. He was right on both counts so I signed an open-end contract. This meant I could keep them as long as I wanted but I needed to give them a week's notice when I was ready to cancel.

When I first heard the word super star, the name seemed to rub me the wrong way. I think it was the connection of Jesus Christ with superstar that did the job. I requested my good Lutheran mother to see the show, but her immediate answer was "No!" The next logical question was "Why?" Her answer was to the point and I almost agreed with her – "Superstar doesn't belong with Jesus Christ." I knew I had a hard sell on my hands after my discussion with my mother so I decided to do something different. Opening night I had 68 customers. The second night it jumped to 172 because I had invited 70 ministers but only 29 accepted the invitation. The first weekend it jumped to 350 on Friday and 450 on Saturday. Word of mouth took it from 69 to 450 where it consistently stayed for nine weeks.

The show was the talk of the area and I started to feel like I was getting good in the entertainment business. This was a BIG mistake and it almost "did-in" my show business career.

TODAY IS A GOOD DAY TO DIE...

After seeing the success of *Jesus Christ Super Star,* I was convinced that I should take a chance with the same musical group, led by Kenny Gordon. The new rock musical, "Today Is a Good Day to Die", was written about the American Indian and his fight to survive in America.

This musical was so new; Bridge Vu Theater was to be the world premier. I was going on my gut feeling that this was a great year for Indians -- how could I miss after twelve weeks of a full house with *Jesus Christ Super Star*.

Kenny
Gordon
and the
Sound
Gathering
"Today Is A Good Day To Die"
An Original Rock Opera

It didn't take me long to come up with a PR plan (not quite a gem, but a plan). My idea was to employ a true American Indian to stay at our Holiday Inn for a week while I used him, dressed in full battle garb. I called my agent "Honest Hal Monroe" with my unusual request; (1) one true American Indian with authentic costumes and, (2) one very large teepee.

Hal didn't seem to be shocked at my request. In twenty-four hours I was shaking hands with Frank Fast Wolf, a full-blooded Cherokee, out of Chicago, complete with a huge 22-foot white teepee. I asked Frank to set up the teepee on the theater patio next to the main entrance. It looked great as both local newspapers snapped pictures of Frank standing near the opening of the teepee.

I had always heard the tale about Indians not being able to handle firewater (liquor). I wish Frank could have met my Dad early on in his life so maybe his theory "It's made to sell, not to drink" might have helped him. I picked Frank up at

10:00 am at the Holiday Inn on Monday morning to start my PR plan. I was reminded of the old wives tale, "Indians and liquor don't mix" because, you guessed it, Frank was as drunk as you could ever imagine.

I finally got Frank, dressed in full Indian battle garb, into the front seat of my station wagon. Our first appointment was Lori Woycik's special education class at North View Elementary School. I decided to call Lori and give her a heads up on Frank Fast Wolf's condition. As we discussed the problem of how to handle a drunken Indian, Lori informed me, "The kids have been looking forward to seeing a real Indian and I know how disappointed they will be if he doesn't show up."

I felt it was time to make an executive decision. "Lori, in order to avoid disappointing your class, I will pull my wagon into the parking lot in front of the school. You have the kids walk around the car checking out Frank through the windows. It will be just like the Indians attacking the wagons of the cowboys, only in reverse."

The excitement of Lori's special education kids made my decision worthwhile. They moved around the car peering through all of the windows, as Frank Fast Wolf looked straight ahead, looking like a hood ornament on a 1969 Pontiac. Lori had one young boy by the hand as I approached her to see how long she wanted me to keep the chief on display. The young boy looked at me and said "F_ _ K YOU." Lori quickly put her hand over his mouth and apologized by saying, "He gets a little too excited and cuts loose with a few naughty words." It didn't bother me and I was sure Frank didn't hear a thing. He was still looking straight ahead.

The first appearance of Frank Fast Wolf ended on a high note. We didn't disappoint the special education class, and Lori said the kids told everyone they talked to about their meeting with a real live Indian.

It became obvious to me that using Frank to help me promote the upcoming World Premier of the musical, "Today Is a Good Day to Die" was going to be short-lived. Our next appointment was supposed to be the Valparaiso Rotary luncheon, and I had a problem seeing those Rotarians walking around my station wagon peering through my windows.

Saturday afternoon a strong windstorm hit Valparaiso. I was walking across the theater parking lot when I saw the large white teepee rise up and down several times. I looked into the opening and saw Frank wrapped around the main pole riding it like a bucking bronco. Once again, he was overwhelmed with liquor. This turned out to be Frank Fast Wolf's last day. I never said that all of my P.R. ideas were winners!

The World Premier was a great night, but the musical, "Today Is a Good Day to Die" did just that, it DIED!

One month after Superstar closed at Bridge Vu, I booked the show for twelve weeks as a traveling unit. What a mistake! I used a friendship with another agent to book theaters and nightclubs throughout the Midwest in cities like Columbus, St. Louis, Indianapolis, Pittsburg, Louisville and Cincinnati. By the way, the nickname of this agent was "Crazy Charlie." My ego got the better of my logic and at the same time I was promoting Superstar I was in a partnership with a nightclub (the Rat Fink) owner from Indianapolis named George Salieba. We had booked six weeks with a risqué comedian, Rusty Warren.

We advertised the show, as the wildest MAD-MOD show ever conceived. A swinging evening with Rusty Warren, the sensational singer of sinful ballads. Rusty had sold over 5 ½ million LP's over a ten-year period. How come? The titles of some of Rusty's big selling albums provide a pretty good clue: "Knockers Up," "Rusty Rides Again," "Banned in Boston," "Songs for Sinners," and "Sex-X-Ponent."

For some good clean, dirty fun, come see Rusty Warren!

Rusty called me several weeks before our road trip was to start to insist she needed a certain back up trio out of Canada to really make her show. I didn't fight with her over this request. I was to find out later that two of the three from the trio were Indiana boys. They were from Munster and their father was the famous "wire-bender" dentist, Dr. Tilka. His one son, Patrick, will be mentioned in later chapters of my life.

RUSTY RIDES AGAIN

RUSTY WARREN

I'm starting to feel the financial squeeze with two shows on the road at one time and both were not doing well. My partner is very gay and we are promoting a lesbian comedian. If my mother knew her Lutheran son was involved in this type of show business she might have had a heart attack. That is the main reason I didn't tell her about all of my promotions! I also didn't explain to my wife, Liz, about these two shows.

When the Rusty Warren show started to lose money I left Superstar in St. Louis and drove to Columbus, Ohio to see what I could do to brace up the advertisement and promotion for the Rusty Warren show. It was too late, but I needed to know what mistakes we had made so it wouldn't happen again. I arrived in Columbus early in the morning and I went straight to the old hotel where the two shows were booked in a very old banquet hall.

My first meeting was with my partner, George Salieba. He really didn't have a clue why we weren't making the money we had forecasted so I suggested we start with the room we were booked in. My first thought was to see how many people we could seat in our "show room." The conclusion was if we sold every seat for both shows, we would lose $1250 in one night. I had trusted the agent from Indianapolis with his "booking ability." I should have known anyone with the nickname of "Crazy Charlie" couldn't be trusted!

I also received a long distance call from a New York attorney who informed me I was doing something completely illegal by taking Jesus Christ Superstar on the road and I should "cease and desist" immediately or I would be sued. My answer was, "Damnit, I wish you had called me six weeks ago." He answered with, "You mean you are not making any money?" "No," I said, "I'm losing on every show." That was the last time I heard from anyone from New York.

When the tour on both shows was completed, I was financially bankrupt so I had to negotiate a sale of my holdings in Wellman's and Bridge VU to pay off my debts. I tried to look for financial help from Dr. O'Neill, but since he was such a good businessman he could smell an opportunity to take over the entire operation and give his son the chance to run the show.

Dr. O'Neill soon realized that the new management needed to have some reinforcement so he partnered with Jerry Kauffman, operator of Mill Run Theater in the Round, located in Niles, Illinois.

It looked like my days in show business were coming to an end. I paid all of my debts and I obtained the money for my parents' part of Wellman's, but I was looking for a new challenge and a job.

Chapter Eight

THE COURT

My new challenge was, I was fifty years old, financially very close to being broke, but I still had the responsibility to pay for educating our two daughters.

Dawn was finishing law school at Valparaiso University and Kim was just handed her high school diploma from the president of the Valparaiso School Board (1973). He was better known as Kim's father! Kim had the desire to enroll in Purdue's Veterinarian School and my son Scott was working on construction, but was very heavy into the "party mode." The only positive things I really had left was my reputation as a restaurant operator, a maverick show business entrepreneur attitude and the fact I was a workaholic looking for a challenge.

I ended up with two and one half choices – (1) Pete's Offer and (2) Gene Hicks Restaurant – the ½ offer came from Dean White, but I turned it down.

PETES OFFER

I received a telephone call from Judge Frank Stodola asking me to have lunch with him at the famous, internationally known restaurant, Phil Smidt's, located in the Northern tip of Hammond, Indiana. I accepted, but I didn't have a clue why I received the invitation because I really didn't know the Judge very well.

The two of us met and as we were just finishing lunch the owner, Pete Smidt, joined the table. I had met Pete a

Phil Smidt's Restaruant - 1950

couple of times through the major league bowling league held in the 12/20 Bowling Lanes in Gary, Indiana. Other than those two casual meetings I knew very little about him.

The story was Pete Smidt's wife really ran the restaurant while he was on safaris in Africa or fishing in South America. Mrs. Smidt was well known for being the hostess, greeting almost every customer entering Smidt's. She was also known for the bright, round circles of red rouge on each cheek.

When Mrs. Smidt passed away, Pete was thrown into the breach of actually having to run the restaurant on his own. After we finished our lunch, I started to catch on to why Judge Stodola had asked me to lunch and why Pete had joined our table. The Judge was acting as a "restaurant cupid." In other words, he knew that his very good friend, Pete Smidt, really didn't want the responsibility of running a very busy restaurant and he was trying to put the two of us together in some type of partnership.

Pete talked about the building and the history of the restaurant and why it was located in its present location. It seems his folks got off the train in Roby, Indiana thinking they were in Chicago and didn't have enough money to take the next train back to Chicago, so they settled in Roby (later named Hammond) and started their restaurant business.

During a lull in Pete's conversation he looked me in the eyes and said, "Bill, would you like to take a tour of the building?" I always enjoyed looking at other restaurant owners' kitchens and hearing their comments about their problems, so I accepted his invitation. The tour lasted about thirty minutes, then we returned to the Judge and more conversation.

Pete finally put his cards on the table and came out with the full reason the Judge was playing "restaurant cupid." "Bill, I love the restaurant business and I really enjoy the people but I don't want to know when the sewer backs up." This last statement told me exactly how Mr. Pete Smidt felt about running a restaurant. His next statement really threw me a curve. "Bill, I will give you fifty percent of my restaurant if you will take over the responsibility of operating it. I will not ask you to put any money into the business I just want someone to give the restaurant some "tender loving care" as my wife did."

I came up with some small talk but my mind was mulling over the pluses and minuses as I thanked Mr. Smidt and Judge Stodola for the offer. I then told them I needed to have a conversation with my partner (Liz) and I would let both of them know in three days.

The trip back to Valparaiso took close to 45 minutes since I-65 was still on the drawing boards of INDOT. Liz and I stayed up past midnight marking down the pros and cons. Our three kids were really entrenched in Valparaiso and we didn't want to move to Hammond, but the main point that convinced me to turn down this offer was the distance I had to drive home after closing up a bar and restaurant six nights a week. The fact that in 1973 I was still drinking (not alot) and the drive home was literally a "killer," was the top reason for turning down a great opportunity.

Three days later I stopped into Phil Smidt's and informed Pete, "I really appreciate the very generous offer and I may have just made the biggest mistake of my business career, but my wife and I have decided to turn down your offer." He seemed genuinely surprised with my decision and I think he was disappointed.

I followed up with a call to Judge Stodola who also was disappointed and really couldn't understand my logic but accepted my decision.

It wasn't long after our meeting when Pete Smidt decided to give the restaurant to Calumet College as a gift. The quality of the restaurant seemed to start a downward slide after the Smidt family gave up their ownership and that slide has continued to the present time.

It has gone through my mind many times, trying to figure out where I would have ended up if I would have accepted that offer in 1973. Of course, I would have missed all of the fun at the Holiday Star Theater and working for Dean White for thirty years - decisions, decisions!

GENE HICKS RESTARUANT

In 1974, I was approached by Gene Hicks of Ogden Dunes to help him put together a restaurant in downtown Valparaiso.

I discovered a bar for sale called The Club Royalee. It was nothing fancy, but the owner had a three-way liquor license legal for two buildings located on the square in the downtown.

The original name was the Seafood Restaurant, owned by the Pappas family. One member of this family was a well-known wrestler and this was before wrestling became a national joke and a sideshow.

The business was for sale because the present owner was an undertaker from East Chicago who had purchased the bar for his girl friend. Their romance ran into hard times following a fight in his car in which he pushed her out of the front seat while the car was still moving. She ended up in the hospital and of course, the local newspaper gave the story front-page treatment.

I'm sure the newspaper story was hard to explain back home to the undertaker's wife. So the timing of buying the Club Royalee was ideal.

The day I approached the undertaker about looking over the building for a possible purchase turned into an unusual day.

I was standing on a tall ladder with my head poked through an opening in the false ceiling on the second floor checking out the rafters. I spotted a box neatly tied with string about six feet away from my roost.

My curiosity got the best of me as I moved the ladder within range of the large suit-size box covered with dust. As I untied the big box and lifted the lid off, I saw sixteen small paper bags neatly placed in rows of four.

I was just ready to open one bag when a voice below said, "Are you finding everything you are looking for?" It was the undertaker and I'm sure he had no idea that he had just scared the hell out of me. I said, "Yes," as I put the lid back on the mystery box.

The next two days my imagination took me in many directions. I could picture hidden money, old documents, or maybe photographs of the original opening of the Seafood Restaurant.

It took several visits to the funeral home in East Chicago before I struck a deal to buy the restaurant, but during one of our negotiating meetings, I heard an employee talking to a prospective customer about the package deal that the funeral home was promoting to customers. If you made a contract to bury a loved one, they would invite all the family members back to the funeral home for a hot lunch served by the undertaker's wife.

It seemed odd to display the body in one corner of the large room during the service and then 45 minutes after the casket was lowered into the ground, bring people back to the same room for a big meal.

The day all parties signed the agreement to allow Mr. Hicks to purchase the building I broke all speed records to get back to where my mystery box was waiting.

I pulled out one of the neatly wrapped and tied paper bags. The excitement reached a pitch as I cut the string with my knife. The light was very dim but my eyes caught the many bright colors as I looked at 16 bags of confetti saved from some ancient New Year's Eve party. What a letdown!

Planning a restaurant can be much more fun than operating one. Our choice was Design Organization with Chuck Bone and Doug Pierce to work our way through the plans, along with my wife Liz. Choosing the name "The Court" was easy because of the location, across the street from the Porter County Courthouse.

Harry Brown of Merrillville supplied the old stained glass windows, but the real treasure was a portable double jail cell that he discovered on a scrap pile in Illinois. It was made of strap iron and still had the metal bunks that folded up to the sides. So we made "The Jail" into a unique table for six. It turned out to be the most popular requested location in the restaurant.

It was during this time Liz and I attended several interesting auctions. The first at the South Shore Country Club where we purchased so much equipment it was necessary to hire Landgrebe Trucking to carry everything back to The Court in a huge semi truck.

There were 356 stuffed velvet dining room chairs in lots of eight. I won the bidding at $5 per chair on the first offer when the auctioneer said, "How many lots do you want?" It set him back when I said, "I want all of them." This started a ruckus because a lot of ladies wanted to buy four to six of these antiques and have them repaired just to say to their friends, "These chairs are from the South Shore Country Club."

We also bought dishes and silverware; in fact, some of the dishes were brand new still in their packing cases.

The auction lasted two days and the crowd was really not paying much attention when we entered a lower level of the building. The first item was an upright piano on a cart. The auctioneer asked me quietly, "Are you interested in the piano?" I said, "yes," and the next thing he did was really unusual. He said, "Sold for $25. Folks, you have to stick with me and pay attention. This man just bought a piano and cart for $25." It got their attention and I made a great buy.

Before we started to tear off the décor of The Club Royallee and start the remodeling process, I decided to have a "Demolition Ball." Our guest list received the invitation to the right:

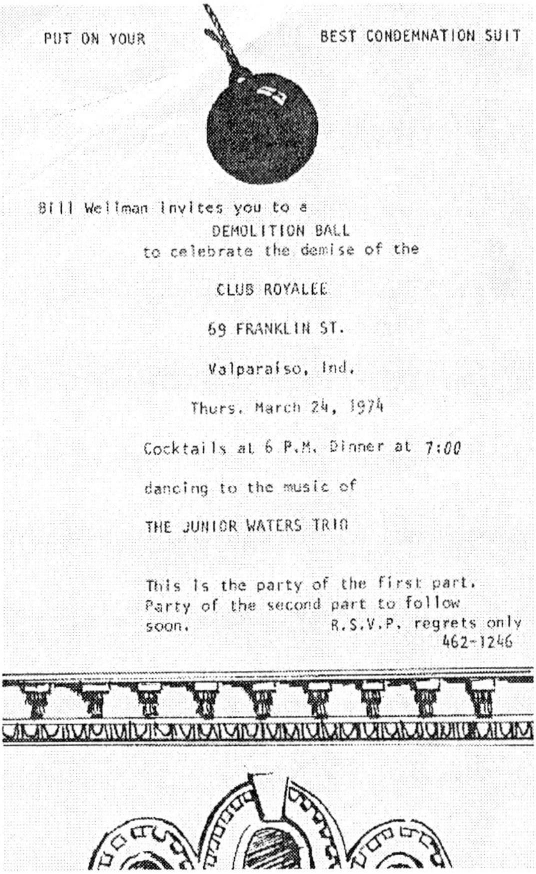

PUT ON YOUR BEST CONDEMNATION SUIT

Bill Wellman invites you to a
DEMOLITION BALL
to celebrate the demise of the
CLUB ROYALEE
69 FRANKLIN ST.
Valparaiso, Ind.
Thurs. March 24, 1974
Cocktails at 6 P.M. Dinner at 7:00
dancing to the music of
THE JUNIOR WATERS TRIO

This is the party of the first part.
Party of the second part to follow soon.
R.S.V.P. regrets only
462-1246

The ball was a great success and the remodeling began. Mr. Hicks was educated as an engineer so the remodeling process took on major structural changes. The upstairs banquet rooms could hold the weight of 5000 people (200 at a time), however, the cost of remodeling also got heavy, but we finally opened the doors.

Len Dryfus put together a beautiful brochure by using the sketches of Dale Fleming.

"Len, did I ever pay for this job?"

The JUDGE'S CHAMBERS

Authentic materials and artifacts recreate the mood of a turn of the century court.

All woods are really wood, copper is copper. Even the plants, which have been pinched time and time again on suspicion of being impostors, are real and are serving for life. The bricks, though renewed by sandblasting to expose their rich color, have served the building throughout previous aliases as a livery stable, a funeral home, the old Tivoli Theatre, a barber shop, and several taverns.

Some day, when the service is particularly slow (rarely, rarely) and you feel you've been waiting a long time, just remember the building has waited over 100 years for good food.

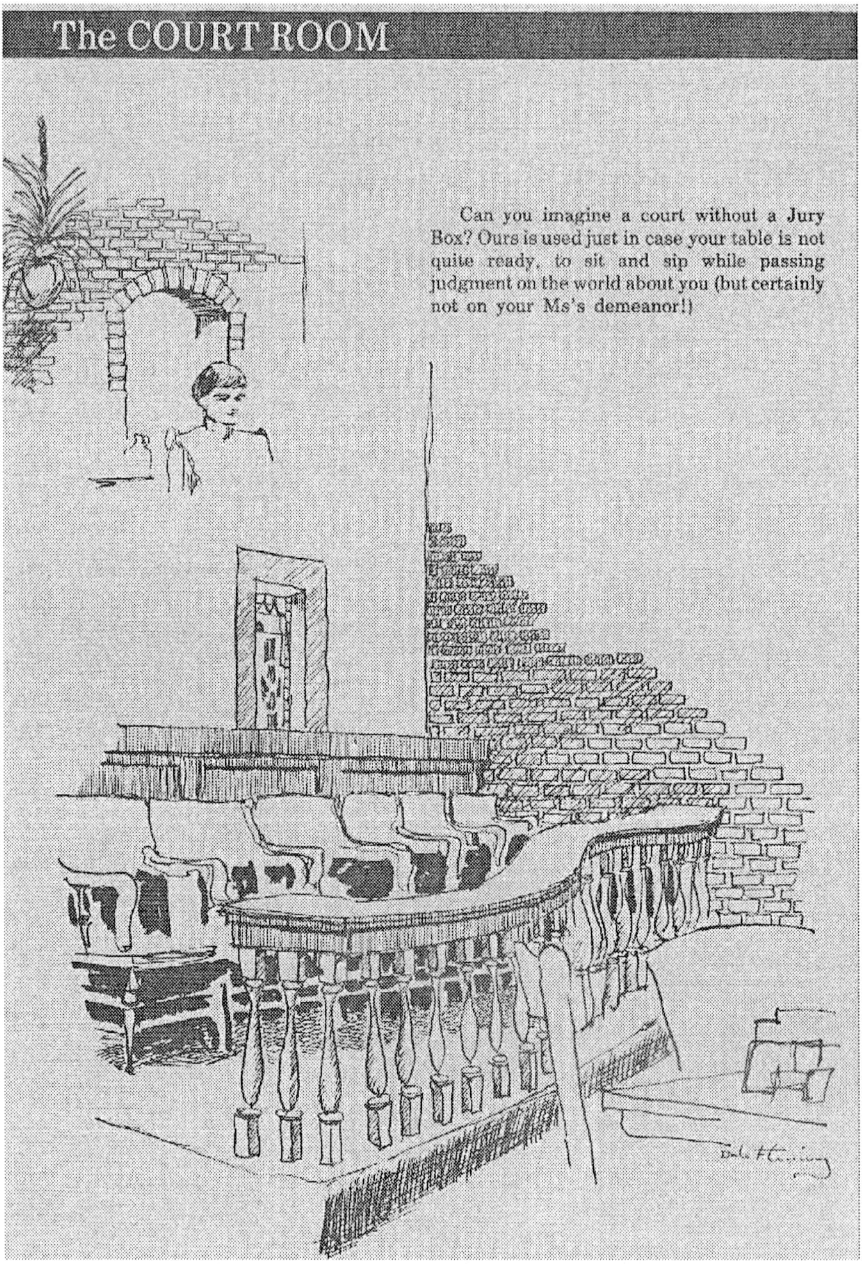

The COURT ROOM
Can you imagine a court without a Jury Box? Ours is used just in case your table is not quite ready, to sit and sip while passing judgment on the world about you (but certainly not on your Ms's demeanor!)

The Jury Booth was used as a neat place to have a drink and wait for a table!

The Court was a beautiful restaurant full of antiques that seemed to fit the theme. It's first year we won national menu honors in the National Restaurant Association's annual show held at the McCormick Place in Chicago. The menu and holder were unique. It was patterned after the manner in which court records were maintained in the 1800's.

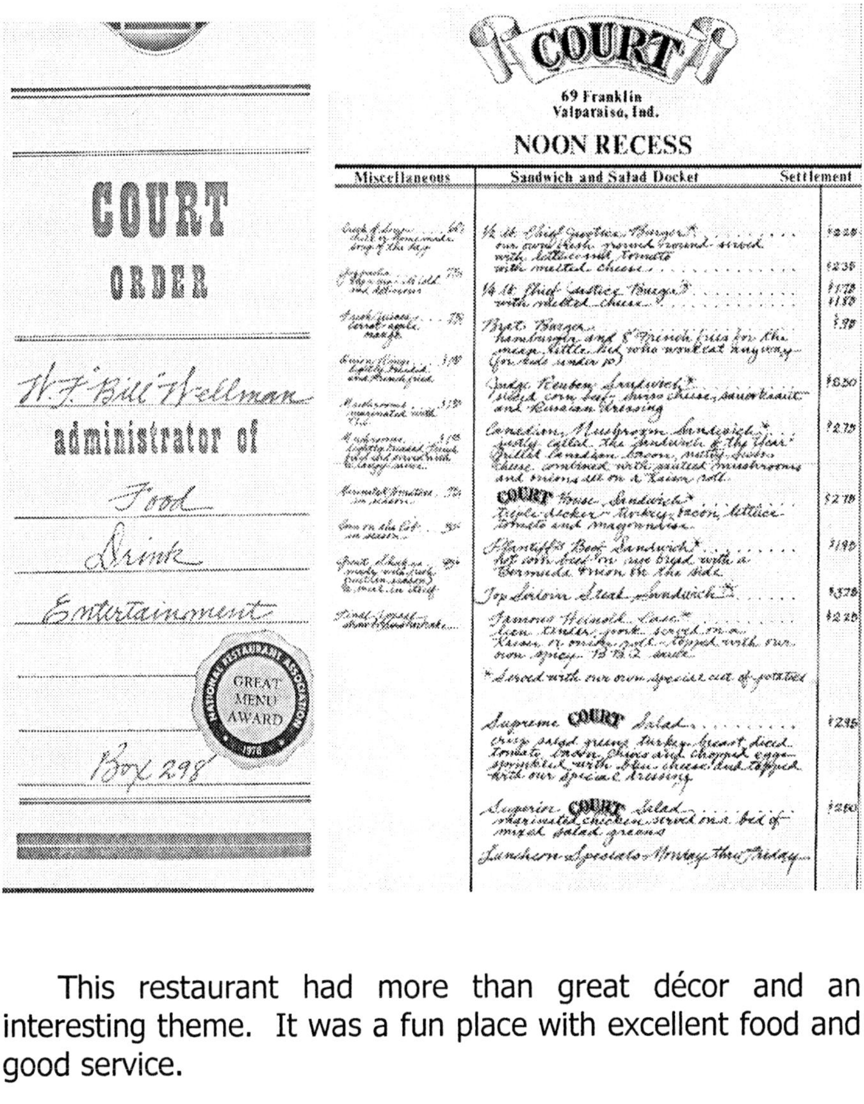

This restaurant had more than great décor and an interesting theme. It was a fun place with excellent food and good service.

From brick to brick . . . that is where the **Court** started and that is where it has returned. It seems fairly certain that the many masons whose work went into the two buildings that now house this distinctive restaurant never expected their work to be the center of attention. Nor would they have appreciated the warmth and beauty of the brick as we do in today's world of plastic imitations. The buildings are now nearly 100 years old and have served many functions over the years including a livery stable, a funeral home, the old Tivoli Theater, a barber shop and several taverns.

Court owes its namesake to a buffet located on the West side of the Court House in 1894 called Court Buffet and was suggested by the architects as they sifted through old photographs of that era.

The restaurant's decor depends on realism rather than imitation. W. F. "Bill" Wellman, his wife Liz, and the staff of Design Organization (Douglas J. Pierce and Charles H. Bone), Architects, used authentic materials and artifacts to recreate the mood of a turn of the century court. All woods are really wood, copper is copper, plants are real and so on down the line.

We will try to list some of the more interesting features for your enjoyment and so that you may know something of the planning process. Starting with the two aforementioned buildings, everything was stripped to the wooden frame members and brick walls. All structural members were analyzed and strengthened or replaced when necessary. All floors were resurfaced as was the roof. With that, all surfaces were sandblasted to expose the rich color of the native brick. That was followed by new plumbing, electrical, heating and air conditioning. The front of the building was then closed by a brick entrance facade made of nine arches, constructed by mason contractor, Joe Clifford and is certainly among the best works in any era of Valparaiso's building history.

Much of the more conspicuous trim and accents are the choice of Liz Wellman, working with Harry Brown of the Carriage House in Merrillville. The huge walnut entrance doors once graced a Springfield home not far from the Lincoln residence. Harry's many cut glass windows are either refurbished originals or new construction from old glass. Liz and Peg Fuller of Tulip Antiques in LaPorte came through with much of the antique furniture including the hutch in the south dining room.

Other items to notice include the **Court** logo used on all the paper products. The design of the logo and the design of the paper products, including menu, napkin rings, cocktail napkins, etc., are the work of Christine Probasco of Design Organization. The menus and envelopes are fashioned after court documents of the time and are stored in the document holder mounted over the salad bar which came from an old Indiana court house.

The plants, silver, and china all bring back the feeling of the era, but perhaps not as well as a meal served in the old jail cell, circa 1809. The wood blade fans are authentic and the dumbwaiter is from the Red Star Inn, Chicago. A look into the "Gentlemen's" facilities reveals a great free-standing lavatory sink with brass fittings and an ornate Greek column for support, courtesy the old Gary Hotel. Long time Valparaiso residents will remember the white rest room tile and hand painted trim as once adorning Allen's Bakery, formally the "Farmer's" Restaurant. And if you had ever been inside the South Shore Country Club of Chicago in its glory, you are sure to see something familiar . . . . Bill bought a truck load at the auction.

That is not all, as you can plainly see, but it is a start and you may discover more on your own. Our objective is to capture a time gone by without being garish. We will be continually adding and subtracting things and so our advice to you is to come often and maybe . . . "take a friend to Court!"

W. F. WELLMAN – PRESIDING

COURT

69 Franklin Street
Valparaiso, Indiana
462-2141

THE
DESIGN
JURY

COURT

69 Franklin Street
VALPARAISO, INDIANA

The restaurant was coming together and we were within a few days of actually opening our doors, but I had given clear instructions to my still "number one chef", Karl West, "Karl, the vent system to your stove in the basement is not hooked up yet, so don't use it." I either wasn't heard or not too clear.

It was the day before we opened our doors when I received a call from the fire department at 6:00am telling me we had a problem at The Court.

Karl had started his famous stockpot to obtain a good supply of stock for the opening, but he didn't heed my warning and set off the sprinkler system, soaking him from his chef cap down to his shoes! He then ran out of the kitchen door to the fire station, a half a block away to get help. In doing so, he locked himself out of the building.

When I arrived to open the door I spotted Karl, his eyes like silver dollars and soaking wet! The sprinkler system had automatically shut off, so there was no real damage, but I immediately had Homer Burrus finish the final work on the vent system for the stove.

It was during the early days of The Court's existence, a young man was learning some practical cooking skills under Karl West's wing. It was a very young Russ Adams, who is now the proud owner and operator of Strongbow's Restaurant, one of the best in Indiana!

If you asked Russ what was the main experience he remembers from his days of instruction under Karl's teachings, it would be, "Karl, can I buy you a bottle of Schlitz Beer?" Karl's answer was always short and to the point, "Schlitz is pee pee, Beck's is good German beer!"

The Judge's Chambers
The Court Room showing the jail
Cozy - a perfect spot for Courtship
Entrance to the Higher Court
W. F. "Bill" Wellman, Presiding
69 Franklin
Valparaiso, Indiana 46383
Telephone 219 - 462-2141

ELEPHANT STORY

It was during my days at "The Court" that some one talked me into becoming a fundraiser and financial advisor for Valparaiso Chief of Police, Kelly Gott, in his campaign to run for the Republican candidate for Sheriff of Porter County.

I remember getting a call from Mr. Horn from Kouts. Mr. Horn ran a chocolate candy operation packaging candy for fundraisers. He called me and asked: "Bill, have you heard Casbon's Electric commercial on FM 101 out of Chicago?" I had not, so I asked what was this about? His voice was really excited as he said, "You will really enjoy it when you hear it?"

I was on my way to pick up some fresh fish at Ludwicks in Michigan City when I turned my radio on to FM 101 when I heard the commercial. It sounded like a circus barker talking very fast and loud as he said, "That's right folks, bring your Pachyderm to our store before 10 a.m. next Saturday and you will win a Pioneer stereo absolutely FREE. That's right...just bring your elephant to our store before l0 a.m. next Saturday and you will win a free Pioneer stereo."

I must say Mr. Horn was right when he said I would enjoy hearing Casbon's commercial. Casbon's Electric was being run by Dave Casbon and his partner, Charlie Poloreck. They specialized in televisions and stereos.

Upon returning to Valparaiso, I called Casbon's and Charlie answered the phone: "Casbon's Electric, Charlie speaking." His voice was full of excitement after I told him about hearing the commercial on FM 101. "I don't know if it will help our sales, but Tom Allison and Dave put it together and we are having a lot of fun with it." I then said, "Charlie, that's the reason I'm calling to give you a leg up on getting the media to cover this event because I will be there at 9 a.m. with my elephant next Saturday."

There was dead silence on the other end of the line, until Charlie said with a very different tone in his voice, "You're not kidding, are you?" Of course, I responded: "No, I'm not kidding, but I wanted to give you plenty of time to get some real great press out of this. We will be in front of your store about 9:00 a.m. Saturday."

There seemed to be a lot of sadness in his voice as he said, "Well, Dave wrote the damn thing so I suppose we will have to follow through." I tried to convince Charlie this was a great public relations opportunity and while it may not be as good as Bill Veck's midget pinch hit, but it was close.

The reason Mr. Horn called was to tip me off about the commercial. He was a Republican from Kouts and he knew I was helping Kelly run for Sheriff on the Republican ticket. But he also knew I had made arrangements to rent an elephant for the Valparaiso Homecoming Parade on Saturday. The commercial, the elephant, and the parade all melded into a great public relations opportunity.

That Saturday morning just before 9 a.m., Paul Lewis from Peru, IN pulled up to the south side of the "Almost" famous restaurant – The Court – with his trailer holding the elephant called Linda.

After Mr. Lewis backed Linda out of her trailer, he said, "Pee Linda, pee." Linda let go of a stream that would have made Paul Bunyan smile. I was happy Linda was not on the grass, but in the street.

Linda, Mr. Lewis and Bill Wellman taking a walk

I explained my situation to Mr. Lewis about the "free stereo" and that we needed to walk over to Casbon's Electric with Linda to pick up our prize. As we approached Casbon's, I estimated there were several hundred people waiting to see Linda. The story flew around Valparaiso that an elephant was going to show up in front of the store on Saturday morning. Of course, I helped move the story around as much as possible.

It turned out even better than I had hoped. Dave and Chuck followed through by having the stereo boxes piled high on the sidewalk. We arrived on time to the applause and laughter of the crowd. The media turned out to record this historic moment.

"Did you think I wouldn't have my elephant on Saturday morning?"

Associated Press picked up the story and sent it across the country with this headline: "Just Put it in the Trunk." It made the papers all across the country. Pioneer loved the story. In fact, the company reimbursed Dave and Chuck with a stereo to replace the one they gave to Kelly Gott for the sheriff's campaign. All in all, it was a win-win situation.

After leaving Casbon's we lined up for the Homecoming Parade for the "real" reason Linda was in town. I had convinced my son Scott that I really needed some extra special help for the parade. I asked him to wear a tuxedo with tails, a top hat, a white face, a red bulb nose, and red clown shoes. He was ready and he did a great job of following Linda with a wheelbarrow, a push broom and a shovel. The streets of Valparaiso never

Scott at his best!

looked better and the health department really appreciated our thoughtfulness.

If you have never ridden an elephant, you know they are not an easy ride. My old friend J.R. Waters and I carried a 12-foot ladder. We used it to get Kelly on and off Linda. The plan was that he was to get on at the old post office and after he passed the reviewing stand, J.R. and I would follow with the ladder and get him down near Sievers Drug Store.

Gott for Sheriff!

Kelly Gott was a little over 6 feet tall and weighed about 210 pounds. For a man with one eye, he was a very good athlete. He was a former Golden Gloves Champion and a punter on the undefeated football team at Valparaiso High School in 1939. So riding an elephant was a piece of cake for Kelly. In fact, he was enjoying the ride on Linda so much that he rode the entire route of the parade. The change in plans made some extra work for Scott, J.R. Waters and me.

The next day's newspapers devoted great stories about "Just Put It In the Trunk." One paper also stated there was no truth to the rumor that J.R. Waters and Bill Wellman won first prize with their "Ladder" for the most unusual float in the Homecoming Parade.

It ended up a win-win situation for everyone. The "Gott for Sheriff" Committee sold the Pioneer stereo and put the cash in the committee's general fund. Pioneer received national publicity. Casbon's Electric was reimbursed for the give-away. Charlie got over his "little snit" when he realized he wasn't out of pocket any cash for the stereo as a result of the commercial that his partner, Dave Casbon, had written. And I ended up with a great picture of Linda and me receiving our gift. Even better, I have a great story to tell my grandchildren.

WELL WATERS PRODUCTION

In 1974 Junior convinced me that he had enough original material to do an album. It did not take me long to say: "Yes, we can do this." I always had the feeling that once I had the idea in place, I could come up with a way and the money to accomplish this task. With this in mind, I convinced Charlie Ashton and my attorney, Dennis Hoover, on the sale of Wellman's, to invest $1,000 each. Then I added $2,500, for a total of $4,500 invested into Well Waters Production Company.

A very young Bill Porter-check the hairdo!

The first chore was the soundtrack. I called my good friend, Bill Porter, and told him we wanted a sixteen-piece orchestra, and we wanted him to handle all of the orchestration. Bill was familiar with Junior Waters' work, so on a Saturday morning in Vern Castle Studios in Lake Geneva, Wisconsin, the soundtrack was cut. I had given Bill Porter $1,800 in cash to dole out to the musicians. The musicians loved this kind of work, and I am sure that Uncle Sam never saw any of that money reported on anyone's tax forms. It was a great gig for a musician. (Don't worry Bill, that was twenty-five years ago. The IRS will forgive you!)

The surprise of the day came when the three back-up singers showed up at Junior's request. I did not pay them, because I was out of cash, but they did perform, and they performed really well. Junior handled their compensation. I never heard how he did it, but he told me that I should not worry; all three were satisfied. I didn't ask any questions, but I always wondered what their pay was.

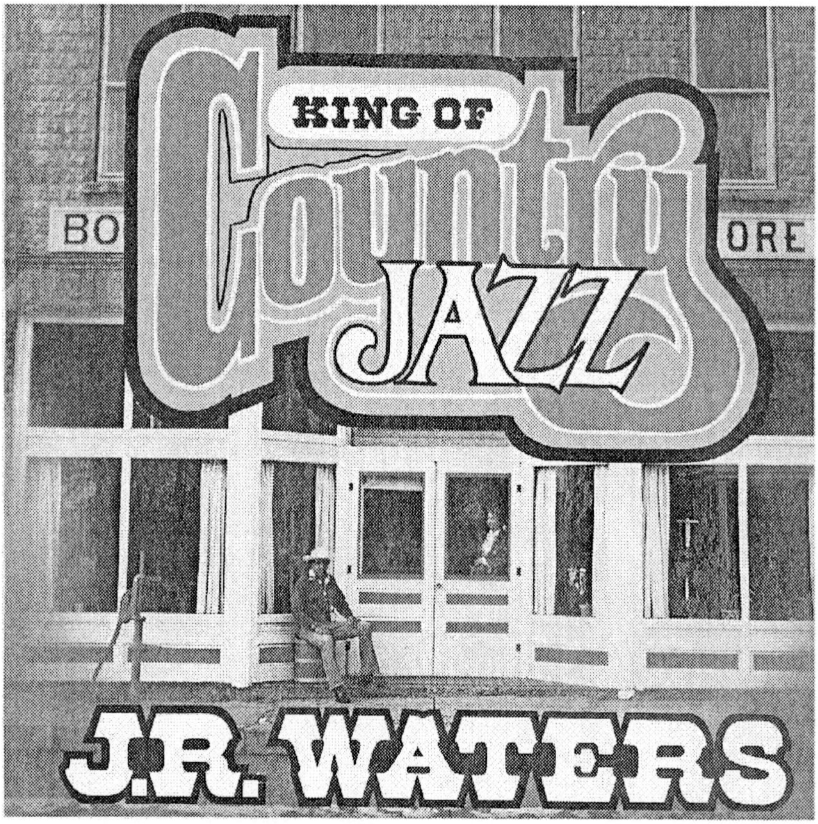

I got Lenny Dryfus involved with the artistic layout of the album and David Thon to handle all of the photo work. The terms were "pay later." Things fell into place, and after two months, Junior Waters and W.F. Wellman headed to New Jersey to a record company with a master cut of the Junior Water's album, "King of Country Jazz." The layout looked great.

The two "hard hats", Carl Hallberg and J.R.
This picture was taken in Walter Luchts Blacksmith and Welding Studio located next to Duffy's bar (formerly Jackson's bar)

The "Hear Ye, Hear Ye!" picture was taken in the Indiana Dunes State Park. It was a fast take by David Thon because of J.R.'s seating arrangement!

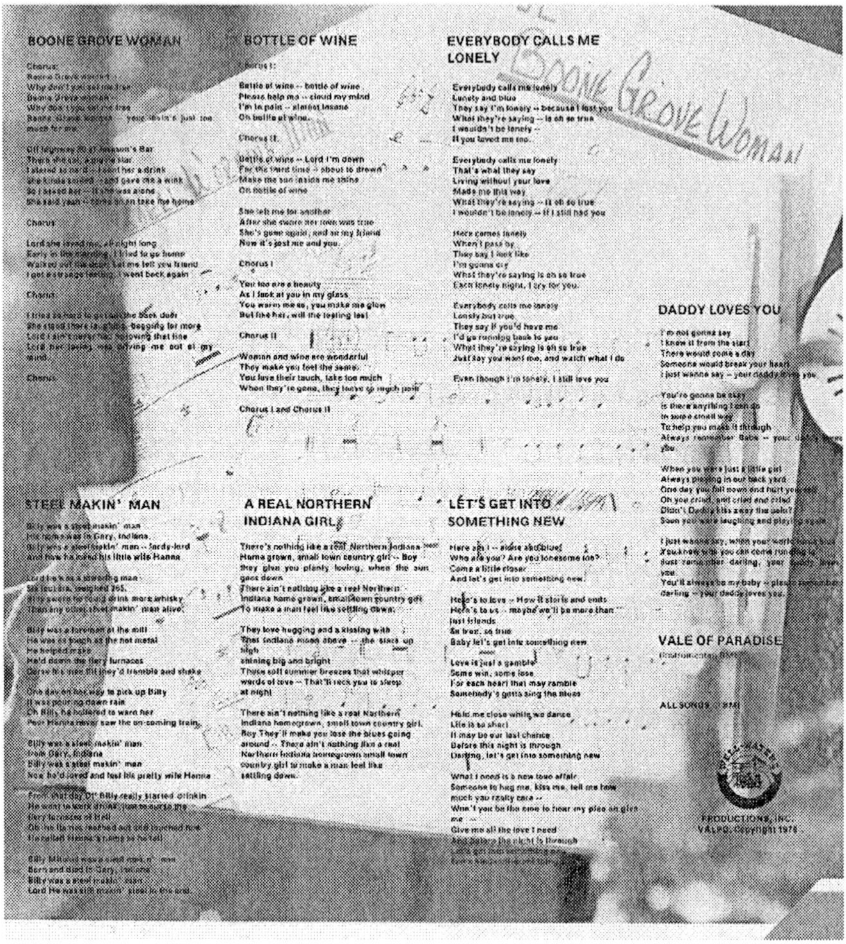

We stayed at Junior's wife's house for the night. No one ever knew if he was married or divorced. I think that they had a mutual agreement that so long as he sent a weekly check, they were still friends.

That night, Junior's half-brother, Zachary, picked us up in his brand-new Caddy and drove us to our first bar. It took us forty minutes to get there, and as Zack parked his new "hog," Junior explained that if we had taken the direct route, we would have arrived in less than ten minutes. But Zack wanted as many people as possible to see him driving his new car, so he really took the scenic route. The entire evening was spent in three bars, but the last one proved to be the most interesting. The music was great and lasted until three in the morning. The lubricant was also great, and I knew that I was headed for a huge hangover. The couch was my bed for the night.

The next morning we had our appointment at the plant that had produced the album. I was surprised when Junior appeared in a light tan summer suit, brown cowboy boots and a brand-new dark tan Stetson. He looked sharp, but I was puzzled. It did not take me long to solve the puzzle. The production plant had several hundred employees and 98% of them were young ladies. Junior had been on a previous tour of this plant, and he knew what the percentages were, so he dressed for the occasion.

The tour was great, and the ladies made Junior feel like a Superstar. We probably could have finished the complete tour in forty-five minutes, but Junior did not want it to be over. We completed the deal by ordering fifty boxes of fifty albums per box, to be delivered to my home in Valparaiso, Indiana within forty-five days.

Not long after this, at noon one day, Liz called me at the Court Restaurant and asked me what she should tell the truck driver who was sitting in front of our house with fifty boxes of "King of Country Jazz" albums. I told her to ask him one simple question: How far will he take them into the house? The answer was also simple: "I unload them on the sidewalk in front of the house, no further."

Trying to find room for fifty cartons that weigh over twenty pounds each in a very old house with three kids was a problem. But when I saw the cartons on the sidewalk, I made one of those executive decisions: Put as many as possible into Liz's walk-in closet.

At our last inventory in January 2004, we still had twelve boxes left. I am hoping that these last 600 albums become collector's items. If they do, I will see too it that Charlie Ashton and Dennis Hoover finally get their money back—without interest, of course.

In June 1994, I received a telephone call from Mrs. Lydia Hall, informing me that her brother, Junior Waters, had passed away. She told me that Junior was performing on a Carnival Cruise ship, and that he had fallen in his cabin. He was not found for twenty-four hours. They dropped him off at their next stop, and it took him three weeks to get strong enough to fly back to the United States. He stayed with his sister, in New Jersey, and seemed to be getting better each day, until he had a setback and was rushed to the hospital.

They said that he died because of a liver problem, but I think Johnny Walker Black Label was really the main cause of Junior's death. I could not make it to his funeral, but I sent a blanket of flowers that looked like piano keys. I treated Junior with show-business style right to the end.

At Christmas time, 1994, I asked the stage manager from the Star Theater in Merrillville, Jim Holly, to make up three-dozen tapes from Junior Water's album. Each tape began with my voice wishing every one a Merry Christmas, and then telling them that although we lost a dear friend, I wanted them to have a tape of Junior's work.

I then sent them to our friends and relatives. My brother, Guy, told me that he had everyone sitting around the Christmas tree to listen to the tape. They were expecting some fun and games from his talented brother, but he said that in one minute of hearing me talk about losing a dear friend, his happy occasion had turned to tears.

Junior Waters was a true friend, and we all miss his humor and great smile.

MARRELL'S RESTAURANT AND MY 50TH BIRTHDAY

It was June 16th, 1974, Liz and J.R. Waters were helping me celebrate my 50th birthday at Ray Marrell's "Almost Famous" restaurant called Marrell's. It was supposed to be just a dinner and few drinks along with a small birthday cake until all hell broke loose.

Valparaiso's Chief of Police came over to our table with the shocking news, "Bill, we have a drunken sixteen year old in hand in your restaurant and he has done a lot of damage, I think you should come with me." I didn't hesitate as I got into his squad car and headed down town.

The chief had me hook, line and sinker as we pulled up to the side of The Court. I started to wonder about his story as he double-parked on the south side. There were cars parked on both sides of the street and it was Sunday afternoon.

J.R. Waters and Liz planned a surprise birthday with about 150 friends and relatives. It was a complete surprise including J.R.'s homemade spaghetti, which included the wings and legs of chicken in his sauce (New Jersey Style).

J.R. Waters, Abe Gibron, Guy Wellman Sr. and a fifty year old "birthday boy"

To top off the surprise, my friend Abe Gibron was a great master of ceremonies. When Abe took over the mike he presented me with a beautiful floral arrangement nestled in an old toilet seat! Abe started with "I didn't know there were going to be ladies in the audience but if you think I'm changing any script because of that, then you don't know me!"

It was a GREAT BIRTHDAY PARTY!

J.R. Waters spent a lot of time on The Court's small stage, including a Saturday afternoon show for the younger set. We even made trips to the elementary schools to give shows to the "future customers."

It's "Kids Day" at The Court – the 1806 jail is in the background

ROSEMARY CLOONEY

J.R. Waters and I were shocked, but very proud when Rosemary Clooney walked into The Court to give us a big hello on October 2, 1975. It was even BIGGER when she sat at the piano with J.R. and did a half dozen of her great standards.

A very young Rosemary Clooney visits friends 10/2/75

Can you imagine a lucky customer telling a friend or relative, "I was entertained by the great one, a skinny Rosemary Clooney at The Court Restaurant last night!"

Friendships are great, when they are real!

One lesson I learned from the years at Wellman's and Bridge VU Theater was a small newsletter like "Wellman's Review and Forecast" or The Court's, "Court Recorder" was worth the effort. Our mailing list ended up being some of our best customers. Take the time to read our Court Recorder from December 1975. It has humor woven throughout the four pages. After looking it over, your curiosity will be heavy about who won the "name the boat" contest. It was a lady from Calumet City with the winning name, "Who Gives A Ship." I must repeat: the story in the Court Recorder reminded you, "Make the name a little humorous because our judges are a little funny!" They were warned!

The COURT RECORDER

December, 1975 Telephone A.C. 219 - 462-2141 Valparaiso, Ind.

O-FISH-L BOSTON SEA PARTY FRIDAYS

BOAT A-GROUND IN COURT

It seems fitting that the Court would start its O-FISH-L BOSTON Sea Party at the beginning of our bi-centennial year.

When we use the line "Eat fresh sea food from our own boat" we are not telling an untruth. The presiding judge bought a wooden boat from Lefty's Coho landing in Portage and proceded to cut it completely down the middle. This operation took place at Nostalgia, Inc., next door to Valparaiso's No. 1 fire station. I'm sure the local fire fighters are still puzzled why anyone would cut a perfectly sound boat down the middle. If there is anyone interested in buying half of a boat please contact Bill Wellman. I'm sure the price will be more than fair. In fact the price will be reduced 50%.

The boat (½) will be placed on the dance floor to handle the chafing dishes for the many different types of special sea foods.

If a customer is interested in joining the O-FISH-L Boston Sea Party he or she will first try our "Almost famous salad bar" and then our boat deck, that will feature steamy clam chowder or gumbo, smoked trout, fresh oysters on the half shell, steamed clams, corn on the cob, fresh shrimp in shells, broiled white fish with a mild cheese sauce, herring in wine sauce and herring in sour cream, sardines in tomato sauce, caviar, and a few other of our specialties.

After finishing the second course your waitress will tie a bib around your neck if you are having the live lobster. The bib won't be necessary if you have chosen the New York Strip steak.

The final catch on your Boston Sea Party will be a choice of Boston Cheese cake, fresh strawberry shortcake, grasshopper pie, or brandy alexander pie.

The cost of the O-FISH-L BOSTON SEA PARTY is $12.50.

There is a warning on the bow of the boat similar to the warning on cigarette advertisements: WARNING: The Sturgeon General has determined that overeating is dangerous to your health. There is also another sign on the dance floor giving out another warning: Poachers and Shrimp Lifters will be charged.

As you arrive on Fridays, you will be greeted at the front door by a salty old fisherman wearing a yellow rain slicker and rain hat, holding his oar.

P.S. I'm sure someone will start a rumor unless we specifically spell out the last word of the previous paragraph: OAR — a wooden lever with a broad blade worked by the hands to propel a boat. — Websters Dictionary. It's always wise to be cautious when you live in a small town.

Our O-FISH-L BOSTON SEA PARTY should be fun.

NEW YEARS EVE PARTY

Sure, its the most expensive package in the area but its also the best. Make your reservation early for Courts Millionaire (give or take 999,000) New Years Eve Party.

Arrive at 8:00 for cocktails and hors d'oeuvres, have your dinner any time from 8:00 til 10:30. Dance to the music of Jr. Waters and his trio. Drink as much as you like of any type of drink and then have champagne to welcome in 1976.

The dinner will include a choice of onion soup or shrimp cocktail, our almost famous salad bar, choice of New York Strip steak or a one pound lobster tail. Dessert will be fresh strawberry short cake or Boston cheese cake.

Coffee and fresh donuts will be served at 2:00 a.m.

Jr. Waters will be the main attraction but dancing will be the theme featuring Jr. and his trio.

Who else offers you the opportunity to ring in the New Year in COURT.

The most expensive package in town $29.75 per person — including Court costs, taxes, tips, entertainment, and all you choose to drink. Pick out your table and make your reservation now.

NAME THE BOAT CONTEST

The boat used as a serving area for our O-FISH-L BOSTON SEA PARTY needs a name. If you have a good name drop us a post card and win a complete night in jail for four people.

The complete night includes cocktails and choice of the menu. Get your legal minds working and drop us a card. Make it a little humorous because our judges are a little funny.

SPECIAL SUNDAY STYLE SHOW

Our Sunday Brunch was really brightened up recently with a style show by Lowenstine's Department Store.

All of the models were Lowenstine's employees and we must add very attractive models.

This show was a first with other shows to follow.

BAR OF JUSTICE IN HIGH COURT

The Bar of Justice is higher in Court than was originally planned. In fact, there was no bar planned until the crowds on week-ends made it very obvious to all that a lounge area was needed where people could wait for a dinner table.

The old banistered stairway winds upstairs to a very friendly and warm atmosphere with the 1880 sand blasted bricks to the old fireplace (it really works). The brass rails around the well mirrored backbar make the wait just a little easier on all.

Hors d'oeuvres are served from silver chafing dishes (from the South Shore Country Club). Add this to the beautiful view overlooking the skyline of the Vale of Paradise (a little humor) and you will enjoy the Bar of Justice. Oh, by the way, it is located in the Higher Court.

The electronic brain of the fantastic David Thon, V.T.I.C., B.S.V.U. and L.T.O.B.V.U.T., will be used to give The Bar of Justice one of the finest sound systems in the loup (of Valparaiso).

During the first part of the week all drinks in the higher court will be everything but high. The Judge's decision to price all drinks at $1.00 will prevail until a higher court reverses this decision.

JAPANESE NIGHT INVADES COURT

Court will feature Roy Murakami as the head chef of the night and let him bring a little of his home land to Valparaiso every Thursday night during the month of January.

GOVERNMENT MAN MOVES IN ON COURT

The Higher Court was invaded Friday, November 28 by The Old Fashions featuring Valparaiso's own Postmaster, Bill Pennington on the piano. The dance was called "Songs of the Forties" and had to be one of the more successful events of the year. It brought out some of the better dancers of the 40's. I'm sure there were a few sore muscles the next day.

Get yourself in shape and join in on the fun January 9th from 9:00 'til 1:00 at the next Songs of the Forties.

There is a cover charge of $1.00 per person. Please use cash — no stamps.

SCHULTZ HOSPITAL SAVES FERNS

If there is one question that is asked more than any other in Court, its: "Are your ferns real," and "How do you keep them so nice."

The answer is simple, but the care is loving and tender. We have a full time fern nurse, Maritta Mann, who is in complete charge of alternating, watering, and talking to each and every one. If this type of care fails Dr. Anthony Schultz (Schultz Floral) is called in for consilmantation. We also have four of our larger ferns in Dr. Schultz's hospital (green house) for a complete rest and relaxation period before returning to court.

Its not easy being green.

BANQUET ROOMS GIVEN TRIAL

If you're having a party that is in need of banquet facilities, call 462-2141 and ask for Sue. We have two beautiful rooms with a capacity of 120 in one and 70 in the other. A large movie screen is built into the ceiling along with a very good P.A. system. All of the chairs are the original dining room chairs of the late South Shore Country Club on the south shores of Lake Michigan. The brass rails on the stairs come from the Morrison Hotel in Chicago. The washstand in the men's restroom came from the Gary Hotel.

LEGAL LUBRICANT LIKES LOCAL COURT

Court is alive and living on Sundays with one of the finest brunches in the area. The doors swing open at 12:00 (high noon) and serves its, almost famous, Brunch until 4:00 p.m. At this time the regular menu takes over and the kitchen stays open until 9:00 p.m.

The following letter is handed the first member of a Brunch party and really explains the Sunday Brunch:

Congratulations!

You have been chosen as foreman of your jury and it is now your duty to inform the other members of your party about the regulations pertaining to COURT's Sunday Champagne Brunch. That's right — rules and regulations!

1st — Relax and enjoy the imported Champagne (well, it does come from San Francisco).

2nd — After the champagne go to the left side of the salad bar and pick up your plate (small isn't it?); carefully examine the herring and relishes. If you look in the metal box above the salad bar you should find Bagels. Now, as you come to the fruit, your container is in the wooden ice box. Assorted cheeses will be on the old side board in front of the dance floor. Return to your table and if you pass by the jail you will not collect $200, but you are ready and entitled to more champagne.

3rd — By this time you are ready for your main course. Go to the left side of the hot line where the smiling (she'd better be) young lady will explain all the assorted hot dishes. She has the plates and will help you in your selections. Return to your table and enjoy brunch.

W. F. "Bill" Wellman
Presiding

P.S. Have another cHampagne. . . It's rEally quitle good, and It;s suPrizxing how it wille r ealLy reLaX yxolu . . . .

P.P.S. We haven't had a hung jury yet!

AUNT ETHEL'S BOY — JR. WATERS

Jr. Waters' Aunt Ethel started her nephew in show business at an early age. Jr. has always told me that being her nephew didn't put bread on his table but he is very proud of his aunt.

Jr. is the kind of entertainer that has been discovered ten or twelve times a year. His talent has always kept him high on the singles wanted list from buyers of entertainers. Catch Jr. in the right mood and let him play his own composition. I know you will be pleasantly surprised at the high quality of his own work.

Jr. has played Valparaiso for the past twelve years and as he tells his audiences, "I finally made it to downtown Valparaiso."

Rumor has it Wellman and Waters have legally formed a new corporation called (are you ready for this) Wellwaters Production, Inc., for the purpose of producing and promoting a record album entitled, Valparaiso. The cover of the album will be a picture of Jr. standing in front of a local restaurant drawing a few hearts on the building with J.R. loves Valpo inside of the hearts. All of the songs will be Jr. Waters own work with musical arrangements by William Porter. A twelve piece orchestra will back up Jr. in such songs as Let's Get Into Something New, Daddy's Girl, Boone Grove Woman, Steel Making Man, Everybody Calls Me Lonely, My Old Friend Bill, and Valparaiso.

Wellwaters Production, Inc., hopes to be recording during the month of December with the first records coming out during the first part of 1976.

WATERS-WELLMAN HIT ROAD

Jr. Waters and Bill Wellman have been the featured program at several Rotary, Kiwanis, and Lions meetings in the area. They have been called "Salt & Pepper," "The poor man's Win Schuller," along with some names censored even for this news media.

Bill Wellman has informed service clubs that this notorious team is available for meetings. They not only do it for free, but the musical trivia by Mr. Waters makes for fun and free dinners in Court.

DUNCAN TIMES HITS COURT WITH "5" STARS

The great restaurapnteur Duncan Times gave Court "5" stars on his last visit to Valparaiso. This famous eater-outer thought the decor of Court was worth "6" stars but he had not handed out over five stars since World War II. Marrell's restaurant was the only other local establishment to reach this high plateau.

A.Z.: Re lease

VALPO'S WELLMAN KEEPS AN EYE ON DODGER PROSPECTS

SCOTTSDALE, Ariz. — Guy Wellman (Valparaiso, Ind.), chief scout for the Los Angeles Dodgers, also handles the winter instructional league in Arizona. As Guy says, "its called coconut snatching" — moving a player from one position to another. Walter Alston, Dodger manager says it's one of the most important programs we have. Products of the program have been such greats as Steve Garvey, Davey Lopes, Ted Sizemore, and Joe Ferguson.

COURT
69 FRANKLIN ST.
VALPARAISO, IN 46383

BULK RATE
U.S. POSTAGE
P A I D
PERMIT NO. 344
VALPARAISO
INDIANA 46383

This advertisement shows what a typical Millionaires New Year's Eve Party looked like in 1975:

BAD VIEW

It was during my short stay at The Court my number one son, Scott, was having difficulty controlling his use of drugs and a drinking problem. He had been picked up for three DUI's within a two-week period.

It was during one of his DUI pick-ups by an Indiana State Trooper that Scott took the troopers pistol away from him and barricaded himself in his apartment on Jefferson Street. I was called to intervene and the trooper told me, "It's a wonder one of us wasn't killed during the tussle." This incident landed Scott in the local jail directly south of The Court.

Our small office was located on the south side of the building facing the north side of the county jail. Liz was doing a lot of office work for me at The Court when she noticed someone waving to her at the top of a jail cell window. It was Scott.

For a couple weeks he managed to give his mother a wave on a regular basis! It was sad, but that was Scott.

During his short stay in Porter County Jail, he wrote an interesting poem called, "What In The Hell Is A Gazing Ball?"

IT'S MADE TO SELL-NOT TO DRINK!

GAZING BALL

by: Scott Robert Wellman

I got a satellite dish
Right next to my gazing ball

I got flamingos in my yard
and my grass is left kind of tall

I got some plaster paris deers
Some trolls and elves and a concrete frog

Just what in the hell are you supposed to do
with a gazing ball?

I got a black red silken jockey
Holdin on to nothing but a ring

And wooden peckers and ducks
That have never been on the wing

I got rusted crap piled high
and weeds out of every orifice of them things

And I haven't cleaned the yard
cause my rake's been overgrown since fall

Just what in the hell are you supposed to with a gazing ball?

I got a Mary Kay pink leisure suit
White shoes and a belt to match

I got the Shriner's saber swords
On my bumper and on my cap

I got a black velour print of the King of Rock and Roll in the hall

Just what the hell are you supposed to do with a gazing ball?

Scott also wrote a great letter to his grandmother during his stay at the Porter County Jail. I needed to get his permission to use his letter because it was very personal, but it was a great letter.

3/27/87 1:20 P.M.

GRANDMA,

I KNOW THAT I SHOULD HAVE WRITTEN SOONER, BUT I GUESS I WAS MORE EMBARRASSED THEN ANYTHING.

EVERYONE HAS HEARD ALL OF MY EXCUSES BEFORE, AND ARE AS TIRED OF THEM AS I AM. ALL I CAN TELL YOU GRANDMA, IS THAT I AM SORRY THAT I HAVE HURT YOU AGAIN.

I BELIEVE I'LL BE LEAVING FOR LOGANSPORT STATE HOSPITAL TUESDAY OF NEXT WEEK. THE PROGRAM DOWN THERE WILL BE FROM 60 TO 90 DAYS. ALL I CAN TELL YOU IS THAT I'LL GO THERE WITH AN HONEST AND OPENED MIND.

THIS WILL BE MY THIRD TIME IN A HOSPITAL. SOMETHING, I'M NOT TO PROUD OF, BUT THEN AGAIN, I'M MUCH MORE ASHAMED OF WHAT I PUT MY FAMILY THROUGH.

WHEN MY SON WAS BORN, I COULDN'T HELP BUT THINK THAT I WANTED

HIM TO BE NAMED AFTER GRANDPA. AND NOT JUST FOR THE FACT THAT I LOVE HIM. BUT ALSO WHAT HE HAD ACCOMPLISHED IN HIS LIFE. THE RESPECT AND THE HONESTY THAT HE INSTILLED IN PEOPLE... THE ZEST! FOR LIFE.

THE SAME HOLDS TRUE FOR DAD, AS WELL AS FOR UNCLE GUY. TWO PEOPLE WHOM I ADMIRE AS WELL AS I RESPECT AND ENVY VERY MUCH.

AT THIS POINT GRANDMA, I DON'T SEE MY KIDS SPEAKING OF ME AS I HAVE JUST DONE ABOUT MY DAD. WHICH I DON'T BLAME THEM. I AM NOT MY FATHER. I AM ME I AM A MIXTURE OF MOM AND DAD, YOU AND GRANDPA EVERYONE IN OUR FAMILY.

AND I LOVE ARE FAMILY VERY MUCH I CAN REMEMBER GROWING UP AND BEING SO PROUD OF THE FACT THAT I WAS BILL WELLMAN'S SON AND GUY WELLMAN'S GRANDSON. WHEN I WOULD TELL PEOPLE THAT I WOULD BE GIVEN A SLIGHT EDGE IN WHAT EVER I WAS DOING. EITHER IT BEING A JOB

INTERVIEW OR JUST THE SIMPLE
ACT OF MEETING SOMEONE NEW.
WHEN I WOULD MEET SOMEONE THAT
DAD OR GRANDPA KNEW, IT SEEMED
I WAS TREATED WITH MORE RESPECT.
AFTER I WOULD TELL THEM THAT I WAS
THE SON OR THE GRANDSON OF THE
WELLMAN FAMILY. FROM WHAT GRANDPA,
DAD, AND UNCLE GUY BUILT, BECAME RESPECT
OF OUR NAME. AND I AM VERY PROUD TO
BE INCLUDED IN THAT.

I LOVE YOU GRANDMA VERY
MUCH. I LOVE AND THINK ABOUT
GRANDPA ALOT. I'M SURE HE WOULD
NOT BE TO PROUD OF ME NOW, BUT I
KNOW IN MY HEART, THAT HE WOULD
GIVE ME LOVE AND THE ADVICE WHICH
HE ALWAYS SHARED WITH ME.

WHEN I GET TO LOGANSPORT
I'LL WRITE AND GIVE YOU MY ADDRESS.

MY LOVE IS WITH YOU AND
GRANDPA ALWAYS.

SCOTT

Scott was incarcerated in Logansport followed by a transfer to Richmond, Indiana. When he was sentenced, Judge Billings told him, "Scott, if you can make it through these two institutions you have a chance to get your life back."

Liz and I made many trips to Logansport with a picnic lunch with Scott's two children, Guy and Drew, in hand to spend a Sunday with their dad.

The judge's statement proved to be accurate. Scott made it with flying colors and to this day he is as clean as the board of health. I'm as proud of his accomplishments as I am of Dawn becoming a great trial attorney and Kim managing a hematology department at Indiana University Hospital. Kim also does experimental work with Eli Lilly.

IN-HOUSE BANK ROBBER

In 1975 The Court had a visit from two young FBI agents requesting a meeting with J.R. Waters and Bill Wellman. Once again, it was de'ja vu all over again, reminding me of that Saturday when my wife woke and informed me the FBI wanted to visit with me in regards to the late Tommy Morgano and his deportation case.

This meeting was requested to inform us one of my waitresses was a suspect in two (successful) bank robberies.

I loved J.R.'s first statement, "Beverly a bank robber – No Way!" I felt the same way, but when they caught up with Beverly she confessed and showed them where she had stuffed the money in her golf bag and hid it under her bed in her apartment.

The two successful robberies were conducted in Valparaiso. Beverly wore a wig and sunglasses and used a note each time to inform the teller she was armed and wanted all the money the teller had in her drawer. Beverly was caught on her third try when one of her fellow waitresses recognized her as she was standing in line. She bolted and the FBI took over the case. It was solved in less than one week and Beverly was sentenced to 2-4 years in prison, but she really was released in less than a year because of her three young children.

I tried to tell J.R. Waters, "You can't tell a waitress by its cover!"

VALPO SCHOOL BOARD

During my six years on the Valparaiso School Board I was not very popular with my fellow members. In fact, I was so unpopular they made me Vice President two terms in a row! This was the first time in the history of Valparaiso that the school board didn't take automatic step-ups from one office to the next. By doing this they forgot I took over as President in 1975, the year the new high school was dedicated. Check out the plaque in the hallway of Valparaiso High School.

Homer Jesse was the principal of Valparaiso High School for years and he could, and would, scare the beJesus out of you. During his last days before he died, I decided to visit him at Porter Memorial Hospital. I was trying to make small talk when I came up with, "Mr. Jesse, when I was in high school did you ever think I would end up on the school board?" He immediately raised his head from his pillow and literally screamed, "You would be one of the last ones I would pick!" I knew he meant exactly what he said. He died the following week.

STEALING A PIZZA RECIPE

It was during the construction of The Court when Liz and I traveled to Chicago almost every weekend looking for equipment for the kitchen and dining room, but we also worked on finding a pizza recipe.

Geno's East was our target. It was located ½ block east of Michigan Avenue on Superior. We would park in the alley early in the morning to write down the names of the purveyors delivering their wares.

The key name was Anachine Brothers located on Wells Avenue. They furnished their sausage to almost every successful pizzeria in downtown Chicago.

Once I had the list of purveyors I started to investigate how I could get the recipe to make the dough. I found a small bar located next to the sausage maker and after a couple of hours I had the confidence and the names of the brothers. Both Anachines were good customers of the bar, and I learned they made several visits to the bar starting with a lunch break.

Before the day was over I had met the brothers and one of them arranged a meeting for me with the dishwasher from Pizzeria Uno, who happened to be the early morning dough maker. The meeting occurred and a date was set for me to pick up the nameless dishwasher at Jose Vaga's house in East Gary, Indiana. The nameless dishwasher didn't want to know where he was going. The agreement was, I would pay him $100 and he would spend four hours (including travel time) with our people teaching us how to make the dough and explain the procedure of making a deep dish pizza similar to Gino's East, Pizzeria Uno and Due.

The mystery man and I arrived and we entered the back door of The Court restaurant and headed to the basement kitchen where Leigh Lyle and my wife, Liz, eagerly awaited our visitor. Liz had a clipboard and copied his every move. His Spanish accent was good enough, but at times he seemed fearful that what he was doing could get both of us stuffed in a trunk. At this time I was very happy that he had no idea what town he was in!

The recipe was really never used too much at The Court, so I took it with me when I finally decided to make a BIG move. My decision was easy when I realized Gene Hicks really wanted to run The Court more than I did.

It was time to get back to my real love – Entertainment and promoting show business.

Dean White asked me to come to Merrillville and help him plan and develop a theater. I accepted and quickly resigned from The Court!

Chapter Nine

HOLIDAY STAR THEATER

I joined Whiteco Industries on Wed., July 28th 1976.

THE HERALD, Wednesday, July 28, 1976

Wellman joins Whiteco staff

W. F. (Bill) Wellman, has been named Special Projects Manager for Whiteco Industries with emphasis focused toward aquisitions in the food and lodging industry.

In making the announcement, Dean V. White, president of Whiteco, said that Wellman's experience in the food and lodging business will add a new dimension toward Whiteco's continued growth and diversification.

A resident of Valparaiso since 1933, Wellman has been in business there since 1946, most recently operating the Court Restaurant. He will retain a minority ownership position and his seat on the Board of Directors but will no longer actively participate in the Court's management.

Wellman, a Marine Corps veteran, attended Valparaiso and Indiana Universities. He is a member of the Valparaiso Rotary Club and a past Director of Valparaiso Chamber of Commerce which, in 1973, presented him with its Distinguished Service Award.

In 1972 he was named Indiana Restaurant Man of the Year by the Indiana Restaurant Association, a group he has served as president, and in 1974 was voted "Boss of the Year" by the Kenwaunee Chapter of the Calumet area American Business Women Association.

A member for six years, he is a past-president of the Valparaiso School Board.

Mr. White gave me several chores but the main thrust was to start working with an architectural firm from LaPorte, Indiana, Fleck and Hickey, to help them plan and design a world class live entertainment theater. Tom Hickey was the lead architect chosen by Mr. White because of his past experience in designing the Twin Towers in Merrillville.

My first three months were spent studying Mr. White's operations and creating a report on all of his divisions at the Holiday Inn and Admirals Health Club and Bar.

The Health Club Bar turned out to be a den of down right thieves. I watched the bar operation for about a month when I informed Mr. White I would like to put the word out to the employees I was asking for a lie detector test on everyone working in the Admirals Health Club Bar.

In 1976 it was still legal and there happened to be a firm in the Twin Towers giving the tests. The final results were shocking! The bar manager confessed before she was hooked up to the machine. She stole cash, coffee, orange juice, liquor and even traded her hair products with the "in-house" barber for bottles of scotch.

Her husband was a Brinks driver who had a free lunch five days a week, which included his partner.

I knew she was stealing, but the real surprise was her drinking. She always had a pleasant smile but I later discovered she was smashed by eleven o'clock every day. It was straight vodka in a coffee cup. She forgot the cash register after lunch and operated out of her apron pockets. I explained the test results to Mr. White and we both decided to ask her to resign. I estimated she stole more than $20,000 a year for two years. She was so brazen she had the coffee man put the coffee in the trunk of her car without even bringing it into the building.

Typical Len Dryfus advertisment

I eventually named this bar The Sub Pub and it turned into a neat hide-away lounge. If you were sitting at the bar, the back of the bar was made up of glass windows over-looking the health club's swimming pool with entrances from both the men's and women's locker rooms. Therefore, the pool was used by both genders. It was a typical co-ed pool, except from the bar side it seemed like you were looking at a fish aquarium with live people instead of fish.

My dad was 81 years old when he decided to join the health club even though it was sixteen miles each way from his home in Valparaiso.

I heard about an embarrassing incident involving my dad but I waited a couple of weeks before I approached him with, "Dad, did you have a problem at the health club a couple of weeks ago?" He didn't hesitate when he answered, "Yes I did. The young fellow who signed me up and gave me the tour of the place didn't tell me there was a women's dressing room on the other end of the pool. I took it for granted it was a men's health club so I was walking around the pool like a "bank walker." (When we were little kids we swam in Salt Creek bare-assed and when the girls would come by most of us "little fellows" would jump in the cold water to hide our manhood, but there was always a proud boy and we called him a "bank walker.")

I then proceeded to tell my dad the rest of the story. The Sub Pub was opening for lunch and two waitresses were doing their side work when one girl said to Iris Pratt, "Oh my, there is a naked man walking around the pool!" Of course, Iris took a GOOD look and followed with, "That's Guy Wellman, Bill's dad. He is 81 years old." The other waitress responded with a classic statement, "For an 81 year old man, he's not half bad!"

Dad took in the rest of the story then followed with a classic of his own when he asked, "Which waitress made that statement?" That is exactly what I would expect to hear from Guy Wellman Sr., my "bank walking" father.

My report also gave Mr. White a warning about his general manager at the Holiday Inn. I'm sure he realized I was writing a report for Mr. White, but he continually asked me to have lunch with him. And I did on several occasions.

The summary on the young GM was, he was a drinker and he had a loaded 45-caliber pistol in his top drawer of his office desk. He pulled the 45 out one day and waived it around exclaiming, "No one is going to rob this place without a fight."

I explained what a 45 would look like going into a body, but I emphasized how large the hole was when it exited. I also told him, "When you pull a gun on someone you must have the courage to use it or they might just stick it in your ear and blow you away."

The young GM didn't last much longer in the hotel business. He returned to the much calmer outdoor billboard business.

The report also told about a chef in the main kitchen who required sexual favors from the waitress staff if they were to get their orders out in a timely fashion. The waitress staff had been there for years, so their neat trick was changing the percentage of the tips on house charges. The big mistake they made was tampering with the assigned tips signed on by Mr. White. It was time to clean house!

The report wasn't very positive, but it could be straightened out with a lot of tender loving care!

Working with Tom Hickey on the Star Theater was a pleasure, especially when he took some advice from Richard Pick, David Thon and Homer Burrus, experts from past experience at Bridge VU Theater in Valparaiso.

ENOUGH ICE FOR LAKE COUNTY

In the planning of the theater, I asked the general manager of the hotel to give me an idea of what he thought was the correct number of ice cube machines we should have to handle 3400 people for two shows on a full house. In three days I received a five-page report from the manager regarding my request.

After spending the time reading the report twice, I decided to take it to an expert. I once again called Homer Burrus for his opinion on the so-called "ice cube report." Homer read the report and looked at me with a half smile on his face. I then asked him, "Homer, is this guy a bull shitter?" His answer was quick and short, "Yes he is, but he is a good one, and if you follow everything he is requesting you will be able to supply enough ice for all of Lake County in a hot summer!" It was at this point I realized that my experience at Bridge VU and my contacts with "REAL" experts was the way to go.

The Holiday Star Theater opened on a Sunday night with the Four Girls Four, made up of four individual stars; Rose Marie, Helen O'Connel, Margaret Whiting, and the super, super star, Rosemary Clooney.

Four Girls Four

It was a great feeling to see my good friend Rosemary. The last time I saw her was the night she surprised J.R. Waters and me by coming into The Court Restaurant and giving our customers a musical treat.

I still remember standing in the last row of the balcony, watching and listening to the first rehearsal. One of the girls, Margaret Whiting, was singing a cappella. When she stopped I heard her say, "The acoustics are great!"

That statement by Margaret Whiting made my day. Every word she said from the stage was distinguishable without amplification. The Star Theater was off to a good start with the stars.

I received two telephone calls from nearby restaurants on Monday after our first performance. They both asked the same question, "Can you send us your schedule of shows?" We got hit last night and we were not prepared. Your show gave us great business, but we were not ready for anything like what happened." The two restaurants were Tiebel's and Strongbow's. These calls proved to me that the Holiday Star Theater had the ability to not only spin off restaurant and bar business to all of Mr. White's business, but the spin off to other restaurants and hotels was huge.

We did a survey and found out that 95% of the people attending the Star Theater for a show on a weekend ate some place other than home the night of the performance. This meant that, on a sold out show of 3400, our restaurants could only take about 15% of the total, meaning over 2700 people were eating at other restaurants within a twenty-five mile radius around the Holiday Star Theater. The economic impact to Northwest Indiana from the theater was HUGE.

The picture of one of Dean White's billboards shows how we opened the theater during the month of December. We started strong and we had a very large variety in picking entertainers for the first month.

The following article, written very well by Bob Kostanczuk, on the 20th anniversary of the opening of the theater, appeared in the Post Tribune explaining what happened on opening night twenty years ago:

It was going to be the night that proved Northwest Indiana could play with the big boys! December 19, 1979.

The Holiday Star Theater (now the Star Plaza Theater) was heralding its grand opening with a performance by Donna Summer, the undeniable "Queen of Disco," who was the biggest pop singer in the country at the time.

Hundreds of business leaders, media types and VIP's had arrived that night for a pre-show dinner celebrating the official kick off of a six million dollar Merrillville venue that aimed to be a respected showcase for big name "Las Vegas style" entertainment. Put to rest would be those jokes about an "iffy" theater in the "corn fields," located – as one Chicago newspaper snidely put it – "ten miles from nowhere!"

But it appeared something was going to go horribly wrong for the upstart venture on that all-important grand opening night. "During the dinner, someone whispered in my ear that Donna Summer was sick and was not going on," recalled Bill Wellman, who was the general manager of the theater. "I lost my appetite in a hurry," he laughed. Scrambling, Wellman enlisted the aid of a doctor/friend of his, who happened to be at the gala dinner. (The doctor was Dr. Martin O'Neil, Wellman's former partner at Bridge VU Theater.) Wellman remembers hoping that the doctor would be able to convince her she's not as ill as she thinks she is.

Wellman said an ear problem had befallen the disco diva who was seen backstage by the doctor. "He looked at her and convinced her that she had an earache," said Wellman.

The physician, he added, was able to get the point across to Summer that there was nothing seriously wrong with her.

"She decided to go on," said Wellman. "She accepted his theory that she had an earache and he was right because she was all right the next day."

A different account from another theater official suggested Summer had perhaps been bothered with a throat problem that night. But which ever story is more accurate, Summer's performance was certainly in doubt for a while because she felt ill.

Wellman cringes at the thought of Summer bowing out and disappointing a sellout crowd that night. "It would have been a disaster..." he predicted.

That assessment is essentially echoed by Bruce White, a key member of the powerful family which built the theater and the surrounding Star Plaza. "It would have been very negative – quite devastating," said White. "People in Chicago and people in the industry, I think, were really looking for us to fail. There really was a stigma attached with being in Merrillville, Indiana – the image of being in the middle of a cornfield. Everybody was obviously quite surprised when we got Donna Summer and would have loved to have seen us not do a great job with her. But it turned out to be great! It was a great learning experience. We built a lot of strong relationships. It was really a springboard to bigger and better things as time went on."

When Summer first came to the Merrillville theater in 1979, she reserved 25 rooms for herself and her entourage in the nearby Holiday Inn. Her opening night at the Star was both tense and exciting for the local people responsible for pulling it off.

Highland's Judy Bronowski, who was in charge of marketing for the theater, said she felt "pretty overwhelmed with everything." Now the vice president of marketing for

White Lodging Services, Bronowski expanded on what she was feeling on opening night, "There was naturally a huge amount of excitement and apprehension about what was going to happen with this theater. Everything was just like passing in a blur. Wellman, the theater's general manager at the time, was sweating the details, concerned about everything from the temperature to whether the same seat had been sold twice!" As for the show itself, Bronowski remembers, "a lot of glitter and flash!"

Summer also proved to be a little steamy, serving up what White recalls were "gyrations with the microphone stand" as she sang "Love to Love You Baby." Sitting next to his grandmother, whom he described as having a strong Puritan background, White was admittedly uneasy during the song and remembers "hoping that my grandmother's vision was not good enough to see what was going on up on the stage!"

Roy Leonard, a former film and arts critic for both WGN and TV in Chicago, summed up his impression of Summer on opening night, "She just turned the crowd on – I remembered that!" Leonard was one of the key members of the Chicago media that the White family was trying to impress on grand opening night at the new theater. They apparently succeeded!

"I remember feeling very positive about it at the time, mainly because of the people who were running it", Leonard recently recalled. "I was particularly impressed that opening night with the auditorium itself – the acoustics and the site lines. There wasn't a bad seat in the house." Leonard downplays the theory that the Chicago entertainment industry was looking down on the upstart Indiana theater during its early days.

Rather, there was a current of underlying concern, he speculates. "I think they looked at it with some apprehension mainly because a lot of big acts that ordinarily would play Chicago wound up playing at the Star Plaza," he said.

The Star Plaza Theater had indeed established itself as a major venue, not only holding its own with Windy City theaters, but also securing a national reputation as one of the top-grossing venues of its size drawing and estimated 500,000 patrons annually, according to the theater calculations.

A plus: No seat is more than 110 feet from the stage. On Wednesday there'll be a gala cocktail reception for VIP's in celebration of the return of Donna Summer, and this time theater officials won't have to be anxious about making a big impression.

"I think this time we can enjoy it," said Bruce White. "Instead of just being so consumed with the anxiety of making sure things happen, we'll just be able to enjoy the evening for what it is."

The Post Tribune article seemed to capture almost everything that occurred on our VIP opening night except the rest of the story on Roy Leonard.

W.F. "Bill" Wellman, Dean White & Roy Leonard

I remembered my lesson at Bridge VU Theater of how hard it was to get the critic from the Chicago Tribune, Will Leonard, to write a review on my theater, but the results were really worth the effort. So I thought up another P.R. GEM.

It was a coincidence in 1969 I was working with Will Leonard from the Tribune and then ten years later I'm trying to get another critic to give us a good review and it happens to be another Leonard. This time it's Roy Leonard (as far as I know there is no relation between the two.)

This time I decided not to take a chance. I hired Roy Leonard to be our MC for the evening and we even got him involved with the ribbon cutting.

The reviews were great in the Chicago Tribune and WGN radio. The Holiday Star was off to a great start!

GLADYS KNIGHT & THE PIPS

It was Saturday night, March 29, 1979 and we had two sold out shows with Gladys Knight and The Pips at $10.75 per ticket.

I was standing at the back of the house during the warm up act and I noticed a section on the main floor of about 150 seats vacant. It didn't really cause me too much concern because on all African American ticket selling shows, coming

Gladys Knight and the Pips

late to a show seems to be the thing to do especially if the seats are near the front where the customer can be seen as he or she makes their entrance.

When Gladys finished her first number I became concerned with the empty section of seats. I looked up the ticket numbers and found a bus operator out of Chicago had purchased six busloads, three for the first show and three for the second. Their plan was to have dinner at the same restaurant in Chicago with three busloads eating before the second show and three busloads eating after the first show. I decided to call the restaurant.

The young lady heard my story and quickly came back with one of her own, "That explains why we have an overload on our buffet, we have all six buses eating at one time."

The bus promoter decided not to show up at the theater when he discovered the mistake, but I decided to call for extra security realizing I would have close to 150 people looking to see a show at 10:30pm when their ticket said they should have been in their seat for the 7:30pm show.

I have seen angry people before, but 150 at one time was a scary scene. They would have hung the promoter if he had the courage to show up, but once he realized his mistake he decided to avoid the problem and return to Chicago.

The crowd was hard to contain and explain what had happened, but the uniformed police from the Sheriff's department wrote a full report and gave several copies to each leader on the bus.

I heard the bus promoter closed his business and was looking for some other type of work. It wasn't long after five show performances that Gladys did a bit of firing herself by breaking away from The Pips! She was then booked as "Gladys Knight."

This next story didn't seem to fit in my book, but after telling you about Gladys Knight I decided to follow with a true story on my favorite basketball coach "The General" Robert Montgomery Knight!

BOBBY KNIGHT

It seems as though everyone has a story about Coach Knight, so I will spin my yarn to keep up with all of you. It starts in 1989 when I came home from watching a basketball game at the Lutheran School in Valparaiso.

The game was between Immanuel and a Lutheran school from East Chicago. I told my wife, "Liz, I just saw a skinny 7th grade kid from Valpo's Immanuel Lutheran School play ball and I think he could be the star of Valpo High School's varsity team right now."

That was the beginning of the Bryce Drew era. I followed his career and saw his energy level go down, as his heart problems seemed to get worse during his junior year in high school.

It was his junior year that Coach Knight first saw him play so, I clipped results from his senior year games, when Valparaiso High School stayed undefeated until the final game in the state tournament, when they lost in a double overtime to South Bend.

I continued to send these clippings to Coach Knight and I even wrote him explaining the difference in Drew's energy level was like night and day after the doctor solved his heart problem.

Coach Bobby Knight

The coach sent the following letter to me on November 14, 1993. I was so proud of receiving a letter from the coach, I had it framed and it hangs on my "walls of fame" in the Whiteco corporate office.

INDIANA UNIVERSITY

DEPARTMENT OF
INTERCOLLEGIATE
ATHLETICS

December 17, 1993

Bill Wellman
Whiteco Industries, Inc.
Suite 700
1000 East 80th Place
Merrillville, IN 46410

Dear Bill:

Thank you very much for taking the time to drop me the note on Drew. He is a fine player but we have one coming in just like him in Neil Reed and will not be doing any more recruiting.

Once again, thank you and best wishes to you and your family for a most enjoyable holiday season.

Sincerely yours,

Bob Knight
Basketball Coach

BK/bjm

Assembly Hall
Bloomington, Indiana
47405-1101

812-855-2794

As you can see, Coach Knight is telling me that Bryce Drew is a fine player, but he has found a young man named Neil Reed he is interested in.

Now, in case you do not remember the name Neil Reed, he is the young man on that "almost famous tape" where the coach (allegedly) choked Mr. Reed at a practice and unfortunately someone got it on tape.

In the year 2000, Bob Knight was flown into Valparaiso airport in Dean White's jet to speak at a fundraiser for Boys Town of Schererville, Indiana. It was at this dinner I had a chance to get a couple of basketballs signed, but more importantly I had ten minutes to do a one on one with the coach.

It went something like this: "Coach, I received a letter from you in 1993." The coach responded, "Is that right? What did it say?" "I happen to have a copy with me," I said as I handed it to the coach. He read the letter and looked at me and said, "You know, I do make mistakes, and this was one of my bigger ones. I would have loved to coach Bryce, he is my type of kid."

It takes a BIG man to admit a mistake like this and Coach Knight's stock went up in my book. That is my Coach Knight story and I wish he was still in Bloomington.

BILL COSBY

My first experience with a top-notch comedian came when I booked four shows on February 23rd and 24th with Bill Cosby all by himself. The ticket price was $10.75.

Mr. Cosby came in on Friday with two performances on Saturday and two on Sunday. The first request was, "Do you have a tennis court available?" I had an early warning about this, so I had made a reservation for all three days on the new indoor courts in Merrillville (now it's Hobart).

The first show on Saturday was scheduled for 7:00pm but our entertainer didn't show up until 7:30pm, when he walked onto the stage still in his sweat suit and carrying a banquet chair. There was no announcement. He just parted the curtains and walked out! He stood there without speaking for several minutes and finally put the chair down and said, "Why – why is this theater located here?" It broke up the full house. He then did fifteen minutes on why he was late.

He explained he finished his last tennis game when he realized he hadn't eaten anything all day, so he was standing in line at McDonalds when the young lady working the line he was standing in recognized him. He did ten minutes of great comedy demonstrating how cool she was as she waited on him. He then introduced the girl in the audience and brought her up on stage to finish off the late bit. She told the audience she spotted him because of the sweater he wore under his sweat suit jacket. It was a bright red knit sweater with the word JELLO in bright yellow letters.

He finished the bit by also introducing the young girl's parents he had invited to attend his first performance. Mr. Cosby just did 15 minutes of good, clean humor by tying everything to a local happening.

The limo driver attending to Mr. Cosby's every need was a young, sharp African American about the size of a professional jockey. Bill seemed to have almost adopted our driver because they had room service for every meal, including Chinese and pizza. The room service jumped to three after the first show on Saturday when a Chicago taxicab delivered a tall, very good looking young blonde lady to the Holiday Inn desk where she asked for Mr. Cosby's telephone number. This was the last time I saw her.

It was just before the early 4:00pm show when a rumor flew around back stage that Mrs. Cosby was on her way from Chicago to Merrillville. It didn't take long to OK a trip to the airport with our limo sending the beautiful young blonde on her way to catch a plane to "wherever!"

What happens in Merrillville stays in Merrillville – well, almost!

Mr. Cosby's contract was a guaranteed contract with a percentage bonus if he did well in attendance. He did well, so I met him in the Green Room to do my first settlement with a percentage. I was a little nervous but the two of us were alone when I said, "Mr. Cosby, I would like to show you the results of your four shows and I'm ready to write you a check." He took away all of my fears with, "There is no need to show me anything." I was a little shocked and followed with, "Don't you want to see how well you did?" "No, you trusted me that I would show up and I trust you on your figures. Just send the check to my agent; I know you have his address."

My fears were not warranted and our deal was completed as I said, "Thanks for coming and I hope we will be doing business again."

The entire meeting took less than five minutes as he finished off our conversation with, "I like your facility and the acoustics are exceptional."

The end of my Cosby story is, Mrs. Cosby didn't show up, it was just a rumor!

TOM JONES

The first time Tom Jones appeared at Holiday Star Theatre was May 13th, 14th and 15th in 1980. He was there for eight shows and the tickets were $12.75.

He was a ticket seller and I considered him at the peak of his career. To give you an idea of his age, his 20-year-old son accompanied him on this trip.

The "Pointer"

Now, you might think having his 20-year-old son traveling with him might cramp the senior Mr. Jones' style, but it did not. In fact, I think it added to the overall mystique of this "ticket seller."

Tom Jones was, and still is considered one of the top party men in the entertainment field. When it came to the (almost) nightly party, the elder Mr. Jones seemed to have a plan of attack that reminded me of the way a Marine Corps general would plan his attack on a South Pacific island. He just did not allow any small detail of the plan to escape his notice.

The nightly plan went something like this: first, all traveling band members (there were five) would, on a daily basis, scout out a bevy of good looking single ladies and invite them to come to the late performance (free Celebrity Circle tickets); next, the ladies received a party invitation to the Star Suite of the Holiday Inn immediately following the show.

The Star Suite was designed to take up four rooms facing the swimming pool / hot tub atrium. The upper two rooms were two bedrooms, while the two rooms downstairs were designed like a large party room with wet-bar, nice chairs, a dining room table and chairs, and a baby grand piano. This room was added to the hotel to make Liberace feel at home and comfortable on his many visits to northwest Indiana.

The band members were pros when it came to picking good looking ladies to attend the parties, and the reputation of Tom Jones' parties is well known and famous in the entertainment field. I think the batting average was about 99% of the guests invited also attended.

At the rehearsal, Mr. Jones really did not need too much time because that "almost famous" trombone and orchestra leader from Chicago, Bill Porter, put the other eleven members of the orchestra together. When Bill Porter was assigned to have a 16 piece orchestra ready for a rehearsal at a certain time on a given day, you could count on having nothing but top musicians from the Chicago-land area on stage.

Bill has been in charge of all the music needs at the Star Theatre since before the grand opening featuring Donna Summers. He is also known for doing the orchestration for the late J.R. Waters album, "King of Country Jazz," which had the almost famous hit song, "Boone Grove Woman." According to the charts at Fetla's Bargain Center, located on State Road 2 in Valparaiso, this song still holds the record of being in the top 10 for over 8 years and holding the number one spot for 56 straight weeks.

It was during this first rehearsal that I got a surprise. Mr. Jones approached me by saying, "Mr. Wellman, I would like to invite you to attend my first party tonight after the show, in my suite." I was really shocked that I was invited, and I am sure it showed when I said, "Thanks for the invitation; I'll be there."

The first performance went exceptionally well, in front of 3,250 screaming fans. This show was the first time we had to have extra security guarding the stage. It was also a first for me to see flowers thrown on stage, along with envelopes containing motel room keys. Several fans tossed their panties in his direction with notes attached. The ever-present "Tom Jones Fan Club" had reserved seats early and often. They were large in number, loyal, and full of fun, however, none of them passed the test by the five band members to be invited to any of the parties that took place in the Star Suite. I am sure the five young members of the 'party approval invitation committee' put looks and age into the formula. It was close to midnight when I entered the bi-level suite and found the famous Tom Jones party in full swing as about 18 very attractive young ladies sipped champagne and sampled the variety of hors d'oeuvres that were ordered nightly for the party.

I had just finished a vodka and tonic with a lime and was about to order my second one when our host shocked me again. Mr. Jones said, "Mr. Wellman, this will be the last time that you will be invited to one of my parties." I think it was the false courage of the first drink that made me respond quickly: "What did I do wrong? Did I offend you in any way?" His answer was, "No, but if you look around, the only males here are my son and my band members and a couple of our roadies. We never invite outsiders, but since you are new to the business and this is my first visit to your great theatre, I invited you out of courtesy. But, as I said, this is your last invitation."

After my host had finished his speech, and I was half through my second drink and feeling very relaxed, comfortable, and little bit cocky I said, "Tom, I really appreciate the one-time invitation and I think that if I was in your shoes I would use the same logic." It was my next statement that may have given Mr. Tom a little shock. I said, "You remind me of a bird dog that I once had. He would point his prey with great accuracy. In fact, you are so good I can tell which young lady you are pointing at tonight." I had my host's full attention and interest when he came back to me with, "OK Mr. Wellman, which one is it?" I did not hesitate when I pointed out a very attractive young lady, Judy B.

The shock seemed to be reversed when he came back at me with this remark, "I now have a second reason for not inviting you to another party."

I left the party about 1:30 a.m. under friendly conditions after I thanked him for my one and only invitation. I understood he wanted to keep his famous parties within the fraternity of his people and I respected that position. The very next day Judy B. came to my office for some advice. Judy was the very attractive Vice President of marketing for the theater and she had been swallowed up in the party net that the band members had thrown throughout the area, when they were looking for invitees to the first famous party. When I made my statement to Tom Jones about my bird dog and the fact that I could pick out a certain girl in the room he was pointing at, I really had a leg up in the selection process because I knew Judy and she was, by far, one of the most attractive girls in the suite on that night.

The "after party" look!

Judy's problem was this: Mr. Jones had invited her to have dinner with him on the weekend and, since I was the general manager, she did not know how to answer the invitation. At this point I went back to my father's theory and used a little of "Guy's Law." My logic went something like this: we were brand new to this theater and we had not set a policy that would cover this type of situation, so I asked Judy, "Do you want to go out to dinner with him?" Judy did not hesitate when she answered a resounding "Yes I would." I thought a minute and said, "There is nothing in our policy handbook that covers this and he will probably have some of his band members with him at the dinner, so I think you should accept his offer for dinner. But, let me know how it turns out."

The following Monday I ran into Judy, but I did not get a chance to say anything before she said, "You were wrong about the invitation. It was a candle light dinner for two in his suite." I decided that I did not need to know too much information about the dinner party or the rest of the evening.

For the next few years at the Holiday Star Theatre, Tom Jones appeared like clock work twice a year and averaged 2,850 customers per show. That put him in the class of a real "Ticket Seller."

I think that Father Time has almost caught up with Mr. Jones, but I must say his memory is still good. At one of the last performances that I saw him give, I noticed, before he said anything to the audience, he spotted lovely Judy B. seated in the fourth row of Celebrity Circle. I watched him as he held his hand over the mike and he looked right at her and said, "You cut your hair; I like it."

Tom was really sharp and he definitely knew how to point.

NICE HOOKER

George Lindsey, better known as *Goober* on TV's Andy Griffith Show, was one of our better opening acts. Eventually, he got to know the head of Whiteco Outdoor Graphic Department, Jim Kernagis. Jim invited *Goober* to have lunch with him at the Holiday Inn the first day he arrived in town. It was during lunch that the *Goober* got very serious and made this statement, "Jim, when you're on the road as much as I am you get very lonely. Can you head me in the right direction in making a connection with a nice hooker?" This must have flustered Jim, because he immediately bounced back with, "I would suggest you see Bill about that."

Jim did have the courtesy to tell me about *Goober's* request so I asked Jim, "Why did you tell him to see me? He will think I'm either a pimp or a well-connected guy." Jim apologized, "I didn't know what to say, and it just popped out." The next day at 10:00 a.m., I was doing what I did daily, helping the telephone girls take ticket orders. While taking an order, I recognized a voice ordering four tickets to an upcoming Tom Jones show. After taking her order I said, "Katie, it's Bill, how are you doing and are these tickets for you?" She replied, "No, they are for my mother and her poker playing friends." At the same time I was carrying on a friendly conversation with Katie, (a high school date and friend) I got a tap on the shoulder by George Lindsey. I waved to him, but I continued talking to Katie by saying, "Katie, meet George Lindsey, he will be opening tomorrow in our theater." I handed the telephone to *Goober* and he took over the conversation. "Katie this is my first night in Merrillville, why don't you come over and have lunch with Bill and me." He then handed me the phone and Katie said, "Was he kidding?" I followed with, "No, why don't we meet you in the Holiday Inn dining room at 12:30?" Katie agreed so I made a reservation for the three of us.

George Lindsey – "Goober"

Goober and I had just sat down when Katie made a great entrance, dressed in a solid black leather outfit including a wide brimmed leather hat. Katie was, and still is, a very attractive lady. Both *Goober* and I stood up to welcome our guest. George didn't realize that his cloth napkin was not only tucked under his belt, but also under a glass of water, which proceeded to fall right on the *Goober's* pants. This wasn't the way to make a great impression with someone you just met, but George followed the water act with, "That will cool me off."

Lunch went well and the conversation flowed with the help of a glass of wine. After lunch George said, "Katie, I have to go back to my room to do one telephone radio interview and then I would like to invite you to come with me to Chicago to have dinner." Katie agreed to his offer as he headed to his suite to do the interview.

As George left, it hit me that his request from Jim Kernagis in obtaining a nice hooker, which was referred onto me, was evidently what Mr. Lindsey thought Katie was. I explained the situation to her followed with, "Katie, he thinks I have followed through with his request and he thinks you are that hooker. If you want to leave, I will make up an excuse." She didn't hesitate a bit as she said, "I think I will take him up on his dinner offer, and don't worry, I will be able to handle everything."

To this day I never asked my friend Katie any questions about her trip to Chicago. Once again, what happens in Merrillville stays in Merrillville.

CHAUFFER FEVER

One of the transportation problems with the Holiday Star Theater was scheduling limo pickups of all the so-called stars. Mr. White had given the OK to purchase the second limousine, so I figured the time was just right to present him with one of the Wellman P.R. gems.

One of the things that I always admire about Mr. White is he would usually go along with an idea that would fit the theme of pleasing the stars. We always felt the more we catered to the star the more he or she would want to return to Indiana.

The idea I presented to Mr. White went something like this. I would like to hire a girl as our #1 chauffer. This girl was working as a waitress in the new restaurant in the Twin

Towers and her name was Kelly. She was 6'1-1/2" tall and weighed about 145 lbs. with very little body fat and a chest that would get the attention of any O'Hare policeman. The plan was to get Kelly to wear two types of uniforms. One was a dress suit with very high heels and the other was a country outfit with cowboy boots and a Stetson. Both outfits made Kelly look like she was 6'5", especially when she wore the country western outfit.

After giving Mr. White my idea, and all of the vital statistics, he did not hesitate to give me the OK, so I put the plan into action immediately. This is one of the times Bruce White (the boss's son) agreed with one of my ideas.

When I first approached Kelly she seemed a little reluctant; but when I told her about the salary and some of the benefits, she agreed. I asked her to go to Marshall Fields in Chicago to be fitted for her two very classy outfits.

The first time I saw Kelly dressed in her country outfit I knew that I had developed another P.R. gem.

"I'm in love with your chauffer"

Kelly's first O'Hare pickup was Kenny Rogers and his scheduled pickup ran extremely late. When I asked Kelly if she had any problems because she had to wait so long her answer did not surprise me. She said, "The police were really nice to me and allowed me to park my limo in the same spot right in front of the United Airlines." Can you imagine a big Irish policeman looking at Kelly as she opened the door of her new Cadillac limo and starts to pull her body out of the front seat and continues until she puts on her Stetson? No way would he tell her that she had to move on!

Kelly got to know most of the policemen who regularly worked O'Hare, so she never had a parking problem if her pickup star was running late.

Kenny Rogers came into my office about 2:00 p.m. and the first thing he told me was, "I think I am in love with your chauffer and I know this is the first time I have ever said that to anyone." Kelly really did a great job and I want to tell you what a great impression she made for the Star Theater right from the start.

It was working just like I thought it would until Humperdink arrived two days early for his three-show weekend. He was not convinced that the Merrillville life style would keep him interested in staying a total of five days in the Hoosier state, so he asked for the use of our limo to go to Chicago on his first day.

Engelbert Humperdink

Well, the one-day trip lasted a day and a half so our new limo driver had to stay over night. This did not bother me, but it seems as though Kelly's boy friend took offense and he took it out on Kelly by physically working her over. This was Kelly's last trip. She quit the next day.

They say that if good ideas are successful two times out of six you are a winner. Good ideas are not always your own, you steal some to keep your average up. This is the advertisement I put in the paper after Kelly left me.

FOR SALE:

2 – ALMOST NEW, GOOD LOOKING CHAUFFER UNIFORMS. (FEMALE) YOU NEED TO BE AT LEAST 6'1" TALL. IF THEY FIT, A JOB MAY COME WITH THEM. CALL W.F.WELLMAN AT THE HOLIDAY STAR THEATER.

I received no takers on the advertisement so I went back to male drivers. Too bad, the idea was great!

CHARLIE FINLEY

Charlie Finely was another one of my favorite characters. He was brilliant in many ways but just as common as many of my former bar customers.

Mrs. Finley, W.F.W and Charlie (minus the toupee)

I received a call from Charlie wanting to make a reservation for nine people for dinner as well as nine tickets for the Star Theatre. He specifically asked for Celebrity Circle seating to see the late show featuring Humperdink.

Charlie and the Wellman family go back a long way. In fact, both my Dad and Charlie are members of the LaPorte Baseball Hall of Fame, so accommodating Charlie was almost an obligation.

I remember walking into the dining room and hearing Charlie's voice dominating the entire room. His party of nine was feeling no pain as they headed to the Star Theater and the late show.

Humperdink was as good as always in spite of hearing Charlie's voice during several of the romantic ballads. After several curtain calls, I waited as long as I could, but I finally decided to approach Charlie's party hoping that maybe only a couple would want to go back to the Green Room to meet Humperdink. No such luck...Charlie insisted that all nine be taken back for an introduction.

I had no choice but to be gracious. The party followed me back and I introduced Charlie with his new toupee and his new girl friend, along with seven of their friends to Mr. Humperdink.

Charlie had difficulty pronouncing Humperdink's name, but before the evening was completed, he hired Mr. Humperdink to sing the National Anthem at opening day in Oakland. All this happened in one hour.

The party of nine was finally ushered out of the lobby of the theatre when Charlie turned to me and said, "Bill, I can't remember where I parked our cars." I respond, "Charlie, can you give me a clue, or maybe a landmark." It took a little time but Charlie finally came up with this insightful comment: "I think I went down a ramp."

Opening day singer - Oakland

The only ramp on the property was the loading dock off the kitchen so Charlie and I walked to the east end of the Holiday Inn and sure enough, there were two cars parked at the bottom of the loading dock.

Charlie and I got into the first car and he didn't hesitate or turn his head. He hit the gas and we flew backward like a shot. "Charlie, hit the brakes before we crash," I shouted. His reaction time was good because we just missed two parked cars.

I then made a management decision and asked for the key to the second car. He gave it to me without a question. Two teenagers then approached our cars and said, "Mr. Finley, we watched your cars all through the show." Charlie gave them each a $20 bill and pulled up to pick up his party. I drove the other car.

The last thing Charlie said to me was this: "Bill, it was a great night and I have part of the Opening Day Ceremonies completed. But you know those two kids didn't watch our cars. But I liked their thinking."

There were several other times I ran into Charlie at 6 a.m. eating breakfast at the Big Boy Restaurant in Valparaiso. The first time I saw him I was curious why he was in town so early when he lived just outside LaPorte. "Charlie, are you just getting home from a long night?" His answer was simple. "I love their buffet breakfast and if you get here early when they first put it out, it's great."

Charlie was well known as the owner of the Oakland Major League Baseball Team, but he was also well known locally. At Christmas time he always had a live nativity scene in his front yard. It lasted for an entire week and it was free to the public.

It always attracted thousands of people but Charlie hired a bunch of Deputy Sheriffs to control the traffic so everyone could stay in their cars and make the circular drive through Charlie's front yard.

Chicago's Channel 7 interviewed Charlie one night during the Christmas holidays. Interviewer Jeanie Morris, wife of former Bears wide receiver Johnny Morris, asked Charlie this question: "Charlie, isn't this live nativity scene a very costly week considering the live animals and all the people involved?" Charlie's answer was this: "No it's reasonable because Shepherds go for only $5 per hour."

It must be in the genes because Charlie Finley Jr. was just as interesting as his father and I would put him among the great characters I have met in my lifetime.

My first year working for Dean White was 1976 and I told him that I noticed that his Holiday Inn never had a successful New Year's Eve celebration. But we could change that in a hurry if he was willing to spend $10,000 for entertainment. He asked me whom I would hire. I'm sure my answer more than confused him: "Dr. Bop and the Headliners featuring the White Raven." I must have built my case well because he approved the band, even though he had never heard of them.

We sold everything in advance. Charlie Finley, Jr. bought three tables of eight and rooms for 12 couples. The only disaster during the entire evening happened when Charlie Jr. did a solo dance on one of the round banquet tables and it collapsed with Jr. landing flat on his back. Fortunately, he had no serious injuries. But I sure wish we had a video of young Charlie doing his impression of Fred Astaire.

HOLLYWOOD SQUARE

My first meeting with Paul Lynde came on the Saturday before we opened with "*The Best of Neil Simon*" starring this very funny man. I was on my way home, driving past the theater, when I saw something in the weeds across the street. I stopped my car as this person dressed in true African safari clothes – mid-length shorts, long knee-length socks, and a pith helmet – was coming out of the under-brush, leading a large poodle on a leash.

The best of Neil Simon, Paul Lynde

I introduced myself as the general manager, and asked him if there was anything that I could do to make his stay in Merrillville, Indiana as comfortable and as painless as possible. He was cordial, but not the friendliest actor I had been around. There was one thing I picked up on: he was *shit-faced, smashed, drunk*! I found out later that Mr. Lynde was in one of his very heavy drinking periods, but I also found out that no one would ever know because it did not seem to affect his ability to act with great humor.

Two days into the play, I had a visit from a young African American from New York who worked for American Express. He came to pick up Mr. Lynde to take him to Chicago to do an American Express radio commercial. I told him where the actor's suite was located in the Holiday Inn, and he left in his rented limo and pulled up in front of the Inn. In only twenty minutes the young man returned. I could see by the expression on his face that he had not experienced a pleasant visit with Mr. Lynde.

I asked, "What is wrong?" When he answered his voice was very high, fast, and full of excitement, as he quoted Paul Lynde. "There is no way I am going to Chicago, and there is no fu... way I am doing any kind of commercial; sue me if you want to."

The young man's next statement was, "I could loose my job over this. I have a director flying into Chicago from New York to handle this commercial, and now I don't have a star!"

I felt really sorry for this young man, but I had two days experience trying to please Mr. Lynde while keeping on his "good" side. I could assure him, with utmost confidence, that if Mr. Lynde said "No way," there was nothing anyone could do to change his mind. The young man then shocked me by asking if "I" would do the commercial. I did not hesitate one second, and I answered, "Why certainly I will do it."

I called Jim Kernagis, our Vice President of Marketing, and told him what had happened. I asked him to make the trip with us. I think I was really looking for moral support while I entered a field in which I had very little experience. Jim and I, and my newfound friend from American Express took the limo and ended up in the 100 block of Illinois Street in a recording studio.

We were introduced to Harry L. Johnson, the hired director from New York. I sat on a stool inside the studio with my script in hand. The director, Jim, and my good old buddy and newfound friend Robert Marks, the young executive from American Express, sat in the next room. They were looking through the window at me, like I was a fish in a bowl.

After reading through the commercial three times, the director's voice boomed over my head; "Mr. Wellman, you make it sound like it is a threat when you say 'don't leave home without it'." I, being the "star" bounced right back with, "Isn't that the way Carl Mauldin says it?" His answer was also quick, "No, I want you to just say it like you would normally, without the threatening tone!" By this time I felt comfortable on my stool, so I read it like Bill Wellman would say it:

"Hi, you don't know me, my name is Bill Wellman and I am General Manager of the Holiday Star Theatre in Merrillville, Indiana where Paul Lynde of Hollywood Square Fame is staring in the best of Neil Simon. We welcome you to use your American Express card. Don't leave home without it."

The director said, "That's a take!" and Jim and I were back in the limo while the director and the smiling Robert Marks took a taxi to catch their plane back to New York. The commercial I made was on three radio stations for a total of 152 times. My mother heard it one night and almost fell out of bed. My brother, Guy, heard it twice and couldn't believe it either time.

They sent me a $1,150 check for doing the commercial and $39.00 each time it hit the airwaves.

Three weeks later I had a surprise visit from young Mr. Robert Marks (still with American Express), and he presented me with an AMY, which was a very attractive crystal award given to stars who have produced a "Don't leave home without it," commercial.

The moral of this story is do not use a threatening tone when you do a commercial!

PERRY COMO

The charming Italian American, whose name became synonymous with mellow, performed through seven decades starting in the 1930's. His idol, the late singer Bing Crosby, once called Como, "the man who invented casual."

His first trip to the Star Theatre was August 25th through the 31st 1980, for nine performances and the tickets sold for an average of $17.00. It was easy to see from the beginning that taking care of Mr. Como's needs would be a piece of cake.

"He invented casual"
Bing Crosby

The first performance was like a Como reunion, because one of his sons worked at Notre Dame University and the entire family came to Merrillville six hours before the show started. One granddaughter brought an unexpected guest, a very young raccoon named "Rocky." You would think that this might upset Mr. Como but he was the one who suggested that Rocky stay in the star's dressing room during the visit.

All of Perry Como's shows were sellouts and they were all outstanding performances, in part because in the 1970's his career was going through resurgence. Some of his songs during that period included "It's Impossible," and "I Love You So Much," and several best selling Christmas albums.

Perry Como was well known as a steel town barber, but in the 1930's he stopped cutting hair to sing with big bands. By the 1940's his songs were a mainstay of radio and jukeboxes. He helped pioneer variety shows on the new medium of television in the 1950's and performed on television specials over the next four decades. His music has remained popular in recent years on easy listening radio.

In 1945, Mr. Como had his first million selling hit with "Till The End of Time." It was among many love songs including "Prisoner of Love," that topped the charts. He competed with Frank Sinatra and Bing Crosby to be the era's top crooner.

Mr. Como emulated Crosby in his earlier years, but some of his best-known numbers were light novelty songs like "Hot Diggity," and "Papa Loves Mambo." He took a shot at the movies, but decided to pursue a career in radio and television. He often said he far preferred singing romantic ballads to some of the lightweight numbers, but the novelty songs were a frequent audience request. "They got tired of hearing Melancholy Baby and those mushy things," Como said in a 1994 interview. "But those are the songs that as a singer you love to sing."

Perry Como made his television debut in 1948 on NBC's "The Chesterfield Supper Club," and in 1950 he switched to CBS for "The Perry Como Show," which ran for five years. Como then returned to NBC for a variety show that ran for eight years: first on Saturday nights opposite Jackie Gleason, then on Tuesday nights.

In 1963 he gave up the regular show and began doing occasional specials. After one of the evening performances, one of Mr. Como's back-up singers became ill and she was taken to Broadway Methodist Hospital in Merrillville. The next morning Mr. Como checked with the front desk at the Holiday Inn and asked directions to the hospital. The desk clerk offered the services of the van and a driver, but Mr. Como said he needed some exercise and since it was only about ten blocks away, it would be okay if he walked. When he returned, he came to my office to inform me that he had given away 32 tickets (promises), to the nurses on the fifth floor, for that evening's performance. Naturally, I told him I would take care of it, but I knew I would have a problem because we were completely sold out. We took care of it by bringing in banquet chairs. After he told me about the tickets, he said, "By the way, there are no sidewalks in your town."

There were several letters to the editor the following week talking about Perry Como sightings on U.S. Highway 30. One lady said she was sure it was him because he had a jacket that had "Captain and Tennille" on the back of it, a golf hat, and sunglasses; but what really puzzled her was that he was walking on dangerous U.S. 30. She turned the car around to make sure she was not seeing things, but by this time he was cutting through the White Castle parking lot.

In his later years, Como lived in a private semi-retirement with his wife Roselle, whom he met at a picnic when he was 16 and then married in 1933. They divided their time between North Carolina Mountains, and the Palm Beach County of Jupiter where he played golf, took long brisk walks, and entertained his great-grandchildren. Roselle Como died in August 1999 at the age of 84. Perry Como passed away on Saturday, May 14, 2001. The crooning baritone barber, famous for his relaxed vocals, cardigan sweaters and television Christmas specials, died after a lengthy illness.

In the entertainment business, there are only a few entertainers that fit two important categories; being 'a real nice guy,' and filling the ticket seller's till. Selling tickets is the key to make the cycle work. The entertainers always make big money, but if they have the ability to sell tickets, then the operator can make a profit too. Mr. Como was a fine entertainer and a "TICKET SELLER." There are no replacements in the present generation of entertainers to take his place.

LIBERACE, MR. SHOWMAN

This man was the BEST showman that ever appeared at Holiday Star Plaza Theatre. I don't mean he was the best talent ever, but as far as pleasing the audience, there was none better.

My first experience dealing with Liberace came when I told Mr. White that we had a good chance of signing Liberace for twelve days, fourteen shows, BUT... The BUT shocked me, and it was a HUGE shock to Mr. White. Liberace wanted to come to the Theatre, ...BUT he wanted a $50,000.00 advance check, and he wanted it six months in advance of the engagement.

I told Mr. White that this would be a first, but if we wanted a true "TICKET SELLER," Liberace was it and, since we were new to the business, we needed a sure winner. Mr. Liberace's agent was a man named Seymour who loved the six months of having Mr. White's fifty grand to invest almost as much as he loved show business. Since I have mentioned Seymour, I must tell you that he had the worst toupee in the business, and he was the horniest man in show business. He would hit on every waitress or maid with whom he came in contact. It did not make any difference what they looked like or how old or young they were. He never seemed to make a score, but he also never became discouraged. We nicknamed him the "HIT MAN!"

The advance ticket sales on the fourteen shows started fast. The costs of the tickets were $13.75 Monday through Thursday and $14.75 for weekend sales. This show called "Dancing Waters" was a hot ticket. The "Dancing Waters" came from the fact that the first man the show hired was a plumber to hook up the water show that was synchronized to the piano. The water fountains were always in the background when Liberace played the grand piano. The show started with Leigh sometimes being driven onto the stage in a limo, and making his entrance wearing a full-length mink coat. Showmanship made the excitement that propelled the ticket sales to become the all time record of 14 shows averaging 3,150 people per show, or 44,100 people in 12 days.

The $50,000.00 shock wore off fast when we sold $126,000 the first day tickets went on sale.

"The GREATEST"

After three shows, Seymour flew back to L.A. to replenish the trinket supply. Trinkets were scarves, records, tapes, music boxes, and bad oil paintings of Liberace. Mr. Liberace loved the trinket sales because I'm sure he loved the CASH and he loved to screw the government. It was hard to check on the value of the trinkets vs. the cash that was taken in each show.

The "bad" oil paintings were about 12" x 14" headshots of the man himself. He would only sell 25 per show because he personally autographed each one. When the show ended, the 25 proud owners of these oil paintings would stand in a single line at the Green Room doorway, waiting for the King to call them in. Leigh would change into what I called a Jester outfit that had one green leg and one red, and we would put him at a small table in a hallway. We would give him a goblet of wine and he would say, "OK, let's have them come in."

Leigh always allowed enough time to let the people ask plenty of questions and he would put his arm around the new owner of the BAD oil painting, for a picture with Mr. Show-business himself.

My wife, Liz, was running a gourmet cooking shop located in the Twin Towers that Leigh discovered after a few days in Merrillville. He loved to cook and began spending time in the cook shop. The problem was that once he started to look over all of the cooking toys, or started in a conversation with Liz about cooking classes, he was discovered by his public. Everyone wanted autographs or to have a conversation. There were times when he would go into the men's restroom and lock himself in a stall until the crowd disappeared and then he would return for more conversation and cooking talk.

On one of his last trips to Merrillville, Liberace ordered several thousand dollars worth of unique items from Liz's shop. He wanted the items for a restaurant he had planned, that his brother, George, was going to run in Las Vegas. I am not sure if the restaurant ever opened.

Once, Johnny Carson asked Liberace where he made the most money as an entertainer, and he shocked everyone when he said, "You won't believe it, but I made the most money in a small town called Merrillville, Indiana." He did not say he would sell $200,000 to $300,000 in trinkets and bad oil painting sales; because, this was his 'cash cow' secret from Uncle Sam.

Bob Angerman, a dentist in the Twin Towers, was the designer of the Eagle "T" shirts that our hostages wore the day they walked off the plane in Germany. Bob became Liberace's good friend, as well as Leigh's personal dentist.

When I called Bob to congratulate him on the success of his T-shirts, I told him I was interested in the rights to sell the shirts in Indiana. He said I was the second call. Leigh had called and offered to back him and to be his partner in the shirt sales. I am not sure how they made out, but the sales were huge in stores like K-mart and Sears. It would be interesting to see if Seymour was involved with this trinket sale, like he was with all of the cash sales before, after, and during the sold-out shows.

On Liberace's first trip to the Star Theatre, Bob Angerman invited my wife and me to have dinner with him and his wife Sarah, Liberace, and Dr. Olsen at the White House Restaurant in Valparaiso. My wife really did not want to go, but I convinced her she would really enjoy his company. The White House Restaurant was owned and operated by two Greek brothers, John and Harry Pappas. The restaurant was in their old family homestead, which was a huge white house that took up an entire block. As you can see, they had very little problem in naming their restaurant.

Liz and I arrived a little before 8:00 p.m. and as we walked past the small bar, I said hello to Mayor Kuehl. I thought his being there was a little unusual because the Mayor lived across the street from the restaurant and 8:00 p.m. was almost past his bedtime. The man seated next to him was the local photographer from the Vidette Messenger (local newspaper). Seeing these two together convinced me that the word was out that a star was about to arrive.

Liberace arrived at 8:15 p.m. in a full-length mink coat and blue jeans. After introductions, the Mayor left for home.

At that moment, I was a little surprised that the cameraman didn't snap a picture, but the evening was not over.

We had a great dinner in a private room and my wife had an excellent evening, enjoying Liberace and his stories. After dinner, John Pappas approached Liberace and asked him, "Would you mind if my brother and I had our picture taken with you?" Leigh of course said yes and before you could say White House, John and Harry had Liberace up against the wall and the photographer from the local newspaper took two quick pictures.

The next day on the business page of the local newspaper, was this great picture of John and Harry Pappas with the smiling Liberace in the middle. The best part of the picture was the article underneath it: "...greet their friend." It was great publicity. The Pappas boys not only did a terrific job of P.R., but they also got a great autographed 8 x 10 picture which hung in their restaurant until it closed in 1992.

Where's the piano?

Harry (left) and John Pappas greet their friend, Liberace, who stopped at the White House restaurant Tuesday for a meal and a visit. The Pappases were introduced to Liberace through a mutual friend. Said John of the visit, "I was very impressed. For a wealthy man, he didn't act like one. He has a fine personality." John said his interest in Liberace's music dates back to the late 1950s when he saw him perform live at Chicago's Soldier Field.

(V-M: Jay Jarrett)

As Liberace's health started to fail, his popularity did not. Bob Angerman invited Liz and me to come to Indianapolis to have dinner and be an overnight guest of Liberace while he was doing five shows at the semi-outdoor theatre located on the campus of Butler University, operated by my good friend Phil Walker.

It was easy to see that Liberace was starting to look older and thinner, and it was obvious that his health was faltering. His love life was still high because of his #1 friend Scott.

Scott was about 28 years old, 6'4" tall, blonde, and he weighed about 230 pounds. The weight did not include the weight of all of the gold Scott wore. Leigh bought every ounce of it. Scott was the same friend who sued Liberace for not following through with all of those bedroom promises over the years. After Leigh's death, Scott persisted in his lawsuit, but as far as I know, nothing ever came of the suit and Scott seemed to disappear as fast as he appeared.

Mr. Liberace died in 1987 in Las Vegas, Nevada. The industry lost the number one "ticket seller" and the record still stands at the Star Plaza Theater.

ROY CLARK / JENNIFER FLOWERS

Roy Clark

During this period Bruce White, along with his food and beverage director, Hans Enderlein, made the decision to give a very, very fancy dinner to each star and his crew after the final show. If the star was leaving immediately after the last performance the dinner was held the night before.

The meal was themed to fit the entertainer. In the case of Roy Clarks "Star Dinner" it was country all the way! Hans Enderlein did his usual great job, but I made the mistake of trying to keep up with our guest when it came to tipping up the little brown jugs of Jack Daniels. I didn't show up for work until just before Roy Clark was to walk on stage. When he saw me he said, "Bill, I looked for you today, where were you?" I honestly answered, "I had a terrible hangover." He quickly looked at me and said, "I'm glad to hear someone else felt as bad as I did; I thought life was over, I felt so bad!"

Roy Clark had two very attractive back-up singers with him the first time he played the Holiday Star Theater. One of them became quite famous later on, but not for her singing ability.

It was Jennifer Flowers from Little Rock, Arkansas, better known as a very close friend of President Bill Clinton!

In Ms. Flower's book, she mentions about the time she was on the road singing back up for Roy Clark. It seems there were times when Roy was a little "scary" to work with because of the use of drugs and heavy drinking.

Ms. Flowers not only was a good singer, but she was beautiful. I can see why the president of the United States had such a heavy affair with her.

P.S. – Did you ever take a good look at Hillary?

I started to get the feeling that once again my career in show business was coming to an end. Bruce White was starting to fall in love with show business and I could see he wanted to have his own people involved in the process. It was no surprise to me when Mr. White asked me to come to his office for a meeting.

Mr. White gave me an explanation when he told me I was going to join him within the corporate office and he would have me start to do Whiteco's lobbying in Indianapolis. I was to handle the public relations and do some real estate development for the family fun centers called Celebration Station.

I think I was mad for about twenty-four hours until I realized I would no longer have to "baby sit" some of the so called "stars".

The final carrot Mr. White hung in front of me was also exciting when he said, "Bill, I want you to go to the Cadillac dealer in Valparaiso. Talk to Mr. Hal Heuring and make a lease trade with him for a new Cadillac in exchange for a billboard." It made me feel as though I had arrived on the same plateau as J.R. Waters. I would be the proud driver of a brand new "HOG".

I made the move from the Holiday Star to Whiteco Corporate with very little fanfare.

Mr. White called my secretary, Charlotte Schweder, and gave her the choice of either staying in show business or making the same move to the main office and continuing to work for me. I am very happy that she made the decision to stick with me. Having someone as efficient as Char makes things so much easier. She has been nicknamed "Charlatron" because she continues to sell a ton of theater tickets, both Celebrity Circle and house seats, just like Ticketron!

Chapter Ten

CORPORATE LIFE

Nearly three weeks into my new corporate life I heard about a young executive, Mr. John Peterman, who was working on a project having to do with the corporation's excessive number of automobile leases. Evidently Mr. Peterman did an excellent job on his report because my "HOG" (Cadillac) just got shot down!

This was my first "real" introduction to John and it was obvious to me he was going to be a rising star in Whiteco Industries. In January 1988 John Peterman was named the new president of Whiteco Industries, Inc. He is the engine that makes Whiteco work and of course Mr. White is the engine's source of ideas and fuel.

Over the years John has been well known for his priceless "words of wisdom." While growing up, his children heard a lot of them, but I'm sure the list I have written down over the many Saturday morning meetings will surprise even John:

- If it's not the truth, it ought to be
- If you didn't have bad luck you'd have no luck at all
- Give a man a fish and feed him for a day - teach a man to fish and feed him for a lifetime
- There are no victims, only volunteers
- Hail Hail to old Purdue – you girls should go to Purdue
- The easiest sale is to a salesman

- People who get out of the outdoor advertising (business) want to get back in outdoor advertising
- Time will kill off more deals than attorneys
- How greedy are you? As greedy as you can be
- They are so dumb, it takes them two hours to watch 60 Minutes
- 90% of life is just showing up
- That's like making my wife the head of NASA
- Thank you, Bite me, Next...
- Pigs get fat and Hogs get slaughtered
- Sometimes the dog will eat the dog food
- There are two types of businesses – those who watch their nickels and dimes and those who are out of business
- He has layers of issues like an onion
- Raw land eats and doesn't shit
- Bankers are like clean underwear – you never have enough of them
- When we have a problem it's a challenge – when our competition has one it's a fiasco
- His ego is so big, he couldn't get into the elevator to get it up here
- As sure as a wet dog shakes
- Pretend you are an Indiana farmer and moan half the time
- Only the ripest tomatoes get picked

The "book censor fairy" eliminated 10 of John's better quotes!

THE MIRACLE AT OPTIMIST PARK

I always considered it just part of my job to look for and come up with ideas on finding hotel sites and other development projects.

When looking for a site for the potential Indiana Welcome Center for the Lake County Convention and Visitors Bureau on I-94, the southwest quadrant of I-94 and Kennedy Avenue stood out as the best location, but it also looked great for hotel sites.

I tried to interest Whiteco in the Optimist Park property, but I couldn't get John's attention and interest to visit the property.

I pushed for the purchase of the thirty-three acres located in Hammond, Indiana on the southwest quadrant of I-94 and Kennedy Avenue. I could tell John wasn't too interested until he was stuck in traffic on I-94 east bound for over forty-five minutes. The only view he had was the 18 acre lake and the 15 acres of "undeveloped" land surrounding the east side of the lake.

The first thing John did, when he finally returned to the office, was to look me up and start the conversation with, "Do you think the Optimists are in a mood to sell their property?" I finally had his interest so I quickly responded, "The club house has been flooded two times, and they have high water marks painted on the walls. The picnic business has dwindled down each year and their flood insurance is very costly."

Once John is hooked on a project he really likes to move fast. The negotiations went well and within 45 days Whiteco Industries, Inc. was the owner of 33 acres located smack in the middle of a flood plain.

The next move by Mr. Peterman was genius. The edge of the lake had to be raised eight feet in order to move it out of the flood plain. The service road was out of the flood plain so it was like filling in a piece of pie from the edge of the lake back to the service road.

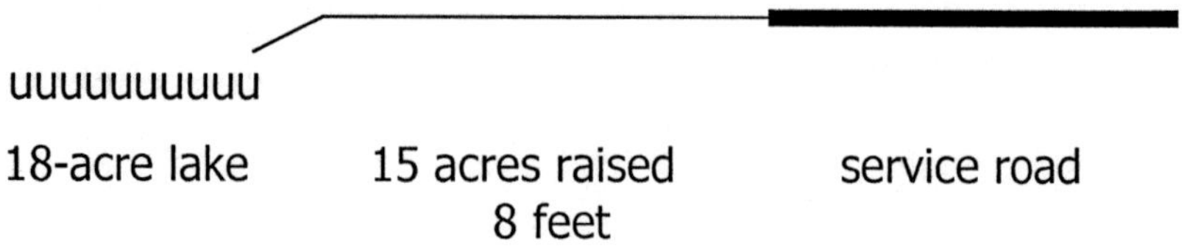

John decided not to bring the fill from outside of Optimist Park but to drain the 18-acres down to 3 acres and then bring the bottom of the lake up with heavy equipment to raise the shoreline by eight feet.

Contractors snickered at this project when they heard what we were doing, but the laughs disappeared when they saw the results of the finished project.

During the construction of the first two of three hotels located on this corner we ran into a unusual problem. The carpenters union got into an argument with the operating engineers on who had the rights to operate the two pieces of equipment used in the loading and moving around the 4 x 8 pieces of drywall.

This argument ended when we found our equipment at the bottom of our 130 foot deep "dry lake". John Peterman and Tony Fleming decided to investigate the mystery, but they got John's car stuck and had to use the local towing service to retrieve the car.

Two unions argue over a dispute and who suffers? The owners! And we didn't have a dog in the fight!

Contractors are still marveling at the final results of raising the shore line eight feet to completely remove fifteen acres from the flood plain without bringing in one load of fill from outside the property.

The development of the high and dry fifteen acres went fast with three hotels, a Cracker Barrel, a Wendy's and Mr. White's donation of the land to the Visitor's Center.

Getting the land ready to build was interesting, but going through the process of obtaining all the permits through the City Council of Hammond was almost impossible.

Whiteco had never asked for a tax abatement on any of our projects until the Optimist Park project. The high cost of raising the shoreline eight feet forced us to apply for the tax abatement in order to make the project financially feasible.

The thirty-three acres was on the tax roles of Hammond for $3,800 per year because of a small oil change business located on a south parcel next to the Little Calumet River.

The rest of the property paid no taxes since the Optimist Club owned the entire property and it is a non-for-profit organization.

The City Council fought us every step of the way, even though with the abatement in place we are paying $250,000 in taxes yearly for the first ten years vs. the $3,800 they received before the sale.

Politics and politicians (especially in Lake County) are interesting. We were approached with many possible solutions to getting our project on track.

One especially eager councilman asked for a manager's job even though he had no background in the hotel business. We were also asked to rebuild the service road from Kennedy to Cline Avenue on the south side of I-94.

Mr. White heard all of the requests offered me and came up with a great decision, "We will give them $30,000 per year for all ten years of our tax abatement and we will give them a check for $300,000 up front to be used for scholarships but we will not be involved in the process of who is to receive them."

The Council accepted the offer but it took them two years to figure out exactly how they would control their newfound scholarship program. Councilman Ernie Dillon finally took the bull by the horns in the second year to organize the scholarship program.

The night we received our final blessing from the Hammond City Council, John Peterman asked me to give him a call with the final results.

It was 2:30am when John received the word we were "good to go." He couldn't believe a council meeting would go into the second day. Only in Lake County, Indiana!

Optimist Park Results
Left to right – Fairfield, Courtyard, Residence Inn, Cracker Barrel, the Indiana Welcome Center and Wendy's

WHERE THERE IS SMOKE - THERE HAS TO BE SOME FIRE

I walked into Mr. Peterman's office for a meeting and after five minutes I said, "Something is burning" as I checked the vents and looked into the false ceiling. Nothing showed up that could produce the aroma. After the fifteen minute meeting I repeated, "John, I smell smoke." He sheepishly handed me one of his loafers. I quickly took one whiff and knew the mystery was solved as John confessed he purchased two pair of shoes at a real fire sale.

We now know John gets "BIG BUCKS" for great ideas but we also know he keeps the biggest percentage by being frugal and keeping up with "fire sales".

BACK TO SHOW BUSINESS (With a Stretch)

I must say I still missed show business, but I didn't miss the late parties or the babysitting of some so-called stars. In order to fill the show business urge I came up with a little Gem to fill the gap.

She was my three and a half year old granddaughter named Drew. What triggered the idea was her red hair, freckles and a husky voice. I took her to Chicago for a photography shoot with a top photographer recommended by (the voice of the Pillsbury Dough Boy) JoBe Cerny. The shoot went well so we produced a single sheet, which I mailed to a list of agencies Mr. Cerny gave me.

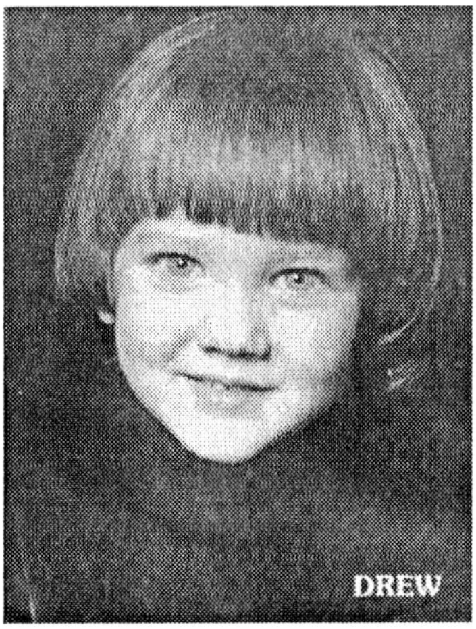

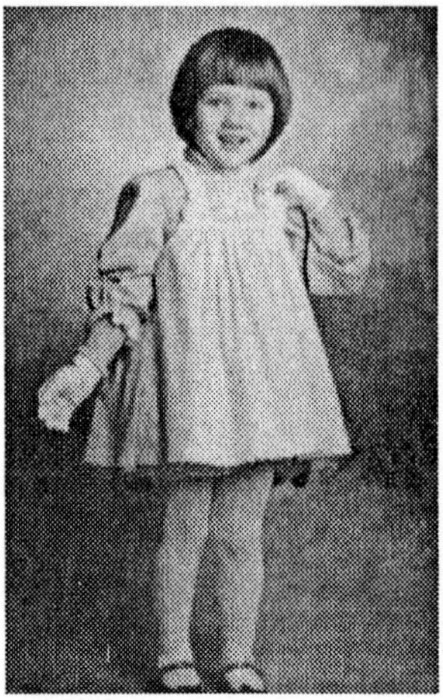

My logic was triggered by seeing too many McDonald commercials where I noticed they usually used little kids, but there was always a red head. That is all I needed to start me back into show business (in a small way.)

The first request I received was from an agency representing the company I targeted – McDonalds. They wanted Drew to be at a specific studio in downtown Chicago at 10:00am for her first interview and tryout for still pictures to be used in an upcoming advertisement campaign for McDonalds.

Taking a three and a half year old granddaughter to Chicago for a three to four hour picture shoot seemed a little scary at first, but Drew was great. She made the final cut and ended up as one of the four kids chosen. There was a cute four-year-old African American boy, a blonde four-year-old boy, a very shy three and a half year old oriental girl and Drew.

Drew at Work

The stage was set for the star of the show to arrive, Ronald McDonald. In the 1980's there was only one Ronald McDonald and of course he flew in from Tinsel Town – Hollywood. Drew was getting her hair arranged along with the oriental girl when one of the two hairdressers asked, "Drew, who does your hair?" No hesitation, "My hair dresser is Gabrielle at the House of Bianco in Merrillville, Indiana." The one hairdresser turned to the other one and said, "At three-and-a-half I couldn't even find the bathroom, let alone know my hair dressers name!"

Drew's first set went as smooth as silk followed by the shy oriental girl. Things went well until Ronald got into the picture and the oriental girl became frightened. Ronald backed off and the young director asked Drew to take the oriental girl by the hand and show her how to open a box of toys and stay with her until she felt comfortable.

Ronald McDonald came back to where I was standing watching and enjoying the entire shooting when he asked me, "How long has Drew been doing this type of work?" I looked at my watch and said, "About forty minutes." He looked as surprised as his "get-up" would allow as he followed with, "Don't let her quit, she is great!"

Show Business!

He told me, "Don't let her quit."

Drew received sixty five dollars an hour for her first job so her mother, Billie, had to get her a social security card and a permit from the schools systems of Chicago to allow her to work in Illinois no more than four hours a day.

Drew's career only lasted a year and a half. She worked for Sears catalog, J.C. Penny, a blue jean company and her big shoots were with McDonalds. Her salary jumped from sixty-five dollars an hour to ninety-five. The balloon popped when McDonalds asked her to do a speaking bit in a TV commercial.

We arrived one hour early for her audition and they gave me the one line they wanted her to say, "Look Grandpa, do you see the pretty butterflies?" We practiced a couple of times and she had it down pat. The camera started to role, Ronald hit the scene and Drew said nothing. She went shy on me and clammed up tight. The only way she would have won the part was if it was a commercial for a silent film!

The trip back to Valparaiso was very quiet for the two of us, except every once in a while Drew would look at me and say, "Look Grandpa, do you see the pretty butterflies?"

At the age of 18 Drew decided to try to give modeling another go. We did another picture shoot but nothing seemed to work out.

DREW WELLMAN

Height: 5' 7" - Weight: 115 pounds - Waist: 27" - Bust: 34" - Hips: 35"
Dress Size: 3 - Shoe Size: 8 - Pix Date: Spring 2001
Birth Date: October 11, 1982 - Talents or Features: Bright Golden Red Hair
Blue Eyes - A few Beautiful Freckles and a Husky Voice

Oh well, I think show business was slowing down in the Wellman family but the flickering flame was still there if I just had someone or something to promote.

PLANET PARK

Mr. White called me into his office and asked me if I would like to attend the Monday night football game in Indianapolis where the Bears would be taking on the Colts. I, of course, said yes, but I could tell there was more to the invitation than just the game.

The invitation got me hooked but his next statement was a surprise when he said "Gary Neale, (CEO of NIPSCO Industries) has approached me with his plan to convince the McCaskey family to move the Bears to a new stadium to be located in Northwest Indiana and he has asked me to allow you to be the lead guy. I told him it was okay with me but it would be strictly up to Bill if he wanted to be involved. What do you think?" I was somewhat surprised Gary Neale would ask permission to have me head up a project like this but I didn't hesitate when I said, "I'm a little puzzled why he would want me to do this because we have never been close, but it sounds like it could be something to promote and have some fun with. I'll do it!"

The visiting team in the Hoosier Dome has a suite and that is where we met the McCaskey family. It was very clear to me Mrs. McCaskey (daughter of the late George Halas) still had a lot to say about what happens to the Chicago Bears, even though her son, Michael, was the CEO of the Chicago Bears.

It was also obvious the Chicago Bears wanted to make a move out of Chicago. The entire family was really ticked at the park department and the Mayor, Richard Daley. They were very serious about moving to Indiana.

I was really surprised when I learned the law office handling the Bears was the same office representing NIPSCO. It gave us a "leg up" on the many questions our volunteers had about the future of Planet Park. The first draft of our plan gave this description:

PLANET PARK

An 1100-acre leisure zone and event park, southern gateway to Chicagoland, with multi-modal access by air, land and water has been selected as the new home of the Chicago Bears.

Our site was located at the southern tip of Lake Michigan, 18 miles south of Chicago, along Interstate 90, just west of the Gary/Chicago Airport and only 25 minutes from the Loop by car. The Planet Park parking lots were planned to contain 25,000 on site parking places convenient to the many attractions of Planet Park. The South Shore Railroad would be to the south, with a new commuter rail stop for both Planet Park and the airport. On

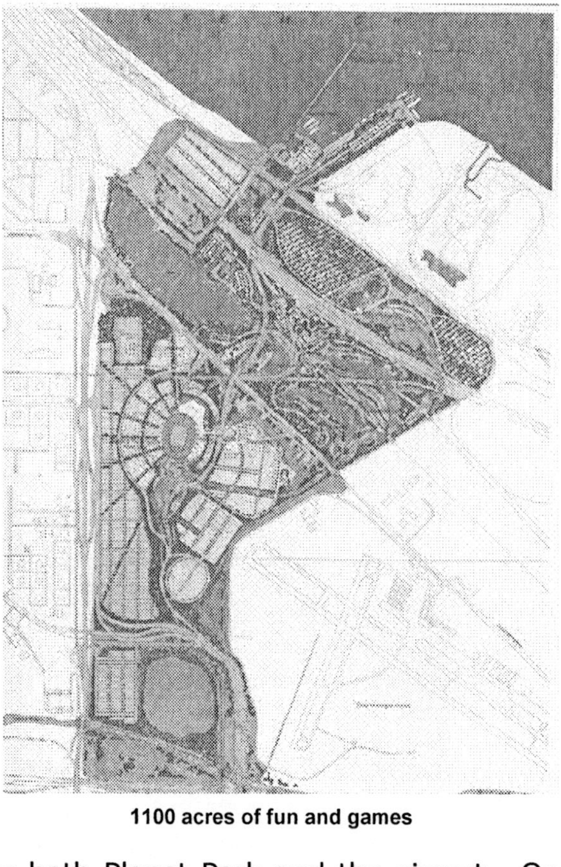

1100 acres of fun and games

the northeastern edge of the site the plans were to use Buffington Harbor for boats arriving from Navy Pier.

The plans for the park included much more than just a stadium for the Bears. It was to be a family resort, where travelers could stop to eat, play and sleep over in accommodations ranging from luxury hotels to lakeside cabins to comfortable campsites for recreation vehicles. The centerpiece of the resort was the Bears Stadium and Midway. The Midway is the heart of the event park, a continuous tent-shaded pedestrian space that is the focus of impromptu and formal events, giving entrance to four major family restaurants around the stadium. The Midway connects a series of small and large event arenas where seasonal concerts or exhibitions would occur. The largest arena is the 75,000 seat, "state-of-the-art" stadium which was to be ready for the 2000 season. The rest of the park would have included a discount mall with over 1,000,000 square feet of retail space and a very large convention center, which would have included the Bears Hall of Fame.

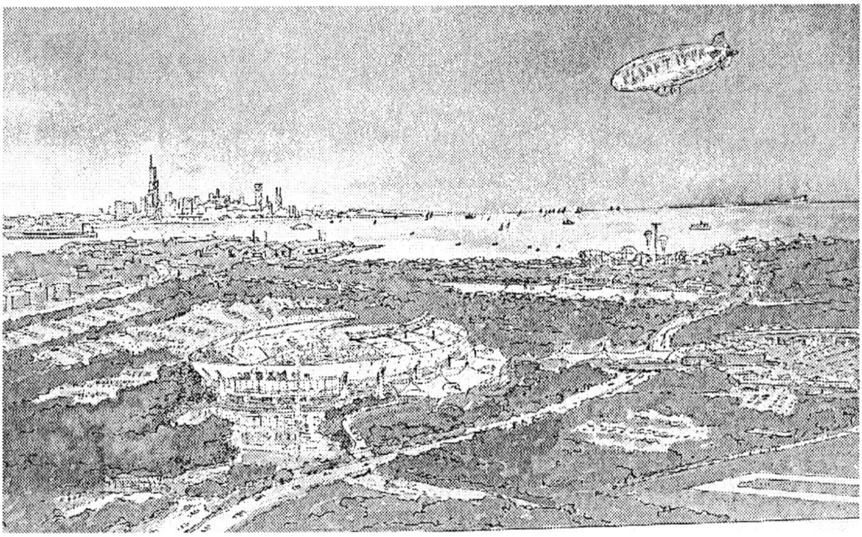

Not far from the loop

Tented Midway

Planet Park would have reflected the prediction of Michael McCaskey, president and CEO of the Bears, who has said, "The future of professional sports organizations lies not in isolated super-structures, but in facilities integrated with family leisure and entertainment. The sports industry will survive and thrive if it blends into continuous entertainment experiences for Americans enjoying their increased leisure time." Planet Park family resort realized McCaskey's vision of an integrated sports and leisure culture experience in an innovative format, appealing to a public as broad in age and interests as America itself.

The entire McCaskey family was ready to make the move to Indiana! They were ready to stick it to Mayor Daley if Indiana was ready for them.

New Bears Stadium

Our plan was good but the job of convincing Lake County to increase taxes to make this project work was impossible. One trip to the Lake County Court House to convince the politicians this was good for Lake County showed me it would never happen. We were lucky to get out of the auditorium without being physically harmed!

Gary Neale gave it a good run but the dream of Planet Park actually happening ended with a thud. It was a lot of fun while it lasted!

GOVERNOR FRANK O'BANNON

Governor O'Bannon called me to set up a breakfast meeting with Dean White even though he knew Mr. White was a very strong backer of Republican candidate for Governor, Steve Goldsmith.

The meeting lasted about an hour but there was no request for campaign funds. After the governor left, Mr. White looked at me and said, "How could you not like a fellow like that?"

My next meeting with Frank O'Bannon was at a very casual bar-b-que in the backyard of the 1890 home his wife Judy had taken on as a major refurbishing job, both exterior and interior. There was a very large tent set up in the backyard to accommodate a couple hundred people.

To Bill, Thanks for your friendship and thanks for your service to the State.
Frank + Judy O'Bannon

Cocktails were served before and during dinner, and evidently conversation was included in the drinks because the Governor cornered me after dinner and came up with his philosophy on life. "Bill, do you know the three things I live by?" Of course I was curious, so I followed with, "No Governor, what are they?" He shocked me a little, but after participating in five knots on the silk handkerchief trick, nothing should shock me! He boldly answered me, "One, never pass up a chance to take a leak – Two, never trust a fart – and Three, never waste a hard-on!"

Coming from the number one man in the State of Indiana I was surprised, but to this day I always think of his number one whenever I'm about to get into a car for a short or long trip. You must admit, the Governor's philosophy was down to earth!

3 Rules of Getting Older
Never pass a bathroom,
don't waste a hard-on,
and never trust a fart

ATTACKING THE JAPANESE – ONE MORE TIME

Mr. White asked me to handle a welcome luncheon for a company called Nippon Iron Powder Co. LTD of Chiba-Ken, Japan. This company was opening a new division in Valparaiso, Indiana called Powdertech. Their entire contingent was staying at Mr. White's Holiday Inn in Merrillville.

To start the plans for the luncheon I was pleased to hear that Powdertech had hired a great P.R. man and an old friend, Al Evans. The same Mr. Evans who played the lead in The Music Man at Bridge Vu Theater in Valparaiso, in 1969.

Al suggested our first meeting to plan the luncheon should be held in the Holiday Inn restaurant, since the President of Powdertech, Mr. Kyoso Hisade, was a guest at the Holiday Inn. I agreed to have a breakfast meeting.

The meeting went well and the plans were made but near the end of the meeting I made one of those smartass remarks that nearly put Al Evans under the table as I said, "Mr. Hisade, I still have a problem with your people." In explanation of this remark I told him of my visitation to Midway Island, Saipan and my Easter morning sermon on Okinawa. Mr. Hisade hesitated a few moments and came back with, "Mr. Wellman, when you were on Okinawa I was only eight years old." This somewhat simmered me down and we finished our plans for a special welcome luncheon to be held in the Holiday Inn Atrium on May 25th, 1989.

After the breakfast, Al expressed his concern about our meeting and how he almost choked on my statement.

When you plan an event with the Japanese there are certain rules to follow. For example: if they are going to have twelve people, we are to have twelve. If there are ten men and two ladies, we were to have ten and two. Gifts are exchanged before lunch and I was to give a welcome speech that was to be followed by a welcome speech from Mr. Hisade.

The luncheon went exceptionally well; however, just before Mr. Hisade gave his speech he approached me with, "Mr. Wellman, I am going to say something special about you in my welcome." I wasn't sure what he was saying, except I did recognize the words, "Midway, Saipan and Okinawa." Each time he mentioned those islands the president of Nippon Iron looked at me and I could hear him say, "Oh" after each name. The president was very close to my age.

The grand opening of Powdertech was show business at its best. Al Evans did an excellent job and Porter and Lake Counties welcomed the new business to northwest Indiana.

As promised, Mr. Hisade sent me my welcome speech translated in Japanese.

Mr. W. F. WellmanのLuncheonに於ける歓迎スピーチ

Whiteco Industries 会社及び私共の社長であります Dean Whiteになり替わりまして、皆様方にノースウエスト・インディアナにようこそおいで下さいましたと申し上げます。

長年に亘って、私共のこの地方は、専ら鉄鋼業が圧倒的に盛んなことで知られておりました。現在でも鉄鋼では全米第一の生産州でありますが、鉄鋼及びそれに関連する産業が多くの失業者を産み出した為に、私共は多角化をすすめなければなりませんでした。Powdertech社のようにこの地方に参入される会社の援助を受けて、私どもは、今 この多角化の戦に勝利を納めつつあります。

多くの異なった国籍の人々がノースウエスト・インディアナ地方を構成している為に、私共は時々ミッド・ウエストの人種のルツボとして知られる事があります。わたくしは、この地方が人種的に多くの人々の混じり合いから出来上がっている事が本当のHoosierを作り上げているのだと思っております。（Hoosierと言うは、インディアナに住んでいる人々のニックネームであります。）
このHoosierと呼ばれる人々は、人なつこく、協力的で経済的基盤の改善、及びそのコミューティに於ける生活の質の向上に大いに積極的であります。

皆様方がこの地方に進出されたタイミングは、正に絶好でありました。私共は皆さん方を歓迎し、友好の精神と協力の手を差し出したいと思っております。

The Japanese translated letter

IT'S MADE TO SELL-NOT TO DRINK!

NIPPON IRON POWDER CO., LTD.

HEAD OFFICE: 217 TOYOFUTA, KASHIWA-SHI
CHIBA-KEN, 277 JAPAN
TEL.0471-45-2126 FAX.0471-46-1445

TOKYO OFFICE: PREMIER KI BLDG(6F)
I MIKURA-CHO, KANDA, CHIYODA-KU
TOKYO, 101 JAPAN
TEL.03-251-8131 FAX.03-251-8134

June 16, 1989

Mr. Bill Wellman
Vice President
Whiteco Industries
1000E. Both Place
#7000N
Merrillville, IN 46410

Dear Mr. Wellman:

I am now back in Japan and wish to express to you my most sincere appreciation for your warm welcome and superb luncheon given to all Japanese visitors on the occasion of Powdertech open house celebration on May 25th, 1989.

Most of Japanese guests, myself included, have been deeply moved and touched by heartfelt hospitalities and willingly offered cooperation by Hoosier people in northwest Indiana.

I as president of Powdertech, am now firmly determined that Powdertech should become a good corporate citizen and should be of some service to the wellbeing of northwest Indiana community.

Meanwhile, I am sending herewith my Japanese translation of your speech delivered at luncheon on May 25th as I promised you to do so.

NIPPON IRON POWDER CO., LTD.

HEAD OFFICE: 217 TOYOFUTA, KASHIWA-SHI
CHIBA-KEN, 277 JAPAN
TEL.0471-45-2126 FAX.0471-46-1445

TOKYO OFFICE: PREMIER KI BLDG(6F)
I MIKURA-CHO, KANDA, CHIYODA-KU
TOKYO, 101 JAPAN
TEL.03-251-8131 FAX.03-251-8134

I take this opportunity to offer you our organization's thanks for your friendliness and generosity shown to our country people and the staff of powdertech. I sincerely hope that we may also count on your goodwill and cooperation in the future.

Thank you again.

yours sincerely,

K. Hisada

Kyoso Hisade
President
Powdertech

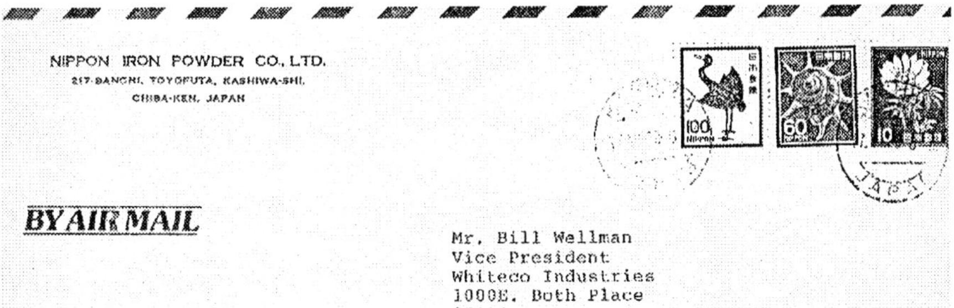
NIPPON IRON POWDER CO., LTD.
217-BANCHI, TOYOFUTA, KASHIWA-SHI,
CHIBA-KEN, JAPAN

BY AIR MAIL

Mr. Bill Wellman
Vice President
Whiteco Industries
1000E. 80th Place
#700N
Merrillville, IN 46410
U.S.A.

P.S. I still have a problem with the Japanese and I know I will not outgrow that feeling.

OVER THE BORDER

I was asked to accompany Bruce White on a trip to Canada with the sole purpose of stealing ideas for the operation of a potential first class nightclub to be located on the southwest quadrant of I-65 and US 30 in Merrillville, Indiana.

The trip was to be no longer than three days, but Bruce became so involved with the investigating process we stretched the trip to five days. The nightclubs were very interesting and we stole many great ideas to take back to Merrillville.

You know you are in a first class operation when you want to run a bar tab and the bartender places your credit card on a clip board and hangs the board on a peg on the back bar. The work was hard and each day was very long and included too much lubricant and a tremendous amount of conversation.

We returned home very late on a Sunday morning and I slipped into the house without disturbing Liz. The next morning I forced myself to spring out of bed early not to let my wife know I was dead tired because of all of the overtime I had been forced to do in Canada!

When Liz told me we were going to Michigan City to see a movie that started at 11:00am I couldn't let on how tired I really was, so I bravely said, "That's great! Who is going with us?" It turned out our daughter, Dawn, and a friend was to go with us.

The movie had just started when I got the funny feeling I was on the verge of passing out. Without saying a word I got up and started to excuse myself as I tried to head for the lobby. The next thing I felt was a person giving me mouth-to-mouth resuscitation and I heard someone say, "A massive heart attack."

The paramedics put me on a stretcher and rolled me into a waiting ambulance. As they strapped me in, they made the mistake of not getting my arm out of the way. I thought they had broken it!

My wife was getting into the ambulance and we were headed to the Michigan City emergency room. I looked at Liz and said, "Liz, I am not having a heart attack. Trust me – no heart attack!"

The emergency room doctor gave me a quick check up and quickly came up with, "Have you been getting enough sleep lately"? I honestly answered, "No!"

Then he asked, "Have you been doing a lot of drinking?" The answer was a loud, "Yes!" It didn't take him long to dismiss me with instructions, "No drinking, and get some rest. Your body just told you not to burn the candle at both ends."

The plans for the new nightclub took an unusual turn when Bruce decided that the nightclub was to be named Second Hand Rosa's, but it was to be a disco. I think this was the last disco in the world, including Canada. Bruce also made another decision by hiring a Chinese manager for Second Hand Rosa's. I could see a Canadian, but a Chinese manager for a disco in Indiana – that was a stretch!

Opening night was a huge affair for Second Hand Rosa's Food Collation and Disco. I decided to catch a ride home with the White Sign Company's leading salesman. As he turned onto U.S. 30 heading east he took a huge sweeping turn that put his car in the westbound lane of traffic going the wrong way. I quickly said, "You're going the wrong way"! He said, "No I'm not!" But he quickly realized I was right as he pulled over and let me drive the rest of the way back to Valparaiso. "It's made to sell – not to drink!"

Second Hand Rosa's had its ups and downs, but really never made it as a disco or a nightclub. It eventually ended up as the first family fun park called Celebration Station.

Maybe Second Hand Rosa's would have been more successful if Bruce and I had spent two weeks in Canada. If that had happened I might really have had a massive heart attack!

CELEBRATION STATION

Dean White sent me out to find land appropriate to build future Celebration Stations (family fun parks.) His instructions were, "Treat the locations like you were looking for hotel sites because when the discretionary dollars start to disappear on family fun parks we will end up with great hotel sites for the future."

With the mission on my mind I took my wife on a work/vacation in the Tampa/Clearwater Florida area looking for a specific piece of ground. Liz and I were driving a rental car through the streets of West Palm Beach when I abruptly pulled off the road as Liz asked me, "What's wrong?" I coasted to a stop and answered, "I just want to take a picture of the hotdog sales lady we just passed." There was little discussion as Liz gave me my instructions, "If you are taking pictures of what I just saw, please leave the car here and walk back."

What a way to buy a dog!

I agreed to take a walk and I snapped the following pictures with the consent of the "Dog Lady." In fact, she even asked me if I wanted to have my picture taken with her. As you can see, I was easily persuaded.

The following article appeared in the local Florida newspaper two days later. When I had the pictures developed Liz Had to admit my photography had improved and the "Dog Lady" had one hell of a body.

Bikini-clad hot dog sellers told to get new sales pitch

WEST PALM BEACH, Fla. (AP) – Roadside hot dog vendors who show off their wares by taking off their clothes will have to set up 4-foot opaque enclosures under a new county ordinance.

The Palm Beach County Commission voted Tuesday night to require vendors who wear G-strings, thongs and pasties to set up the barriers.

At least a dozen scantily clad vendors operate in the county. Last year, county traffic officials studied one vendor, Gloria Gonzalez, and concluded she provoked heckling but no safety problems.

Nevertheless, the commission's ordinance cited safety as one of its justifications, along with "notions of decency."

Violators can be fined up to $500 and jailed for 60 days. The ordinance takes effect next month.

Gonzalez protested the law by attending the hearing in a body-length dress and veil like those worn by some Muslim women. Her lawyer said they plan to fight the ordinance in court.

Commission Chairwoman Karen Marcus said the ordinance was not unreasonable. Vendors can still wear shorts and tank tops, or even bikinis if they cover the buttocks.

"We are not making them dress in black and cover their face like in Iran," Marcus said.

Two to go!

Two with everything!

I'm sure this lady set a record of selling the most "TUBE STEAKS" in the state of Florida. Working for Whiteco was proving to be a lot of fun!

FAMOUS WIVES TALES

The Ron Kittles Golf Outing is considered to be one of the best in Northwest Indiana. Our group won first prize and our celebrity was the Chicago Bears great Gayle Sayers.

Our group consisted of Mike Williams, Scott Bening, Sherm (the "pharmaceutical king"), Pete Reardon, Mr. Sayers and yours truly. Everyone seemed to step up at the right time to eventually make our team the top dog. I had the privilege of having Gayle Sayers ride in my cart so I bent his ear with the story about going to school with the late Chicago Bears coach, Abe Gibron and how my wife and I would go to Abe's apartment on game day to pick up our tickets for the Sunday game. Abe's wife was always in the process of making him three fried bologna sandwiches for half time.

We had just finished the eighth hole when I decided to call Liz and let her say hello to the legend we both watched when he was in his prime.

Gayle was approaching the tee when I said, "Liz, how are you doing?" She responded with, "I'm wringing out the clothes by hand because the washing machine is broken and I have no idea when the repair man will come to fix it." By this time the "GREAT" Gayle Sayers was coming back to the cart so I said, "Liz, would you like to say hello to Gayle Sayers"? There was no hesitation with her next remark, "If he knows anything about how to fix a washing machine I will talk to him, but if he doesn't the answer is NO!" I had the distinct feeling of just being hung up on.

I told my fellow golfers what had just happened and it was the loudest laugh of the day! I decided to check back as we finished an eagle on one of the par five holes. "Liz, did the fellow get the washer fixed?" The answer was yes so I followed with, "Would you like to say hello to Gayle Sayers"? The answer was yes and they carried on a pleasant conversation for several minutes. At no time did he give her any advice about fixing the washing machine.

The evening was complete when we were announced as the winners, including one skin worth $800 in cash and a Ron Kittle golf bag for all six of our players.

Gayle made the statement (after several margaritas), "This is my first time at Ron Kittle's Golf Outing and I have never played on a team like this. I would like to return next year but only if I can play on your team." Mike Williams offered to have our celebrity picked up in a limo and returned to Chicago safe and sound in 2006. This statement would increase the number of Margaritas the Great Gayle could have in 2006. I gave him the nickname of "Gayle the Maytag Washing Machine Man!

NEW YORK, NEW YORK

It was the spring of 2001 when I was invited by Larry Alt, president of Profile Systems, to help run a booth at a regional meeting of Burger King Franchisees to be held in New York.

I had suggested we invite Pat Tilka to fly in from Florida to help us run the booth since he owned and operated over fifteen of his own Burger Kings in the Indianapolis area. Pat knew a lot of the BK franchise people since he had been very active in their association.

Greg Scott, Larry Alt and Pat Tilka

After we set up our booth we had an entire free day before the opening of the Burger King show so Pat and I decided to take a boat trip around New York, which included great photo opportunities. If you make the trip to the "Big Apple" I really recommend a boat trip to become familiar with the city.

Grand Old Lady

This trip was in April and the weather cooperated. The Statue of Liberty was not open to the public but cameras were allowed. I also wanted a picture of the Brooklyn Bridge just because of my older brother's connection and his signing a contract with the Brooklyn Dodgers. Little did I know how great my picture was until after 9/11/01. The picture of the bridge was good, but the two towers couldn't have been more centered. It was as if I actually knew what I

was doing. I used that picture as our featured Christmas card sent to close friends, lest they forget 9/11/01.

Pat and I had our photo taken after the boat docked and his comment after seeing the picture was, "We look like a couple of gay dudes after an ocean cruise!" That was just his opinion!

CHINA TRIP

In October 2002 Mr. White invited six employees to take a trip to China. It was his yearly corporation trip for the board of directors of his sign company located in Shanghai, China.

Falcon 900

Interior of Mr. White's Falcon

When I tell this story I love to start with the line, "I pulled my car into the large hangar at the Porter County Airport for the first leg of our flight to Anchorage, Alaska for an overnight stay and then on to China through Russia".

Our overnight stay was at the famous "Captain Cook" Hotel built in 1965 right after the earthquake. This quake was nine times stronger than the last San Francisco earthquake. The Captain Cook Hotel is a member of the Preferred Hotels and Resorts Worldwide.

We had a great dinner in a famous restaurant called Simon and Seaforts Saloon and Grill. Their dining room overlooked the huge bay so the sunset was as pretty as you will see (except on Kauai). The seafood dinner of salmon and a great Caesar salad was excellent, but the highlight "to die for" was the Key Lime Pie!

The flight from Alaska to China took twelve and a half hours, including a very interesting stop in Russia. It didn't seem to be a very tiring flight because I watched 11 episodes of "Sex and the City". We landed to refuel in a very old military airport in Russia. The landing felt like a very rough corduroy road. The buildings were from the World War II vintage, in fact if a movie director was looking for a spot to do a movie in the 1940's this was the place. None of the buildings have received a coat of paint since they were built.

Russia Airport Building – World War II vintage

As our plane came to a stop we saw five military people headed our way. Two entered our plane, a young officer and a cute young lady dressed in a camouflaged uniform topped off with a fur hat with a small red Russian star in the middle. She didn't speak English, but she had a great international smile.

Our stewardess, Dennis Kackos, A Great Russian Smile and Your Author!

The young officer spoke excellent English and he initially tried to be very serious as he took a seat, but as he opened his briefcase I noticed it only included a clipboard, a rubber stamp and one inkpad. It was obvious his real interest was to see our plane and to get as many newspapers and magazines as we could give him.

We showered him with sandwiches, candy, a six-pack of beer, fruit and all of our magazines and newspapers.

Great Smiles!

I told him some of our people were guessing his age and Eileen had guessed him to be nineteen. He smiled and said, "I'm twenty six but she guessed young because of our beautiful skin." With this he gave me a great smile.

John Peterman asked our guest the most interesting question, "Have you seen the movie Rocky IV?" This is the one where Rocky defeated the huge white Russian. He didn't hesitate when he answered, "I have seen them all." And with his answer he once again flashed his great smile.

Our guests departed and we took off for the last leg of our journey. Lunch was served as we were flying over Osaka Japan at 39,000 feet. The menu consisted of Wagners Ribs from Porter, Indiana.

I forgot to mention the crew on Mr. White's plane consists of the pilot, co-pilot, a mechanic and a very efficient stewardess.

Passengers Coupon

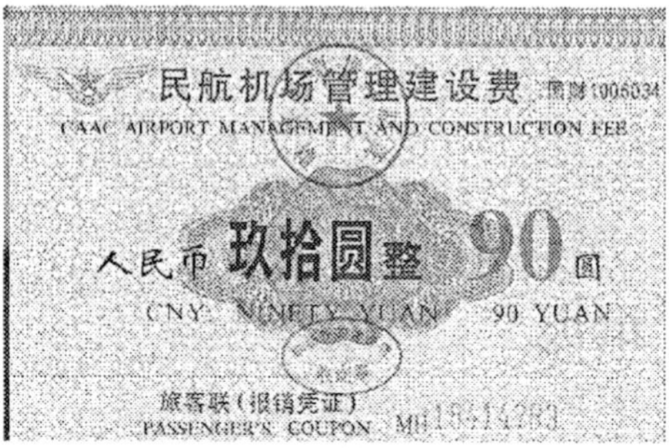
民航机场管理建设费
CAAC AIRPORT MANAGEMENT AND CONSTRUCTION FEE
人民币 玖拾圆整 90 圆
CNY NINETY YUAN 90 YUAN
旅客联(报销凭证)
PASSENGER'S COUPON

It was raining when we landed in Shanghai and we were met by three young ladies from the government customs department. They quickly asked for all of our passports and immediately one young lady looked at each of us and confirmed, by comparing the picture on each passport, we were okay to enter China. It was a very simple procedure.

Welcome to China!

Three SUV's pulled up to the plane with eight people from the billboard office including the "top dog" in China, Jack Dodds. It continued to rain as they proceeded to load the luggage. They must have loaded everything in the wrong vehicle because they had to redo everything. It immediately hit me that I had just watched a Chinese fire drill.

Tourist Guides

Our hotel was the Portman Ritz Carlton located in Shanghai and was first class. The first dinner was in a French restaurant built in a very old church. The building was cute with very expensive crystal chandeliers, but on a scale of one to ten the dinner was only a five.

Mr. White had his usual problem ordering a VO Manhattan. I think he ended up with Jim Beam on the rocks decorated with a cherry.

The second night was hosted by Mr. White's official partner and he chose an Irish Pub. The rating jumped to an eight as we ordered steaks. The after dinner discussion was interesting as they talked through a Chinese interpreter about how well the sign company was doing and the potential of expansion to other cities. The interest level jumped up when Mr. White brought up the possibility of developing a Celebration Station in Shanghai. Mr. White's partner thought it would do extremely well in a city park. Jack Dodds seemed to have the confidence of Mr. White's partner and he was aggressively learning to both speak and write the Chinese language.

Three girls from the Whiteco Outdoor office accompanied Eileen, Terry and me on our first shopping experience. I really enjoyed the negotiating on the final prices of all my purchases. They seemed to encourage you to negotiate; in fact they seemed to look down on you if you don't play their game.

Terry, Anita, Madam Zhu, Dreamy and Eileen

One of the girls accompanied me into a governmental store where you could buy anything made of gold. It was a huge store with over a hundred ladies, all dressed in white, ready to wait on many customers but I only counted four others. There is absolutely no negotiating with the government on gold. The price is set, take it or leave it.

The Gold Store

Next we were taken to the PEARL, which is the highest structure in the city but in order to do this we had to take two taxicabs. Terry and I got in the first cab with a young lady from the Whiteco office named Anita.

The Pearl

A cab ride in China is an experience but this one took the unusual prize. The driver got in the wrong lane and the policeman waved him on so he was forced to make a right hand turn when he really wanted to turn left. In doing so he immediately made a u-turn and drove directly by the policeman who had forced the situation. I applauded the u-turn, but the cab stopped and the driver looked under the hood to see what the problem was. He then came back and got into a loud argument with Anita. I thought he was going to hit Anita, but she stood her ground and asked us to vacate the cab.

We soon found another cab and finished our trip to the PEARL. I had to ask Anita what the argument was about and her response was, "His cab broke down and he didn't fulfill his contract but he wanted a partial payment because he got us half way to our destination. I disagreed and paid him nothing because I was right and he was in the wrong."

Great building!

Our days in Shanghai were interesting and I became comfortable walking the streets at all hours. The only complaint was the heavy smog. It was a daily occurrence.

We moved to Beijing and the Shangri-La Hotel, which was a five star hotel so we could visit the Great Wall of China. The Great Wall was an outstanding experience but the fun of the day was watching John Peterman buy five fur hats similar to the one the young lady wore in Russia. John walked away three times before the deal was cemented with a handshake and John was the proud owner of five (faux) fur hats.

The Forbidden City

At the base of the Great Wall of China

The Great Wall of China

The week in China went by too fast, but the experience will last a lifetime.

The trip back to Alaska was speeded up with a 56 mph tailwind so we avoided a stop in Russia. We arrived in Alaska about 1:30am so all of us were ready for bed. John suggested he and I have an early breakfast, hire a cab and see a moose first hand.

After breakfast we hired an Hungarian cab driver and I told him, "We have one and a half hours before we leave for the airport and we would like to see a moose up close!" His thick accent came back with, "Moose?" I confirmed with, "Yes, a moose."

Trophy Moose!

One and a half hours later our driver dropped us off in front of the Captain Cook Hotel with "Sixty dollars, no moose, sorry." As we checked out of the hotel I took a trophy picture for John.

We arrived in Valparaiso on a Friday night at 9:30pm. My car was waiting for me in the hanger for my short trip home. I had some great memories of my first trip to China. It's really a small world.

INDIANA'S #1 WELCOME CENTER

It is usual to wait until a person dies and then name a building or a room after him, but not in my case. I had served on the Lake County Convention and Visitors Bureau for 22 years, twice as its Chairman, still I was shocked during the dedication of the Lake County Welcome Center in 1999 when our President and CEO, Speros A. Batistatos, made his opening remarks. I could tell he was heading towards honoring (I thought) my boss, Dean White, by naming the Exhibition Hall after him. He really deserved it because he gave the land to the Lake County Convention and Visitors Bureau so they could build the center. I was so convinced it was him, I stepped back a couple of steps just as Speros was finishing his remarks so Mr. White could step up to the podium.

I must say I was completely surprised when he dedicated the room by naming it, The W.F. "Bill" Wellman Exhibition Hall.

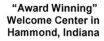

"Award Winning" Welcome Center in Hammond, Indiana

Indiana Welcome Center

Architecture by Design Organization of Valparaiso, Indiana – Lead architect, Chuck Bone

RESTAURANT / HOSPITALITY HALL OF FAME

In 2003 I received a call from John Livengood's assistant. John heads up the restaurant and hotel/motel association for the state of Indiana.

The call went like this, "Mr. Wellman, you have been selected to go into the Restaurant/Hospitality Hall of Fame and we would like to invite you to our luncheon next Wednesday here in Indianapolis." I thanked her and I followed with, "Who is going to be inducted with me?" "Dave Thomas of Wendy's and Arnie Cohen of Arnie's Restaurants from Lafayette." I quickly followed with, "Both of those fellows are dead!" She hesitated but said, "Yes, but both of their widows will be there."

I think my next statement shocked her when I said, "You know I have been invited to play golf at Sand Creek with my good friend Ed Charbonneau and I only get a chance to play at Sand Creek a couple of times a year." The scream on the other end of the line made me pull back from the telephone – "Mr. Wellman, you HAVE to show up because we have to have someone to hand the plaque to."

I did show up to receive the plaque. It was a great honor to be in the company of Dave Thomas and Arnie Cohen, even though they were posthumously inducted. I hope Ed will invite me to Sand Creek next summer for the missed game!

LIFETIME ACHIEVEMENT AWARD

Tom Driver gave me a call in 2005 inviting me to have lunch with Dave Stevenson and him at Café Venezia. I would never pass up a lunch at the best restaurant in Merrillville, so I accepted, not knowing why two bankers would invite me to lunch.

It didn't take Tom long to inform me that I had been selected to receive the "Lifetime Achievement Award" and I would receive it at the annual Entrepreneurial Luncheon to be held at the Radisson Hotel. I really gave the two of them a shock when I answered with, "Tom, I have already received that award." Before the panic could set in I quickly came back with, "I received it several years ago when I sat in for Dean White because he was in China!" They seemed relieved they had not made a mistake.

I felt honored to be in the company of previous winners, Dean White, Charlie Bowman and one of my heroes, Harold Heinold.

Receiving these honors and plaques reminded me of my old friend Walter Fetla who once gave me some advice, "Bill, tell them you would rather have cash instead of trophies and plaques!"

The plaques are all hanging on my office walls, which give you the feeling of being in an old museum.

COMEBACK OF THE KISSING BRIDGE

In August of 2003 I wrote the following letter to Alan Harre the President of Valparaiso University:

August 25, 2003

President Alan F. Harre
Valparaiso University
Valparaiso, Indiana 46384

Dear Alan:

Congratulations! on the "Texas Drew Step". The PR Valparaiso University received from the two moves of the father and son was exceptional. It looked like Valparaiso was sending this clean-cut savior to Baylor to salvage a disaster and bringing back Homer kept the program on the same course.

I would like to talk to you about an idea. This is one of those "dreamers" ideas that I seem to get in the middle of the night while I'm waiting to go to sleep.

The 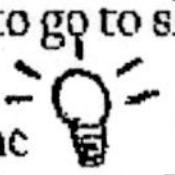 idea has to do with the old student bridge that use to offer the students a safe way over the Pennsylvania Railroad tracks to their housing south of the campus. This was done (before your time) by Presidents Brown and Kinsey back in the 1860's. The university maintained the north part which was all wood and the Pennsylvania Railroad tracks maintained the main part which was made of iron.

The wooden part of the bridge was replaced in 1936 for $400.00 but because the housing south of the tracks seemed to disappear; this bridge was torn down in the 1960's.

President Alan F. Harre
Valparaiso University
Valparaiso, Indiana 46383
August 25, 2003
Page Two

In 1967, I decided to resurrect the "Kissing Bridge" across Salt Creek as a walking access to the Bridge VU Theatre. When the article appeared in my monthly newsletter that sentimentalists would be able to stroll across the gold-leafed structure and reminisce their happy days on the student bridge, the article caught the attention of a very famous alumni "Mr. Lowell Thomas". The term gold-leafed must have hit a nerve so he wrote me a letter congratulating me for saving the historic "Kissing Bridge" but asked me one favor, "Please don't paint it gold, leave it black". In Lowell Thomas's last book he had a picture with two of his lady friends taken on the bridge. I think the picture was 1924.

I answered Mr. Thomas and asked him if he would help us dedicate the bridge and Bridge VU Dinner/Theatre and he surprised me by saying he would love to do it.

Everything went fine until he called me two weeks before the dedication and informed me that he was going to New Guinea on an assignment so he had to cancel.

My substitutes were the radio giant WGN's own Wally Phillips and another famous VU alumni Abe Gibron who attended Valparaiso with me in 1945. We played on the same baseball team and then Abe transferred to Purdue where he was on the All American football team and went on to be All Pro for five years and then he coached the Chicago Bears for three years.

I have given you my story and now I will tell you my idea. The "Kissing Bridge" has a lot of Valparaiso history and I think it deserves a spot on your campus. It could span a small ravine with a large stone and a plaque to explain the history.

President Alan F. Harre
Valparaiso University
Valparaiso, Indiana 46383
August 25, 2003
Page Three

I ran the idea by a couple of alumni and they liked it. If this hits any kind of a excitable nerve, please let me know and I will go to work on the project. If it is a dud idea, you won't hurt my feelings because I have had some dud ideas before.

If you want to see the "Kissing Bridge", pull into Applebee's Restaurant off U.S. 30 and take a hard right (east) to the stream. You will see the stone, the plaque and the bridge.

Thanks for your time and consideration and please let me know if you have any interest.

Sincerely,

Bill Wellman

W. F. (Bill) Wellman
Senior Vice President Communications

WFW/cs

It didn't take the president long to give me a call to inform me he was assigning my idea to a committee. My first thought was the idea would die in committee. I was so wrong.

The committee was made up of students, and their wooden sign told their story:

SITE OF THE NEW VALPARAISO UNIVERSITY STUDENT KISSING BRIDGE

INITIATED BY STUDENTS
PLANNED BY STUDENTS
BUILT BY STUDENTS
CONTINUING THE LEGACY

They not only did the work, they also raised $55,000 to pay for all the material and restoration of the famous "Kissing Bridge".

The "KISSING BRIDGE" has completed a circle: beginning at Valparaiso University in the 1890's, through the junkyard in the 1960's and the Bridge VU Theater and ending finally back to the University's main campus near the two eternal flames (at least one is working) at the new entrance on U.S. Highway 30.

I feel I, too, have very nearly completed the circle of my life-but I still have the imagination, energy and desire to create just one more great P.R. Gem: one that would make Bill Veeck (rhymes with wreck) roll over with glee!

Writing this book – remembering, re-experiencing and researching - has been very hard work and much more difficult than I had expected. It has caused me to relive the past eighty-two years and confront again the many emotions of all the times of my life. I hope my readers have enjoyed the ride as much as I have.

Apologies

"I wish to apologize to my wife Liz, my eldest daughter Dawn, my number one son Scott and my youngest daughter Kim for missing most of your years growing up.

Liz, you did a fantastic job of raising three great children while I used work as my excuse for missing those important years. One day I looked around and realized the kids were no longer kids but were grown up. During this time I was also married to a restaurant and the entertainment business.

I am very proud of how the three of you turned out. Thank your mother for stepping into the breach and being both mother and sometimes father to the three of you.

When the medals are handed out your mother will receive the biggest one!"

Love, Dad

About the Manager

Every project needs a manager. This book has been managed and organized by my good friend, Cindy Misch. Reading my handwriting can be a chore but Cindy amazed me how well she moved through the process. Scanning pictures and following the rules of AuthorHouse (my publisher) was a trying experience, but Cindy expertly plowed her way right to the end! "Cindy, when the medals are handed out, you will receive one of the big ones. Thanks for your help and good work and especially your patience!"

Bill

About the Editor

Editing "It's Made To Sell, Not To Drink" has been an unique education for Marion Heath Dudley, a friend of the author for many years.

Mrs. Dudley, born in Omaha, Nebraska, educated at Brownell Hall and the University of Iowa and its Writers Workshop, has lived in Hobart, Indiana with her husband, John, since the early 1950's.

When their children reached responsible ages, Mrs. Dudley, a journalist, became public relations director and editor of publications of a worldwide executive service organization headquartered in Chicago. The international group held consultative status with the United Nations. For 18 years her responsibilities of fund-raising and project planning for UN agencies took her to many countries and required one-on-one negotiations with government leaders.

In 1988, she was appointed to the Lake County Convention and Visitors Bureau board of directors on which she served 15 years, two terms as board chairman.

Still writing and editing, she has had great fun, and some surprises, learning more about W.F. "Bill" Wellman than she really expected to know.

Acknowledgements

Ramsey Smith – Sketch of Indian Doctors building in Tremont and Grand Trunk Depot

Tom Riggs – Article on Guy Wellman Jr. from the Press Journal, Vero Beach, Florida, March 4, 1989

USS Saratoga – Information from the Dictionary of American Fighting Ships, published by the Naval Historical Center

Bronco John Sullivan – Information from Memories of Bronco John Sullivan by Texas Jack Sullivan, his son

House of David Museum – Benton Harbor Michigan

Ernie Pyle – Article written by Joan Milne, Hammond Times, May 11, 2002

The New Phyllis Diller – by Virginia Thrower, Post Tribune, January 30, 1972

Phyllis Gets Lift Out of New Face – by Sandra Pesman, Chicago Daily News, February 3, 1972

Flyboys – by James Bradley, author of the #1 seller, Flags of Our Fathers

Martha Connelly – author of the Kissing Bridge story from Lake Magazine and her pictures on the history of the bridge

Okinawa photography – courtesy of United States Marine Corps

Prohibition – by Franklin P. Adams, 1931

Indian Doctor of Tremont – Chesterton Tribune, 1991

Blaine "On The Go" Marz – Courtesy of the Gary Post Tribune

Robert Horton's Biography

William Louis Veeck Jr. Biography

Cartoon of Phyllis Diller – by Ken Fallin

"Confessions of a Much Married Man" – by Mickey Rooney

Court Brochure – by Dale Fleming

Cartoon – by Guy Wellman

Opening Night – Bob Kostanczok, Post Tribune

Edda Taylor – Photographie

Gaye Lindsley – Typing Technician

Deb Devine – Typing Technician

Advisors

Jason Weisler (Junk Yard Dog)
Wanda Crumpton
Eileen Plumb
Charlotte Schweder
Karen Kleine
Robert Victor
Andrea Rivera
John Dudley
Len Dryfus
John Davies
Dave Piercy
Ann Bowman

Shawn Spence, Book Cover Photography

Special Advisor

Speros A. Batistatos

Good Listeners

***** *Liz Wellman*
*** *Larry Alt*

Printed in the United States
55179LVS00005B/1-72

9 781425 945435